T0146944

Parecon

VERSO

Parecon

Life After Capitalism

MICHAEL ALBERT

VERSO
London • New York

First published by Verso 2003
© Michael Albert 2003
Paperback editon first published by Verso 2004
© Michael Albert 2004

1 3 5 7 9 10 8 6 4 2

Verso
UK: 6 Meard Street, London W1F 0EG
USA: 180 Varick Street, New York, NY 10014-4606
www.versobooks.com

Verso is the imprint of New Left Books

British Library Cataloguing in Publication Data
Albert, Michael, 1947–
   Parecon: life after capitalism
   1. Macroeconomics 2. Economic policy – Social aspects
   3. Economic policy – Citizen participation
   I. Title
   339'.01
   ISBN: 978-1-84467-505-0

Library of Congress Cataloging-in-Publication Data
A catalog record for this book is available from the Library of Congress

Printed and bound in the USA by R. R. Donnelley & Sons

Contents

Acknowledgments

For every book many people contribute words, style, and ideas, not to mention experiences. When a book calls on decades of collective experience and centuries of history, giving comprehensive thanks is impossible. Still ...

Thanks go firstly to Robin Hahnel with whom my contributions to the participatory economic vision were produced in tandem.

To Andrea Sargent who edited the entire manuscript and is overwhelmingly responsible for whatever clarity it has.

To members of South End Press now and in the past for helping create the practice behind many of *Parecon*'s ideas.

To students at ZMI for their challenging discussions of the vision.

To volunteers and co-workers in current projects, Z and ZNet, and in past efforts as well, for continuous feedback.

To audiences at public talks who have heard and debated the contents herein. To participants in the ZNet forum system, who have pursued the ideas in that venue.

To those who have created institutions employing *Parecon*'s insights and relayed their experiences.

And to a few additional special individuals, as well, whose contributions arrive via all the above routes and are so bountiful that personal mention is mandatory: Justin Podur, Tim Allen, Brian Dominick, Stephen Shalom, Cynthia Peters, Noam Chomsky, and Lydia Sargent.

And of course to Verso Books, for publishing *Parecon*, to Tariq Ali for championing it, to Sébastien Budgen for excellent editorial assistance, to Tim Clark for production work, to Gavin Everall for promotion, and to everyone else at Verso for being there, and for caring about economic vision.

Introduction

> Most everybody I see knows the truth
> but they just don't know that they know it.
> — Woody Guthrie

The British Victorian liberal thinker John Stuart Mill (1806-1873) tells us that we ...

> are not charmed with the ideal of life held out by those who think that the normal state of human beings is that of struggling to get on; that the trampling, crushing, elbowing, and treading on each other's heels which form the existing type of social life are the most desirable lot of human beings.

The American social critic Noam Chomsky says he ...

> would like to believe that people have an instinct for freedom, that they really want to control their own affairs. They don't want to be pushed around, ordered, oppressed, etc., and they want a chance to do things that make sense like constructive work in a way that they control, or maybe control together with others.

If "trampling, crushing, elbowing, and treading" are not the "most desirable lot" for humanity, what is? If humanity should not aspire to create an elite minority joyfully dancing atop a suffocating mountainous majority, what should we aspire to? If the instinct to not be "pushed around, ordered, oppressed" and to do "constructive work in a way that [we] control" deserves exploring, where should we begin?

The United States has about 3 percent of the world's population yet does nearly half the world's consuming. Within the US, about 2 percent of the population own 60 percent of the wealth. Other developed nations are similarly unequal. Less developed countries suffer broadly the same internal distribution, though there the richest are less wealthy and the poorest are more destitute.

Indignity, disempowerment, and hunger accompany capitalism worldwide. No one sensibly denies this, yet even among those who despise capitalism, most fear that suffering would increase without it. While some certainly find capitalism odious, few celebrate an alternative and those who do generally favor "market socialism," "centrally planned socialism," or "green bioregionalism." In contrast, this book rejects capitalism but also the typically favored alternatives. The English humanist William Morris (1834-1896) ...

> [sought] a condition of society in which there should be neither rich nor poor, neither master nor master's man, neither idle nor overworked, neither brain-sick brain workers nor heartsick hand workers, in a word, in which all would be living in equality of condition and would manage their affairs unwastefully, and with the full consciousness that harm to one would mean harm to all—the realization at last of the meaning of the word commonwealth.

But how can we undertake economics to usher in Morris's "commonwealth"? How do we reward and ennoble work? How do we enrich consumption and make it more equitable? How do we make allocation just and efficient? Can we enjoy efficiency, justice, democracy, and integrity simultaneously?

Part I of this book discusses economic values and institutions. part II describes participatory economics and argues its benefits. part III explores daily life implications of a participatory economy. part IV rebuts plausible worries. First, we briefly address how economic vision relates to anti-corporate globalization and other economic aims garnering support around the world.

Parecon and Globalization

Anti-corporate globalization activists favor sympathetic and mutually beneficial global ties to advance equity, solidarity, diversity, and self-management. Globalize equity not poverty. Globalize solidarity not greed. Globalize diversity not conformity. Globalize democracy not subordination. Globalize sustainability not rapaciousness. Two questions arise.

- Why do these aspirations cause anti-corporate globalization activists to be critical of corporate globalization?

- What new institutions do anti-corporate globalization activists propose to do a better job than those that now exist?

Rejecting Capitalist Globalization

Current international market trading overwhelmingly benefits those who enter exchanges already possessing the most assets. When trade occurs between a US multinational and a local entity in

Mexico, Nigeria, or Thailand, the trade doesn't provide greater benefit to the weaker party that has fewer assets, nor are the benefits divided equally. Rather, benefits go disproportionately to the stronger traders who thereby increase their relative dominance.

Opportunist rhetoric aside, capitalist globalization's flow of resources, assets, outputs, cash, capital, and harmful by-products primarily further empowers the already powerful and further enriches the already rich at the expense of the weak and poor. The result is that at the turn of the twenty-first century of the 100 largest economies in the world, almost exactly half are not countries but are private, profit-seeking corporations.

Similarly, market competition for resources, revenues, and audience is nearly always a zero-sum game. Each actor advances at the expense of others so that capitalist globalization promotes a self-interested "me-first" logic that generates hostility and destroys solidarity between actors. This dynamic occurs from individuals through industries and states. Collectively beneficial public and social goods like parks, health-care, education, and social infra-structure are downplayed while individually enjoyed private goods are prioritized. Businesses and nations augment their own profits and simultaneously impose harsh losses on weak constituencies. Humanity's well-being doesn't guide the process but is instead sacrificed on behalf of private profit. Against capitalist globalization solidarity fights a rearguard battle even to exist, much less to predominate.

Moreover, cultural communities' values disperse only as widely as their megaphones permit, and worse, are frequently drowned out by communities with larger megaphones impinging on them. Thus capitalist globalization swamps quality with quantity. It creates cultural homogenization not cultural diversity. Not only do McDonald's and Starbucks proliferate, so do Hollywood images and Madison Avenue styles. The indigenous and non-commercial suffer. Diversity declines.

At the same time, only political and corporate elites inhabit the decision making halls of the capitalist globalizers. The idea that the broad public of working people, consumers, farmers, the poor, and the disenfranchised should have proportionate say is considered ludicrous. Capitalist globalization's agenda is precisely to reduce the influence of whole populations to the advantage of Western corporate and political rule. Capitalist globalization imposes hierarchy not only in economies, but also in politics where it fosters authoritarian state structures. It steadily reduces the number of people who have any say over their own communities, much less over nations, or the planet. And as the financiers in corporate headquarters extend their shareholders' powers, the earth beneath our feet is dug, drowned, and paved with no attention to species, ecology, or humanity. Profit and power drive all calculations.

In sum, capitalist globalization produces poverty, ill health, shortened life spans, reduced quality of life, and ecological collapse. Anti-globalization activists, who might more usefully be called internationalist activists, oppose capitalist globalization precisely because it so aggressively violates the equity, diversity, solidarity, self-management, and ecological balance essential to a better world.

Supporting Global Justice

But rejecting capitalist globalization is not sufficient. What specific global exchange norms and institutions would do better than what we endure? Do anti-globalization activists propose any alternatives to replace the International Monetary Fund (IMF), the World Bank, and the World Trade Organization (WTO)?

The International Monetary Fund and World Bank were established after World War II. The IMF was intended to combat financial disruptions adversely affecting people around the world. It employed negotiation and pressure to stabilize currencies and help countries avoid economy-disrupting financial machinations. The World Bank, on the other hand, was created to facilitate long-term investment in underdeveloped countries as a means of expanding and strengthening their economies. It was to lend major investment money at low interest rates to offset the lack of local capacity. Within then existing market relations, these limited goals were positive. In time, however, and most dramatically in the 1980s, these institutions changed. Instead of working to facilitate stable exchange rates and to help countries protect themselves against financial fluctuations, the IMF's priority became bashing down all obstacles to capital flow and unfettered profit-seeking—virtually the opposite of its mandate. And in parallel, instead of facilitating investment on behalf of local poor economies, the World Bank became a tool of the IMF, providing loans to reward countries that offered open corporate access while withholding loans to punish those that did not, and financing projects not with an eye to enlarging benefits for the recipient country but to seeking profits for major multinationals.

The World Trade Organization that was first conceived in the early postwar period came into being only decades later, in the mid-1990s. Its agenda became to regulate all trade on behalf of the rich and powerful. IMF and World Bank policies were already imposing on Third World countries low wages and high pollution by coercing their weak or bought-off governments. The new insight was why shouldn't we weaken governments and agencies that might defend workers, consumers, or the environment, not only in the Third World, but everywhere? Why not remove all efforts to limit trade due to its adverse labor, ecological, social, cultural, or development implications, leaving as the only legal criterion for regulation whether short-term profits can be made? If national or local laws impede trade—say an environmental, health, or labor law—why not have a WTO that can render predictably pro-corporate verdicts to trump governments and populations on behalf of corporate profits?

The full story about these three centrally important global institutions is longer than indicated above, of course, but even with only the brief overview, it is easy to propose improvements.

First, why not replace the IMF, the World Bank, and the WTO, with an International Asset Agency, a Global Investment Assistance Agency, and a World Trade Agency? These three new institutions would work to attain equity, solidarity, diversity, self-management, and ecological balance in international financial, trade, and cultural exchange. They would seek to direct the benefits of trade and investment disproportionately to weaker and poorer parties, not to richer and more powerful ones. They would prioritize national aims, cultural identity, and equitable development above commercialism. They would protect domestic laws, rules, and regulations designed to promote worker, consumer, environmental, health, safety, human rights, animal protection, or other non-profit centered interests by rewarding those who attain such aims most successfully. They would advance democracy by enlarging the choices available to democratically controlled governments and subordinating the desires of multinationals and large economies to the survival, growth, and diversification of smaller units.

Similarly these new institutions would not promote global trade at the expense of local economic development nor would they force Third World countries to open their markets to rich multinationals and to abandon efforts to protect infant domestic industries. Instead of downgrading international health, environmental, and other standards through a process called "downward harmonization," they would work to upgrade standards via "upward equalization."

The new institutions would not limit government ability to use purchasing dollars for human rights, environmental, worker rights, and other non-commercial purposes, but would advise and facilitate doing just that. They would advocate countries treating products differently if they were made with brutalized child labor, with workers exposed to toxins, or with no regard for species protection.

Instead of bankers and bureaucrats carrying out the policies of presidents to affect the lives of the very many without even a pretense at participation by those impacted on, the new institutions would be transparent, participatory, and bottom-up, with local, popular, democratic accountability. They would promote and organize international cooperation to restrain out-of-control global corporations, capital, and markets by regulating them so that people in local communities could control their own lives. They would promote trade that reduces financial volatility, enlarges democracy at every level from the local to the global, enriches human rights for all people, fosters environmental sustainability worldwide, and facilitates economic advancement of the most oppressed and exploited groups.

The new institutions would encourage the major industrial countries to coordinate their economic policies, currency exchange rates, and short-term capital flows in the public interest and not for private profit. They would establish standards to regulate financial institutions, directing the shift of financial resources from speculative profit-seeking to productive, sustainable development. They would establish taxes on currency transactions to reduce destabilizing short-term cross-border financial flows and to provide funds for investment in long-term environmentally and socially sustainable development in poor communities and countries. They would create public international investment funds to meet human and environmental needs and to ensure adequate global demand by channeling funds into sustainable long-term investment.

The new institutions would also work to get wealthy countries to write off the debts of impoverished countries and create a permanent insolvency mechanism for adjusting the debts of highly indebted nations. They would use regulatory institutions to help establish public control over global corporations and to curtail corporate evasion of local, state, and national law.

In addition, beyond getting rid of the IMF, World Bank, and WTO and replacing them with the dramatically new and different structures, anti-corporate globalization activists also advocate a recognition that international relations should not derive from centralized but rather from bottom-up institutions. New institutions should gain their credibility and power from an array of arrangements and ties enacted at the level of citizens, neighborhoods, states, nations, and groups of nations on which they rest. And these more grassroots structures and bodies of debate and agenda-setting should also be transparent, participatory, and guided by a mandate that prioritizes equity, solidarity, diversity, self-management, and ecological sustainability and balance.

The overall idea is simple. The problem isn't international relations *per se*. Anti-capitalist globalization activists are unrepentantly internationalist. The problem is that capitalist globalization seeks to alter international exchange to further benefit the rich and powerful at the expense of the poor and weak. In contrast, internationalists want to alter international exchange to weaken the rich and powerful and empower the poor and weak. Internationally we want global justice and not capitalist globalization. But what do we want inside our own countries? This is where the link between the profoundly important anti-capitalist globalization movements and the rest of this book derives.

Anti-Capitalist Globalization And Economic Vision

Even if internationalist activists seek alternative global economic institutions as above, a vision problem persists. International structures certainly impose severe constraints on domestic choices. At the same time, however, global relations are propelled by pressures from domestic economies and institutions. The IMF, World Bank, and WTO impose on countries markets and corporate divisions of labor. But likewise domestic markets and corporations around the world propel capitalist globalization.

When activists offer a vision for a people-serving and democracy-enhancing internationalism we urge constructing a very good International Asset Agency, Global Investment Assistance Agency, and Global Trade Agency on top of the very bad domestic economies we currently endure. Suppose we win the sought gains. Persisting corporations and multinationals in each country would not positively augment and enforce the new international structures, but would instead continually emanate pressures to return global relations to more rapacious ways. At an intuitive level people actually understand this. When average folks ask anti-globalization activists "What do you want?", they aren't only asking us what we seek internationally. They also wonder what we seek domestically.

What do we want inside countries that would augment the international gains we seek and make fighting for them more than useless posturing?

If we have capitalism, many people rightly reason, there will inevitably be tremendous pressures toward capitalist globalization and against anti-capitalist internationalism. IAA, GIAA, GTA, and more local alliances and structures sound positive, but even if immense exertions put them in place, won't domestic economies around the world undo the gains? The question is warranted.

Capitalist globalization is markets, corporations, and class structure writ large. To replace capitalist globalization and not just temporarily mitigate its effects or stall its enlargement, don't we have to move toward replacing capitalism as well? If efforts to improve global relations through creating the new international regulatory institutions we propose are an end in themselves, won't they be rolled back? To persist, don't they have to be part of a larger project to transform underlying capitalist structures? If we have no vision for that larger project, if we offer no alternative to markets and corporations, won't our gains be temporary?

So, many people deduce, why should we apply our energies and time to the struggles that you propose when we believe that even if we successfully won all the gains you seek, in time those gains would be wiped out by resurgent capitalist dynamics? You keep telling us how powerful and encompassing capitalism is. We believe you. If the efforts you propose don't lead to entirely new economies, they will eventually be rolled back to all the same old rot. It isn't worth my time to seek gains that will be undone.

This assessment is fueled by the reactionary belief that "there is no alternative." To combat this belief anti-globalization activists must not only offer an alternative regarding global economics, but also an alternative regarding domestic economies. People need to feel that the application of their energies to opposing corporate globalization won't have only a quickly undone short-term impact, but will win permanent gains. So what should replace capitalism?

Summarizing Participatory Economics

Capitalism revolves around private ownership of the means of production, market allocation, and corporate divisions of labor. It remunerates property, power, and, to a limited extent, contribution to output, resulting in huge differences in wealth and income. Class divisions arise from differences in property ownership and differential access to empowered versus subservient work. Class divisions induce huge differences in decision-making influence and quality of life. Buyers and sellers fleece one another and the public suffers anti-social investment, toxic individualism, and ecological decay.

To transcend capitalism, parecon-oriented anti-globalization activists would offer an institutional vision derived from the same values we listed earlier for shaping alternative global aims: equity, solidarity, diversity, self-management, and ecological balance.

Such activists would urge that each workplace be owned in equal part by all citizens so that ownership conveys no special rights or income advantages. Bill Gates wouldn't own a massive proportion of the means by which software is produced. We all would own it equally, so that ownership would have no bearing on the distribution of income, wealth, or power. In this way the ills of garnering wealth through profits would disappear.

Next, argues the internationalist advocate, workers and consumers would develop and express their desires via democratic councils with the norm for decisions being that methods of dispersing information and for arriving at and tallying preferences into decisions should convey to each party involved, to the extent possible, influence over decisions in proportion to the degree he or she will be affected by them. Councils would be the vehicle of decision-making power and would exist at many levels, including smaller work groups, teams, and individuals, and broader workplaces and whole industries, as well as individual consumers, neighborhoods, counties, and larger. Votes could be majority rule, three-quarters, two-thirds, consensus, etc. and would be taken at different levels and with fewer or more participants and voting rules depending on the particular implications of the decisions in question. Sometimes a team or individual would make a decision. Sometimes a whole workplace, an industry, a neighborhood, or a county would decide. Different decisions would employ different voting and tallying methods. There would be no a priori correct, detailed option, but there would be a right norm to implement: decision-making input in proportion as one is affected by decisions.

Next comes the organization of work. Who does what tasks in what combinations?

Each actor does a job, and each job of course includes a variety of tasks. In rejecting current corporate divisions of labor, we decide to balance for their empowerment and quality of life implications the tasks each actor does. Every person participating in creating new products is a worker, and each worker has a balanced job complex, meaning the combination of tasks and responsibilities each worker has would accord them the same empowerment and quality of life benefits as the combination every other worker has. Unlike the current system, we would not have a division between those who overwhelmingly monopolize empowering, fulfilling, and engaging tasks and those who are overwhelmingly saddled with rote, obedient, and dangerous tasks. For reasons of equity and especially to create the conditions of democratic participation and self-management, balanced job complexes would ensure that when we each participate in our workplace and industry decision-making, we have been comparably prepared by our work with confidence, skills, and knowledge to do so. The contrary situation now is that some people have great confidence, decision-making skills, and relevant knowledge obtained through their daily work, while other people are only tired, de-skilled, and lacking relevant knowledge as a result of theirs. Balanced job complexes do away with this division. They complete the task of removing class divisions that is begun by eliminating private ownership of capital. They eliminate, that is, not only the role of capitalist with its disproportionate power and wealth, but also the role of decision monopolizing producer who is accorded status over and above all others. Balanced job complexes retain needed conceptual and coordinative tasks and expertise, but apportion these to produce true democracy and classlessness.

But what about remuneration? We work. This of course entitles us to a share of the product of work. But how much?

The pareconist internationalist says that we ought to receive for our labors remuneration in tune with how hard we have worked, how long we have worked, and how great a sacrifice we have made in our work. We shouldn't get more because we use more productive tools, have more skills, or have greater inborn talent, much less should we get more because we have more power or own more property. We should get more only by virtue of how much effort we have expended or how much sacrifice we have endured in our useful work. This is morally appropriate, and it also provides proper incentives by rewarding only what we can affect and not what is beyond our control.

With balanced job complexes, if Emma and Edward each work for eight hours at the same pace, they will receive the same income. This is so no matter what their particular job may be, no matter what workplaces they are in and how different their mix of tasks is, and no matter how talented they are, because if they work at a balanced job complex their total workload will be similar in its quality of life implications and empowerment effects. The only difference to reward people doing balanced jobs for will be length and intensity of work done. If these too are equal, the share of output earned will be equal. If length of time working or intensity of work differ somewhat, so will the share of output one earns.

And who makes decisions about the definition of job complexes and who evaluates the rates and intensities of people's work? Workers do, of course, in their councils, using information culled by methods consistent with the philosophy of balanced job complexes and just remuneration, and in a context appropriately influenced by the wills and desires of consumers.

There is one very large step left to the pareconist internationalist proposal for an alternative to capitalism. How are the actions of workers and consumers connected? How do we get the total produced by workplaces to match the total consumed collectively by neighborhoods and other groups as well as privately by individuals? For that matter, what determines the relative valuation of different products and choices? How do we decide how many workers will be in which industry producing how much? What influences whether some product should be made or not? What guides investments in new technologies in turn influencing what projects should be undertaken and which others delayed or rejected? These questions and others too numerous to mention in this introduction (but dealt with later in this book) are all matters of allocation.

Existing options for allocation are central planning as used in the old Soviet Union and competitive markets as used in all capitalist economies. In central planning a bureaucracy culls information, formulates instructions, sends these instructions to workers and consumers, gets feedback, refines the instructions a bit, sends them again, and receives back obedience. In a market each actor competitively buys and sells products, resources, and the ability to perform labor at prices determined by competitive bidding. Each actor seeks to gain more than those they exchange with.

The problem with each of these modes of connecting actors is that they impose on the economy pressures that subvert solidarity, equity, diversity, and self-management.

For example, even without capital ownership, markets favor private over public benefits and channel personalities in anti-social directions that diminish and even destroy solidarity. They reward output and power, not effort and sacrifice. They produce a disempowered class saddled with rote, obedient labor and an empowered class that accrues most income and determines economic outcomes. They force decision-makers to competitively ignore the wider ecological implications of their choices. Central planning, in contrast, denies self-management and produces the same class division and hierarchy as markets but instead built around the distinction between planners and those who implement their plans, extending from that foundation outward to incorporate empowered and disempowered workers more generally.

In short, both these allocation systems subvert instead of propel the values we hold dear. So what is our alternative to markets and central planning?

Suppose in place of top-down central planning and competitive market exchange, we opt for cooperative, informed decision-making via structures that ensure actors a say in decisions in proportion as outcomes affect them and that provide access to accurate valuations as well as appropriate training and confidence to develop and communicate preferences—that is, we opt for allocation that fosters council-centered participatory self-management, remuneration for effort and sacrifice, balanced job complexes, proper valuations of collective and ecological impacts, and classlessness.

To these ends, therefore, we advocate participatory planning—a system in which worker and consumer councils propose their work activities and consumer preferences in light of true valuations of the full social benefits and costs of their choices.

The system utilizes cooperative communication of mutually informed preferences via a variety of simple communicative and organizing principles and means including, as we will see in coming chapters, indicative prices, facilitation boards, and rounds of accommodation to new information—all permitting actors to express their desires and to mediate and refine them in light of feedback to arrive at choices consistent with their values.

The internationalist pareconist is in a position to answer "What do you want?" succinctly and compellingly, in an appetite-whetting presentation as above, or, of course, in more detail, explaining the logic of the claims, enriching the picture of daily life relations, and rebutting possible concerns—as in the rest of this book.

The summary is that workplace and consumer councils, diverse decision-making procedures that implement proportionate say for those affected, balanced job complexes, remuneration for effort and sacrifice, and participatory planning, together constitute core institutional scaffolding of a comprehensive alternative to capitalism and also to centrally planned or market socialism.

The ultimate answer to the claim that "there is no alternative" is to enact an alternative. In the short term, however, the answer is to offer a coherent, consistent, viable, economic vision able to generate hope, provide inspiration, reveal what is possible and valuable, and orient and democratize our strategies so that they might take us where we desire to go rather than running in circles or even heading toward something worse than that which we now endure. But are parecon's visionary aims rooted in practice undertaken around the world, or only mental constructs?

Parecon and Visionary Practice

In today's world large movements espousing similar aspirations struggle worldwide to better the lives of disenfranchised and abused populations around the globe. Some undertakings pressure elites to beneficially alter existing institutions. Other efforts seek to create new institutions to "live the future in the present." Some efforts are small and local. Some encompass whole geographic regions. If we look at a selection of visionary practices, we can see many features which have led to the reasoning presented in this book. Parecon doesn't float in space, that is, but arises from the aspirations and the insights of a huge range of activist efforts. Here are a few examples.

Historically almost every instance of working people and consumers even briefly attaining great control over their own conditions has incorporated both in locales and in workplaces institutions of direct organization and democracy. These have been called councils or assemblies, and given other names as well. Their common feature, however, has been providing a direct vehicle for people to develop, refine, express and implement personal and collective agendas. Both the successes of such endeavors, and also the undeniable fact that they have been repeatedly destroyed by counter forces, fuel and inform our advocacy of workplace and consumer councils in parecon and our efforts to conceive a context in which such councils can thrive rather than be thrashed.

Throughout the history of struggle against injustice there has also been great attention to matters of equity and specifically to the idea that people ought to enjoy life possibilities in a fair and appropriate manner. We should be able to earn a bit more or less by our choices, of course, but not for unworthy reasons. In times of upsurge and self-determination such as in Spain during the Spanish Anarchist struggles there, or earlier in the Paris Commune, and at many other moments as well from major national strikes in the West to movements for freedom in the East and South, seekers of economic justice have realized that there is something horribly wrong with remunerating those who enjoy more fulfilling work and who have more say in social life more than those who do more rote and damaging work and have less say in social life. Parecon's priority to remunerate only effort and sacrifice arises from these aspirations and also gives them more precise substance than they have previously enjoyed.

But what about instances from the present? Is parecon connected to current exploratory and innovative economic efforts?

Consider collective workplace experiments around the world, including co-ops, worker-owned plants, and collective workplaces. Workers gain control over their factories, perhaps buying them rather than having capitalists close them down entirely, or perhaps originating new enterprises of their own from scratch. The newly in-charge workers attempt to incorporate democracy. They try to redefine the division of labor. They seek narrower income differentials. But the market environment in which they operate makes all this horribly difficult. By their experiences of such difficulties, workers' and consumers' efforts at creating worker-controlled enterprises and consumer co-ops provide extensive experience relevant to the definition of parecon. Not only co-op successes, but also their difficulties—such as tendencies for old-style job definitions to reimpose widening income differentials and tendencies for market imposed behaviors to subvert cooperative aims and values—teach important lessons. Indeed, in my own experience, the effort to create the radical publishing house South End Press and to incorporate equity and self-management in its logic and practice powerfully informed many of the insights that together define participatory economics, particularly the idea and practice of balanced job complexes. Likewise, a number of on-going current experiments in implementing parecon structures continue to inform the vision and its various features.

On a grander scale, consider the movement for what is called "solidarity economics" that has advocates in many parts of South America (and particularly Brazil), Europe, and elsewhere. Its defining idea is that economic relations should foster solidarity among participants rather than causing participants to operate against one another's interests. Not only should economic life not divide and oppose people, it should not even be neutral on this score but should generate mutuality and empathy. Advocates of solidarity economics thus pursue ideas of local worker's control and of allocative exchange with this norm in mind. Parecon takes their insight that institutions should propel values we hold dear and extends it in additional directions. We want a solidarity economy in the same sense as its advocates do. But we also want a diversity economy, an equity economy, and a self-managing economy. Indeed we want one economy that fulfills all these aspirations simultaneously. Parecon thus arises from, respects, and seeks to provide additional dimensions to solidarity economics.

Or consider the efforts, some years back, in Australia of labor unions to influence not only the conditions and wages of their members' work lives, but also what people produced. They developed the idea of "Green Bans" which were instances where workers in building trades would ban certain proposed projects on the grounds they were socially or environmentally unworthy. Sometimes they would not only ban the proposed endeavors that capitalists sought to undertake, but would also undertake alternative projects of their own design intended to treat environment and people appropriately. This experience of course foreshadows and informs both parecon's norms for deciding work and its apportionment of power to affected constituencies. Parecon extends the logic of Australia's Green Bans into a full economic vision for all facets of economic life.

Or consider the efforts in Porto Alegre and other Brazilian cities and in Kerala and other regions of India to incorporate elements of participatory democracy into budget decisions for cities and regions. Indeed, in Brazil this project is named " participative budgeting" and the idea is to establish means of local direct organization via which citizens can affect decisions about collective investments regard- ing government services such as parks, education, public transport, and health care. Parecon's participatory planning has the same aspirations and impetus, but writ larger, encompassing not only public goods but all goods, and facilitating not only proportionate participation by consumers, but also by workers.

Indeed, for all the examples noted above and many more as well, advocates of participatory economics could be expected, once organized in sufficiently large movements, to pursue similar struggles—the only difference being the way pareconists would explain their actions as being part of a process leading to a whole new economy they would advocate, and perhaps how they would try to create new infrastructure and consciousness by not only fostering the immediate aims, but by also empowering participants to win still more gains in a trajectory leading all the way from capitalism to parecon. Pareconist workers' control efforts would seek to attain allocation gains as well, plus new divisions of labor. Pareconist attempts to institute "participatory budgets" would seek as well to address norms of remuneration and job allocation and to engender participation not only in communities regarding public goods, but also in workplaces regarding all goods. Pareconist union and workers councils would seek to affect not only the conditions and circumstances of members' jobs, but also the worthiness of undertaken projects, and would likewise try to link with consumer movements and spread the efforts to government sectors and consumer behavior.

In other words, the participatory economic vision put forth in coming chapters not only springs from and is consistent with past and present struggles to better people's immediate lives in diverse ways, it also offers encompassing values and logic to link all these efforts and to enlarge each consistent with its own best aspirations but also with the logic and aspirations of others beyond.

And what about the newest and certainly very promising World Social Forum? Here is a remarkable amalgamation of movements, constituencies, activists, and projects from all over the globe linked by an open and experimental attitude, a commitment to participation, feelings of mutual respect, and attention to diversity and democracy, all celebrating the sentiment that "another world is possible." In 2002, at its second incarnation, roughly 50,000 participants began to enunciate features that that better world might have. The most widely shared sentiments were rejection of markets and support for self-management, rejection of vast differentials in income and support for equity, rejection of homogenizing commercialism and support for diversity, rejection of imperial arrogance and support for solidarity, and rejection of ecological devastation and support for sustainability. No doubt WSF 2003 will have taken this agenda many steps further by the time this book appears. And like the WSF, parecon contributes visionary economic ideas in hopes that political, cultural, kinship, global, and ecological visionary aims will prove compatible and mutually supportive.

Participatory economics provides a new economic logic including new institutions with new guiding norms and implications. But parecon is also a direct and natural outgrowth of hundreds of years of struggle for economic justice as well as contemporary efforts with their accumulated wisdom and lessons. What parecon can contribute to this heritage and to today's activism will be revealed, one way or the other, in coming years.

Part I
Values and Institutions

The Devil can quote Shakespeare for his own purpose.
—G.B. Shaw

The civilized have created the wretched, quite coldly and deliberately, and do not intend to change the status quo; are responsible for their slaughter and enslavement; rain down bombs on defenseless children whenever and wherever they decide that their "vital interests" are menaced, and think nothing of torturing a man to death: these people are not to be taken seriously when they speak of the "sanctity" of human life, or the "conscience" of the civilized world.
— James Baldwin

The task of developing an economic vision begins with determining what an economy is, determining what values we aspire to, and deciding what our attitude is to existing options that we could retain. While we don't wish to belabor this type of preparatory work, nor can we rush ahead to vision without any preparation at all. Thus our first three chapters, constituting part I, clear the way for what follows.

1
What Is An Economy?

He tried to read an elementary economics text; it bored him past endurance, it was like listening to somebody interminably recounting a long and stupid dream. He could not force himself to understand how banks functioned and so forth, because all the operations of capitalism were as meaningless to him as the rites of a primitive religion, as barbaric, as elaborate, and as unnecessary. In a human sacrifice to deity there might at least be a mistaken and terrible beauty; in the rites of the money-changers, where greed, laziness, and envy were assumed to move all men's acts, even the terrible became banal.
—Ursula K. Le Guin

In the dictionary an economy is a "system of producing, distributing, and consuming wealth." A typical modern economy thus produces wheat and milk, guitars and garden hoses, medical care and restaurant meals. This activity needs labor, natural resources, and intermediate goods in useful ratios. We can produce no houses without wood, wires, saws, and builders. We can produce no guitars without guitar string, proper tools, and artisans. Work occurs in factories, hospitals, and on farms and is done by assemblers, surgeons, bakers, sweepers, nurses, accountants, and custodians. Depending which type of laborer we are, we do different tasks, shoulder different responsibilities, receive different rewards, and make different decisions or follow different orders.

Sensible production needs its products used. We don't want to assemble too many or too few items of any kind. We don't want a hundred guitars at the hardware store or a hundred garden hoses at the music store, nor do we want to produce more or less of either than people desire to consume. Allocation is the name for the process and the institutions that determine who produces how much, what rates it exchanges for, and where it winds up. From the multitudinous choices an economy could technically implement, allocation chooses what actually occurs. Instead of 30 or 140,000 radios, the economy produces 72,000. Instead of all the radios going to a single Radio Shack, they disperse appropriately around the society. The same goes for food, clothes, televisions, toothpaste, rubber, transistors, screws and nails, and finally for workers themselves. Allocation synchronizes production and consumption, work and leisure.

Once products arrive where intended, they must be utilized. A garden hose or guitar is valueless if no one uses it. Individuals and sometimes families, neighborhoods, counties, or other collective units consume or otherwise make use of what has been produced and allocated.

In short, production, allocation, and consumption define every economy. Each aspect provides the reason for and informs the practice of the other two. It follows, as we will see, that an economy should produce, allocate, and consume in ways that further people's values, that meet people's needs, and that do not waste people's energies or create unfavorable by-products.

Key Economic Dynamics and Institutions

To parsimoniously understand diverse economies, what dynamics should we highlight? To comprehend main features but avoid minor details, what aspects should we prioritize?

Ownership Relations

Production occurs in workplaces that utilize hammers and assembly lines, filing cabinets and computer networks. Private individuals may own these means of production and distribution. The state may own them. The whole populace could own an equal share of all means of production. Or, for that matter, a society could have no concept of ownership of productive property at all.

In contemporary economies, a few lucky property holders come into the world to lead lives drenched in continually regenerated opulence. Millions of working people come into the same world only to wonder how they will afford another week's subsistence. An economy's ownership relations dramatically affect people's incomes, economic responsibilities, and say over economic outcomes. Why are the propertied born already rounding third base headed for home with no catcher trying to tag them out? Why are so many others born standing at home plate, holding a matchstick bat, facing the world's best pitcher, two strikes against them, resigned to failure?

Allocation Institutions

Allocation exists in all economic systems and the institutions which accomplish allocation have a profound impact on all economic life. Allocation institutions include competitive markets, central planning, and horizontal planning. Within markets buyers and sellers enact decentralized exchanges with one another. Each pursues personal interests and the sum of their separate efforts define the economy's overall activity. With central planning a relatively few planners assess society's possibilities and announce the amount of each product to produce and where everything should wind up. Their instructions sum to society's overall activity. With participatory planning all society's members assess their own and others' situations and cooperatively negotiate via their worker and consumer councils their individual and joint actions. Their deliberations and negotiations sum to society's undertakings.

Division of Labor

Economies have divisions of labor. Each person does a job that conveys to him or her different responsibilities and different decision-making influence. The extreme possibilities for dividing labor into jobs are twofold: We can opt for typical hierarchical arrangements that include highly differential access to empowering and quality of life work circumstances, or we can opt to provide people with equally empowering and enjoyable work.

With the hierarchical approach, a person becomes a secretary or a Company Chairperson, a janitor or a doctor, a manager or an assembly-line worker, and undertakes responsibilities pegged at a particular level of skill, knowledge, quality of life impact, and influence over outcomes. One actor may have no say over any outcomes, while another has some modest say over a few outcomes, and a third has immense say over many outcomes.

With the contrasting non-hierarchical approach, we have no secretaries or CEOs. Each person has a complex of tasks unique in its details but nonetheless comparable to every other person's regarding its quality of life and empowerment effects. We each do some rote and some creative work, some mechanical and some conceptual work. The mix gives us a fair share of burdensome and fulfilling and/or boring and empowering tasks. While with the existing corporate division of labor some workers have a preponderance of more pleasant, uplifting, and empowering work, and other workers have a preponderance of more boring, dangerous, and stultifying work, with the proposed balanced job complexes we would all have jobs embodying an average quality of life and empowerment effect. We would each do our own different tasks, but the empowerment and quality of life effects of each of our jobs would be just like those of everyone else's. The upshot is simple. Along with the British philosopher and economist Adam Smith (1723-1790), who penned *The Wealth of Nations* in 1776, we believe that:

> The understandings of the greater part of men are necessarily formed by their ordinary employments .... the [person] whose life is spent in performing a few simple operations, of which the effects too are, perhaps, always the same, or very nearly the same, has no occasion to exert his/her understanding .... and [is] generally [pushed to] become as stupid and ignorant as it is possible for a human creature to be.

Smith understood that a person would do different things and have different circumstances at work depending on whether he or she was a secretary, assembly worker, manager, or owner, and that these differences would profoundly affect life prospects. And we agree. The division of labor matters greatly.

Remuneration

The dictionary says "remunerate" means "to compensate for; make payment for." Remuneration norms and procedures determine what goods and services people can afford from the whole social output. Some people are remunerated a pittance for their labors, such as the man or woman who cooked the flapjacks you ate for breakfast in the local diner, or who cleaned rooms in the local motel. Some people are remunerated a huge ransom such as Michael Jordan or a surgeon or prominent lawyer. Some are remunerated not only for their own labors but also for the labors of others—sometimes the labors of thousands or even tens of thousands of others, such as Warren Buffet and his comrades in capital.

Economic remuneration can occur according to five broad standards. We can pay people for:

- What each person's property produces, or total output

- What each person herself produces, or personal output

- What each person is strong enough to take, or bargaining power

- What each person expends and the sacrifices each person makes, or effort and sacrifice

- What meets each person's needs, regardless of activities

Depending which remuneration norms an economy employs and the exact mechanics of their implementation, who gets more and who gets less will differ, as will people's behaviors and thus their evolving motivations and personalities. Remuneration matters.

Decision-Making

Who or what establishes how work is organized, how long we labor, what goods are available, and at what rates goods exchange? Where does power over economic outcomes reside? What logic justifies existing or alternative distributions of power? What mechanics propel the enactment of particular power relations? How does the distribution of economic power affect people's life prospects? Why do some people rule while others obey and are any other relations possible? Many approaches exist for economic decision-making:

- Economic decision-making can give the most say to those best prepared, most informed, and with the most prior experience or best prior decision-making record.

- Economic decision-making can disperse power among diverse actors and agents according to various but still differentially distributed criteria. For example, people who own property might be given disposition over it because they hold the deed regardless of any past experience.

- Economic decision-making can accord more or less say to people depending on whether their jobs give them more or less control over critical decision-making information.

- Economic decision-making can be determined by a specific singular norm, such as that one actor gets one vote and majority rules or a consensus approach.

- Economic decision-making can be guided by a flexible range of norms so that decisions are made differently depending on each decision's specific nature and likely implications.

- And of course, economic decision-making can combine more than one of these norms—for example, an economy can have a democratic or even participatory norm for decision-making among those who own property or who have elite and empowering jobs, while at the same time completely excluding from decision-making those who don't own property and have rote and disempowering jobs.

At any rate, to carry out one or another norm or combination of decision-making norms, an economy will have associated institutions and institutional relations which will themselves bear strongly on the kinds of information each actor has at their disposal, the leverage each actor has over outcomes, each actor's participation in choices, and each actor's subservience to the choices other actors make. So of course the logic and structures of economic decision-making matter.

Economies

If we examine all modern approaches to issues of ownership, allocation, division of labor, remuneration, and decision-making, we can group economies usefully into some broad types that flexibly summarize their essential similarities and properties.

- *Capitalism* has private ownership, market allocation, corporate divisions of labor, remuneration for property, power, and output, and capitalist class domination of decision-making.

- The two *socialisms* (market and centrally planned), have public or state ownership, market and/or central planning allocation, corporate divisions of labor, remuneration for output and/or power, and ruling coordinator-class domination of decision-making.

- *Bioregionalism*, the goal of some environmental activists, has public ownership, decentralized exchange via face-to-face allocation, and mostly cooperative divisions of labor, plus a lack of clear definition of other features (at least in so far as we have been able to discover).

- *Participatory economics* as proposed in this book combines social ownership, participatory planning allocation, council structure, balanced job complexes, remuneration for effort and sacrifice, and participatory self-management with no class differentiation.

Note that any two instances of one type of economy can differ greatly. Variations can occur in everything from their level of development, to population, to available resources, to specific structures (like a special banking system), to the distribution of power among competing classes or other sectors, to features that derive from a racist or sexist history or special political forms. Thus capitalism takes on different features in the US than it did in the old Sweden, the old South Africa, and currently in Haiti. Market socialism can also differ in its implementation, as we have seen in the old Yugoslavia and old Hungary. Centrally planned socialism is different in Cuba than it was in the old Soviet Union. Green bioregionalism and participatory economics are as yet unimplemented in history, but they can also of course have different features in different instances.

However, despite the possibility of diverse instances any instance of any single type of economy will retain the defining features of that type. To understand the broad properties of capitalist, market socialist, centrally planned socialist, bioregionalist, and participatory economies will therefore tell us much about any particular instance of any of these, even without knowing all that country's secondary features.

Class Structure

Another way to look at types of economies is by how their institutions broadly divide people into opposed groups. Of course in any economy there will be differences in the precise circumstances that any two economic actors have regarding the economy's institutions. You have one job; I have another. You work with those tools; I work with these tools. You have such and such income; I have so and so income. Yet within the spectrum of endlessly different precise circumstances allotted to each and every actor, economic institutions may also differentiate people into relatively large constituencies all of whose members share certain critical circumstances different from those shared by other large constituencies. Regarding the economy, we call such different constituencies classes, where a class is a group of people who by the positions they occupy vis-à-vis production, allocation, and consumption have sufficiently similar circumstances, material interests, and motivations for us to usefully talk about their group conditions and group tendencies as opposed to the group conditions and group tendencies of other classes who in turn share different circumstances, interests, and motivations.

Of course not everyone in an economic class has the exact same situation or inclinations as everyone else in that class. Bricklayers go to different workplaces than waiters do. Pharmaceutical capitalists own different property than automotive capitalists. Still, the point of class analysis is that the circumstances and conditions that everyone in a class have in common are great enough and their implications for people's behaviors are important enough that it is useful to highlight the class collectively in trying to understand the overall dynamics of the economy.

So what divides people into classes? As every economist agrees, having fundamentally different ownership relations certainly divides people into different classes. History shows that ownership dramatically affects one's claims on social product, one's impact on economic decisions, and one's interests and motives. Thus, in a capitalist society the conditions shared by all who own some means of production—whether pharmaceutical, automotive, or computer companies—give capitalists sufficiently similar circumstances and motivations for us to usefully talk about their collective (profit-seeking) behavior. It was owning some means of production that made the Rockefellers capitalists and it is the shared (profit-seeking) motives that ownership induces in capitalists that caused Adam Smith to write that "people of the same trade seldom meet together, even for merriment and diversion, but the conversation ends in a conspiracy against the public, or in some contrivance to raise prices."

Yet despite its importance, ownership is not the sole possible basis for class division. Instead, an economy's division of labor or the role implications of its allocation institutions could also lead to some people sharing conditions systematically different than those shared by others, even with the same ownership situation.

In capitalism, virtually every serious analyst calls those who own the means of production "capitalists" and those who own nothing but their ability to work and who must sell that ability for a wage paid to them for doing a rote and subservient job, "workers." But in going beyond property as a basis for class division, we can also identify a "coordinator class" composed of those who receive a wage for their labors but who, unlike workers, do jobs that have considerable influence over their own and other people's economic situations and who retain their more empowering jobs largely due to monopolizing certain skills and knowledge. And we can note that the class of workers such as assemblers, waiters, truckers, and janitors, and the class of coordinators such as managers, doctors, lawyers, and engineers, regard one another with opposed interests. And that each also opposes capitalists, though in different ways.

So, What Is An Economy?

We have argued that:

1 An economy is a set of institutions concerned with production, allocation, and consumption, and including identifiable divisions of labor, norms of remuneration, methods of allocation, and means of decision-making.

2 Key features are public or private ownership relations; hierarchical or balanced divisions of labor; markets, central, or horizontal planning; and elite or democratic decision-making; each of which can differentiate economic actors into classes whose circumstances give each class shared material interests, assets, and behaviors, opposed to those of other classes.

3 Different broad types of economies include capitalism, market socialism, centrally planned socialism, bioregionalism, and what we call participatory economics. While specific instances of each type can have widely varying development, population, political, family, cultural, and other institutions, among other variable characteristics, within any one economic type all instances will at least share the same broad centrally defining economic institutions and derivative class structure.

4 To study an economic type one should determine its core component institutions and their impact on divisions of labor, modes of remuneration, and distribution of influence over outcomes, and on how all these affect different economic classes.

5 And finally, to judge a type of economy one should ask how its features and aspects impact on human outcomes and prospects and whether we like the impacts or not.

2

Economic Values

There is nothing so absurd that it has not been said by philosophers.
—Cicero

True compassion is more than flinging a coin at a beggar;
it comes to see that an edifice that produces beggars needs restructuring.
— Martin Luther King Jr.

We know that an economy needs to produce, allocate, and consume as people wish. But whose wishes matter? What opportunities to express their wishes should people have? How do people produce, allocate, and consume, and with what impact on their life prospects? What are our preferred values regarding economic outcomes and how do particular economic institutions further or inhibit them?

When examining and evaluating economic systems, there are four main questions about values we must address:

1   Equity: How much should people get and why?

2   Self-management: What kind of say over their conditions should people have?

3   Diversity: Should paths to fulfillment be diversified or narrowed?

4   Solidarity: Should people cooperate or compete?

Our first step in envisioning a new economy is to address these four areas of concern.

Equity

Nearly everyone favors "equity." But controversy arises because different people mean different things by the term. We want fair income and fair situations, but fair in what way?

Equity 1: Income

Regarding income, four distributive norms summarize available options for how people should be compensated for economic activity:

- Norm 1: Remunerate according to the contribution of each person's physical and human assets.

- Norm 2: Remunerate according to the contribution of each person's human assets only.

- Norm 3: Remunerate according to each person's effort or personal sacrifice.

- Norm 4: Remunerate according to each person's need.

Of course, historically the most frequently actualized norm is that people should get what they are strong enough to take, but virtually no one morally advocates brute force bargaining power as our preferred criterion for payment. No one thinks this common approach is ethically superior. No one thinks it is efficient. The idea that society should enrich the thug for being thuggish, though it is typically the rule that markets and many other systems impose, is no one's stated ideal. For that reason it doesn't require treatment in a book about economic vision. So, paying attention only to the four norms that people do advocate, let's first consider norm one.

The rationale for rewarding people for the contribution that their private capital makes to output is that people should get out of an economy what they and their productive possessions contribute. If we think of economic goods and services as a giant pot of stew, the idea is that individuals contribute to how plentiful and rich the stew will be by their labor and by the non-human productive assets they bring to the kitchen. If my labor and productive assets make the stew bigger or richer than your labor and productive assets make it, then according to norm one, it is only fair that I eat more or more delectable morsels than you eat. Since I brought greater assets to the kitchen, I deserve greater reward. You own a hoe and I own a tractor. This makes me more productive than you and enables me to make a greater contribution to society's total food output. It is only fair, therefore, that I be better remunerated than you.

Though this rationale has intuitive appeal to many, norm one's advocates have the "Rockefeller's grandson problem" to deal with. According to norm one, the grandson of a Rockefeller should eat 1,000 times as much stew as a highly trained, highly productive, hard-working daughter of a pauper. And this is warranted, says norm one, even if Rockefeller's grandson doesn't work a day in his life and the pauper's daughter works for fifty years providing services of great benefit to others. The grandson has inherited property that "works" for him since he "brings it to the kitchen" and by norm one we credit the contribution of productive property to its owners. Bringing a tractor or 100 acres of Mississippi bottom land to the economy increases the size and quality of the stew we can make just as surely as having another person to dig or peel potatoes does—only more so. Therefore, if we inherit a tractor or land, then along with this inheritance comes a stream of income that we need do nothing whatever to "earn." On the other hand, the fact that we have done nothing whatever to earn it makes it self-evident that we don't deserve it morally due to some meritorious action on our part. There must be some other explanation than our being "morally deserving" for why we ought to have it.

And, indeed, a second line of defense for norm one is based on a vision of "free and independent" people, each with their own property, who, it is argued, would refuse to voluntarily enter a social contract on any other terms than benefitting from that property's output. We need norm one, in this view, if these people are to freely participate in the economy. But while those who have a great deal of productive property would have a good reason to hold out for a social contract rewarding them for their property, why wouldn't those who have little or no property have a good reason to hold out for a different arrangement that doesn't penalize them for not owning property? And if this is true, then how come those with property get the norm they want, and those without property do not?

The historical difference is that those with property could do quite well for themselves (including buying enforcement of their wills via legislation) while waiting for agreements to be reached, whereas those without property could not avoid catastrophe if they had to wait long for an agreement. Requiring unanimity of all parties drives the bargain to favor the propertied. The unemployed eventually have to give in and seek work even under the conditions that profits will go entirely to owners. To do otherwise leaves them destitute. But that means norm one is established not due to moral desirability, but because of an unfair bargaining situation in which some are better able than others to tolerate failure to reach an equitable agreement (and therefore better able to coerce submission and defend their holdings). Thus, the social contract rationale for earning on property loses all ethical force and has its weight only due to contingent, unbalanced circumstances.

This analysis is nothing new, by the way, though it isn't meant to be publicly discussed by those without property. Consider, for example, Adam Smith's pithy formulation that "It is only under the shelter of the civil magistrate that the owner of valuable property ...

can sleep a single night in security." Or consider this old anonymous aphorism: "The Law locks up the hapless felon who steals the goose from off the common, but lets the greater felon loose who steals the common from the goose."

A related insight is that unless those who have more productive property acquired it through personal sacrifice, the income they receive from owning the property is unjustifiable on equity grounds. Basing income on private property is not equitable and must be rejected if we determine that those who own more productive property did not come to it through greater personal sacrifice. Pursuing this line of assessment in tune with the views of the advocates of norm one, we must now ask how property is acquired?

Acquisition of productive property through inheritance obviously entails no sacrifice by the heir. Consequently, we deny the would-be heir nothing that she has a moral claim to if we prohibit inheritance of productive property. But what about the rights of members of the older generation who wish to bequeath productive property to their progeny? Suppose (against all odds) that those who wish to make bequests came by their productive property in a manner consistent with a worthy conception of economic justice. That is, suppose they sacrificed more than others by working longer or harder, and rather than eating prodigious portions of caviar in the twilight of their lives, they prefer to pass on their hard-earned productive assets to their children or grandchildren. To deny them the right to do so would seem an unwarranted violation of their personal freedom to dispose of their legitimate rights to economic benefits as they wish. It certainly does interfere with this right.

But what about the right of members of the younger generation to equal economic opportunities? If we permit inheritance of productive assets, some young people will start out with advantages and others will be debited—all due to no failures of their own—a disparity that could grow from generation to generation. If members of an older generation when exercising their freedom of consumption have the right to pass along productive property, then they will have created for a younger generation unequal economic opportunities that violate the rights of the latter. On the other hand, if members of the younger generation are to be protected from this inequitable result, their elders must be precluded from dispersing their assets as they choose—a result that also seems unfair.

What do we choose? The right to bequeath means of production should be denied because the right for all generations to equal economic opportunity far outweighs the right of some of the members of one generation to bequeath income-generating wealth to their offspring. While some freedom of consumption for the older generation to acquire property and pass it on is certainly sacrificed by outlawing the inheritance of productive property, doing so is necessary to protect a more fundamental freedom of the younger generation to equal economic opportunities. More generally, con-freedoms of this sort are common in economics and other aspects of society as well, and rather than settling such conflicts by abstractly awarding a property right to one party or the other, thereby elevating the notion of property as the arbiter of difference, the goal should be to give every actor decision-making input in proportion to the degree that person is affected by the outcome, thereby elevating true democracy as the arbiter of difference. In other words, economic self-management—defined as having decision-making influence in proportion to the degree that one is affected—is a far superior norm than that of economic freedom based on the right to do whatever one chooses with one's property.

In these terms, since the younger generation would be much more seriously affected by unequal economic opportunities than the older generation would be affected by limiting their freedom to pass on productive property, it is justifiable to limit inheritance rights. While the conflict between freedom of consumption for an older generation to bequeath their property and the right to an equal economic opportunity of a younger generation is only one of many conflicting freedoms in capitalist economies, it is a particularly important one. Awarding the property right in favor of inheritance is a particularly egregious violation of the principle of economic self-management since it permits those who are little affected (the ones making bequests) to greatly affect the lives of many others. These others, as a result, must start their economic lives with serious handicaps relative to a few of their privileged peers.

A second way—beyond actually sweating for it—that people in capitalism acquire more productive property than others, is through good luck. Working or investing in a rising or declining company or industry involves good or bad luck. Pursuing some line of industry and benefitting from ancillary activities of others or from changing global or domestic boom or bust dynamics involves good luck. Distributions of productive property that result from luck hardly reward sacrifices on people's part. There is therefore no moral justification on their behalf, obviously.

A third way that people come to have more productive property is through unfair advantages such as differences in circumstances and human characteristics. For example, arbitrary factors could allow you to accumulate more productive assets than I because you have information that I do not have, or you operate in a town or country enjoying advantages that my locale doesn't enjoy. Arbitrary differences in human characteristics could mean that you have greater innate intelligence, strength, or dexterity than I do, all through no fault of mine and due to no greater effort or sacrifice on your part, and these could lead to your acquiring more property. And though these differences may seem unlikely to be too large, even slight initial inequalities in ownership of productive property will grow aggres- sively more unequal in economies where owners are paid for the contributions of their property. The initial advantage enlarges itself, providing the means to acquire still greater property. If the initial difference is unjust, still greater differences that result from ensuing accumulation are unjust as well.

But what if some people accumulate more because they work longer or harder than others? Or, what if some people consume less to accumulate more productive property? Most who argue for norm one as equitable would have us believe that this is how inequalities in the ownership of productive property usually arise. And, indeed, if someone accumulated more productive property through more work or less consumption in the past, then greater consumption (or leisure) commensurate with the greater past sacrifice is warranted. But this conclusion is a direct application of norm three—to each according to his or her effort or sacrifice—as long as "commensurate" compensation is the quantity required to compensate for greater past sacrifices, thereby making everyone's burdens and benefits fair over time. It does not justify norm one, with its implications of remunerating for property even when it exceeds what effort and sacrifice warrant.

Most political economists accept that in capitalist economies the differences in ownership of productive property that accumulate within a single generation due to unequal sacrifices are minuscule compared to the differences in wealth that develop due to inheritance, luck, unfair advantage, and profit-making. That was what Proudhon meant when he coined the phrase "property is theft." All evidence about the origins of differential wealth at the end of the twentieth century support the opinion Edward Bellamy voiced (in 1888) in his famous book *Looking Backward*:

> You may set it down as a rule that the rich, the possessors of great wealth, had no moral right to it as based upon desert, for

> either their fortunes belonged to the class of inherited wealth, or else, when accumulated in a lifetime, necessarily represented chiefly the product of others, more or less forcibly or fraudulently obtained.

A turn of the twenty-first century TV ad for the brokerage house Salomon, Smith, & Barney provides a delicious example of ethical doublespeak about property income. A man of obvious taste devoutly informs us that the brokers at Salomon, Smith & Barney believe in "making money the old-fashioned way, earning it." What he means, of course, is that brokers discourage clients from the temptation of high-gain, high-risk strategies, and recommend instead expanding wealth more slowly but with greater certainty— precisely without earning a penny of it. As Ricardo noted: "There is no way of keeping profits up but by keeping wages down." And in the typically pithy words of Groucho Marx: "The secret of success is honesty and fair dealing. If you can fake those, you've got it made."

Norm two for remuneration is less straightforward to assess than norm one: Why not reward each according to the value of the contribution of only our human capital, that is, of only what we ourselves through our own efforts bring to the kitchen? While supporters of norm two generally agree with the case made above that property income is unjustifiable, they hold that we all have a right to the "fruits of our own labor." Their rationale for this is at first review quite compelling. If my labor contributes more to the social endeavor, it is only right that I should receive more. Not only am I not exploiting others if I get more, but since I put the extra amount in the pot myself, they would be exploiting me by paying me less than the value of my personal contribution.

But the obviousness of the claim is a function of its familiarity and not of hard thinking about it. Careful thought shows we must reject norm two—rewarding personal output—for the same basic reasons we reject norm one—rewarding ownership of means of production.

Economists define the value of the contribution of any input (whether labor or machines or some resources) as the "marginal revenue product" of that input. If we add one more unit of the input in question to all of the other inputs currently used in a production process, how much would the value of output increase? That amount is the marginal revenue product. But this means the marginal productivity, or the contribution any input makes, depends as much on the quantity of that input available and on the quantity and quality of complementary inputs, as on any intrinsic quality of the input itself. In other words, the amount that my extra hour of labor can add to output depends on how many prior hours I work, and also on how many other hours others are putting in, and on the quality of their contributions, and on the tools we all use, and on the items we produce and their attributes, and so on. This fact alone undermines the moral imperative behind any "contribution based" norm, such as both norm two and norm one.

To reward differences in the value of personal contributions as norm two warrants is to reward differences due to circumstantial and personal factors beyond any individual's control. When young people flock to the profession that you have labored in for twenty years, your marginal revenue product declines although you may work as hard as ever. When your employer fails to replace machines that other employers upgrade, your marginal productivity suffers even despite there being no decrease in your efforts.

Suppose we set aside or somehow account for the fact that the marginal productivity of different kinds of labor depends on the number of other people in each labor category and on the quantity and quality of non-labor inputs available as well as on technological knowledge. The "genetic lottery" constitutes another circumstance largely outside an individual's control that can greatly influence how valuable one's personal contribution will be. No amount of eating and weightlifting will give me a 6-foot-9-inch frame with 300 pounds of muscle so that I can "earn" the salary of a professional football player 50 times greater than the salary I "earn" now. The noted English economist Joan Robinson (1903-1983) pointed out long ago that however "productive" a machine or piece of land may be, that doesn't constitute a moral argument for paying anything to its owner. And we need only extend this insight to individual human characteristics to realize that however productive an IQ of 170 or a 300-pound physique may be, that doesn't mean the owner of this trait deserves more income than someone less productively endowed who works as hard and sacrifices as much.

Luck in external circumstance and in the genetic lottery are no better basis for remuneration than luck in the property inheritance lottery—which implies that as a conception of equity, norm two suffers from the same flaw as norm one. If a person has the fine fortune to have genes that give her an advantage for producing things of merit, or if she is lucky as regards her field of work, there is no reason on top of this good luck to provide her with an exorbitant income as well.

In defense of norm two, its advocates frequently claim that while talent may not morally deserve reward, employing talents requires training, and therein lies the sacrifice that merits a reward. Doctors' salaries are deemed compensation not for some innate capability the doctor has, but for the extra education they endure. But longer training does not necessarily entail greater personal sacrifice. It is important not to confuse the cost of someone's training—which consists mostly of the time and energy of teachers who impart the training and of scarce social resources like books, computers, libraries, and classrooms—with personal sacrifice by the trainee. If teachers and educational facilities are paid for as a public and not private expense—that is, if we have a universal public education system—then the personal sacrifice the student makes consists only of his or her discomfort during the time spent in school.

Moreover, even the personal suffering that one endures as a student must be properly compared. While many educational programs are less personally enjoyable than time spent in leisure, the relevant comparison is with the discomfort that others experience who are working at paid jobs instead of going to school. If our criterion for extra remuneration is enduring greater personal sacrifice than others, then logic requires that we compare the medical student's discomfort to whatever level of discomfort others are experiencing who work while the medical student is in school.

In short, would you rather be in medical school or slinging hash? Only if schooling is more disagreeable than working does it constitute a greater sacrifice than others make and thereby deserve greater reward, and the additional reward it would then deserve would be commensurate to that difference, but not more.

So to the extent that education is born at public rather than private expense, and that the personal discomfort of schooling is no greater than the discomfort that would be incurred by working instead during the same time frame, extra schooling merits no extra compensation on moral grounds. And if one pays for one's education, then that marks the reward warranted, and no more. And if one's education is onerous and demanding compared to working, that difference marks the extra compensation warranted, and no more.

The problem with the "I had to endure school so long" justification of norm two is the "doctor versus garbage collector problem." How can it be fair to pay a brain surgeon, even in the unlikely event he puts in longer hours than most other workers, ten times more than a garbage collector who works under miserable conditions forty or fifty hours a week? Even if medical school is costly, and in fact even if it is more debilitating and harder than collecting garbage during the same time (which is a ridiculous claim), surely it would warrant far less than a lifetime of much higher pay to compensate the doctor for that temporary sacrifice, particularly since the subsequent job—brain surgery—has exceptional social and moral rewards of its own. The moral basis of norm two collapses.

So what about norm three—remunerate according to each person's effort or personal sacrifice? Whereas differences in contributions from people's labor will derive from differences in circumstance, talent, training, luck, and effort, of all these factors people control only their effort. To reward and punish people for things they cannot control violates the same basic tenet of social justice that says it is unfair to pay differently according to race or sex, for example. By "effort" we simply mean personal sacrifice or inconvenience incurred in performing one's economic duties. Of course effort can be longer hours, less pleasant work, or more intense, dangerous, or unhealthy work. Or, it may consist of undergoing training that is less gratifying than the training experience of others, or less pleasant than the time others spend working. The underlying rationale for norm three is that people should eat from the stew pot according to the sacrifices they made to cook it. According to norm three no consideration other than differential sacrifice in useful production can justify one able-bodied person eating more or better stew than another.

Even for those who reject contribution-based theories of economic justice like norms one and two, there is still a problem with norm three: the "car crash problem." Suppose someone has made average sacrifices for 15 years, and consumed an average amount. She is hit by a car. Medical treatment for crash victims can cost a fortune. If we limit people's consumption to the level warranted by the effort they expend, we would have to deny hurt or sick people humane treatment (and/or income while they can't work).

Of course this is where another norm comes in, norm four: payment according to need. But as attractive as norm four is, it is a norm in a different category from the other three. It is not really a candidate for a definition of economic justice. Instead, it expresses a value beyond equity or justice that we aspire to and implement when possible and desirable. It is one thing for an economy to be equitable, fair, and just. It is another thing for an economy to be compassionate. A just economy is not the last word in morally desirable economics. Besides striving for economic justice, we desire compassion as well. Thus we have our equity value, norm three, and beyond economic justice, we have our compassion, to be applied via norm four where appropriate such as in cases of illness, catastrophe, incapacity, and so on. And those are our aspirations for income.

Of course we know that it won't be worthwhile to attain equity of income and even compassionate humanity about income, if in doing so the total productive output plummets or other nasty side effects cost us considerably in our broader lives. But that is a matter that we address when we assess whether we can institutionally implement our norms for economic reward in ways consistent with other values we hold dear. We shall investigate that as we proceed. First, there is another dimension of equity to consider.

Equity 2: Circumstances

Why should one person have an economic condition at work that is fulfilling and pleasant, and another have a condition that is debilitating and depressing? What justification can there be for this difference? On what moral grounds should Anthony enjoy better economic circumstances than Arundhati?

Arguments regarding income carry over virtually without alteration. Surely it cannot be owning property that justifies Anthony getting better work conditions and circumstances than Arundhati does. Nor can it be due to some innate quality, nor to training. If Arundhati actually suffers a worse work situation than Anthony, we can certainly offset it by giving Arundhati a larger income to make the income/work package equal for her and Anthony.

The point is, in thinking about equitable economic conditions, we have to think in terms of not just equitable remuneration but also equitable circumstances. The only real justification for differential allocation of circumstances is if this benefits output, and in turn everyone. But surely, even if this were the case one would then offset the situation for the party who was suffering worse conditions with a higher income, while the party benefitting from better circumstances would receive a lower income.

This attitude toward making circumstances equitable is already inherent in the discussion of income and in the choice to remunerate according to effort and sacrifice, but it is worth pointing out on its own account for clarity's sake. We will return later to the implications of equilibrating not only the quality of work in different jobs, but also how different jobs empower workers. But for now we consider the next area of concern about guiding values.

Self-Management

The fourth area of great concern we set forth is power and participation: To what extent should economic agents affect outcomes? As with remuneration, here too we have a particular controversial value we favor, so we need to make a careful case on its behalf. What should be our norm for the influence any actor should have over economic outcomes? Three primary options exist.

1 Vest most power in a few actors and leave the rest very little say over decisions that affect them.

2 Distribute power more equally, with each actor always having one vote in a majority-rules process.

3 Vary the way power is distributed depending on the relation of each actor to specific decisions. Sometimes you get more say, sometimes I get more say. The issue then becomes defining the criteria that determine how much say any of us have in one decision as compared to another.

The first option—giving the most say to a few people—is generally and rightly labeled authoritarian because it gives to the few disproportionate power over the many. In the political realm we call it dictatorship or oligarchy and generally reject it as being incompatible with respecting the rights of all humans. But if it is wrong to have a political elite decide our political conditions because we should each have some say in this, then surely it is also wrong for an economic elite to decide our economic conditions—on the same grounds that we should each have some say in this.

The second option, one-person-one-vote majority rule in all things, is often called democracy. But consider me as I was typing this page. Should you have had a vote on what computer I used, or on whether I turned the light on at my desk, or on whether I had my window open? No, I should make all those decisions myself, authoritatively, just as you should decide when and whether to turn to the next page of this book or to instead set this book aside and read something more entertaining, or to take a bath, for that matter.

It doesn't take but a minute of unconstrained thinking to realize that praising one-person-one-vote decision-making says little about a general norm for decision-making. To invoke majority rule universally ignores that out of the wide diversity of decisions that arise in social interactions and economic life only a relative few are properly handled by giving everyone a single vote and tallying the results. Should the workers at GM and Boeing and those at the corner grocery have an equal vote on whether workers at Ford take a lunch break at twelve noon or a half hour later? Obviously not.

What emerges is that to have a sensible decision-making norm requires that actors have a range of decision-making influence, from very little to overwhelming, depending on how greatly decisions in turn affect them. But how do we determine where on this broad range one's power should fall for any particular decision?

Suppose that you have a desk in a workplace. You are deciding whether to place a picture of your child on that desk. How much say should you have? Or suppose that instead of a picture of your child, you want to place a stereo there and play it loudly in the vicinity of your workmates. How much say should you have about that?

There is probably no one who wouldn't answer that as to the picture you should have full and complete say, but as to the stereo you ought to have limited say, depending on who else would hear the music and therefore be affected by your choice. And suppose we then ask how much say other folks should have? The answer, obviously, depends on the extent to which the decision would affect them.

The norm we favor is thus that to the extent that we can arrange it, each actor in the economy should influence economic outcomes in proportion to how those outcomes affect him or her. Our say in decisions should reflect how much they affect us. That's the only norm that treats all actors with equal respect and that accords all actors the same claims on power without reducing decision-making to a mechanical process divorced from the logic of its implications. If an alternative norm is different, then it must be saying that some people should sometimes have disproportionately more say and other people should sometimes have disproportionately less say in decisions that affect them. What moral justification can there be for regarding different humans with such disparity?

But is there a plausible pragmatic argument against our norm? Of course there is. Take a very young child. Do we think that this child ought to have overwhelming influence on decisions that affect her overwhelmingly? Or do we say that due to the child's incapacity to understand and make judgments, a parent must make decisions for her? We all therefore easily recognize that one reason for abrogating the norm that each actor should influence decisions in proportion to how the outcomes of those decisions will likely affect him or her is that someone may be incapable of doing this in his or her own interest and in light of his or her own needs and with an effective understanding of the dynamics involved. As to whether this paternalistic caveat has any bearing on economic evaluations, we would like to wait for specific cases in later chapters. The point here is that if we can describe institutions that allow people to have input into decision-making in proportion to how much they are affected while maintaining the quality of economic functions, then we will have attained a desirable result in everyone's view.

Diversity

For reasons of vicarious benefit as when we enjoy other people doing things we can't do or don't have time to do, and also as a hedge against placing all our eggs in one wrong basket, everyone easily agrees that diverse and varied outcomes are generally better than homogenous ones. We don't want to create a massive investment project ruling out all other possibilities without exploring and even being prepared to create parallel endeavors in case we were in error about our priority preference or in case there are diverse preferences not met by the preferred option. We don't want to regiment life in any respect, cultural or economic.

People vary, on the one hand, and thus benefit from varied options. And on the other hand, without diversity there is a huge probability we will make egregious mistakes, traveling down a single path that turns out to be inferior to others that we failed to explore. Thus, assuming equal attention to other values, surely one economy will excel above another if in fulfilling its functions it also promotes and supports greater rather than lesser diversity. Homogenization of tastes, jobs, life conditions, material outcomes, and thought patterns is not a virtue.

Solidarity

We endorse solidarity. It is better if people get along with one another than if they violate one another. In two economies that equally respect and fulfill all other values we favor, would anyone deny that attaining more solidarity is better than attaining less?

To care about one another's well-being as fellow humans is surely good. To view one another as objects to exploit or with other hostile intentions is surely bad. No one who is at all progressive would disagree. So clearly an economy that enhances solidarity by entwining people's interests is better than an economy that yields precisely the same outputs and allocations, but creates hostility by pitting actors against one another.

Efficiency

Of course, in addition to solidarity, diversity, equity, and participatory self-management, there is one more evaluative norm we must keep in mind. It will not do, for example, to have economic institutions that promote all our economic values but do not get the economic job done. It will not do, that is, to have an economy that does not meet expressed needs, or that does so to a limited degree though delivering fewer or less desirable outputs than would have been possible with more efficient operations.

But that said, having these five values—solidarity, diversity, equity, and participatory self-management, plus meeting-expressed needs without waste—gets us a long way toward being able to judge economies. If an economy obstructs one or more of these values, to that degree, we do not like it. On the other hand, if an economy furthers these preferred values, that's very good, though we must still look further to see if there are any offsetting problems.

In other words, the values enunciated in this chapter take us not quite all the way to a full resolution regarding evaluating economies. They can help us pinpoint severe failings that should cause us to label economies inadequate. But though these values mean to be encompassing and critically important so that not furthering them is a damning criticism, there are many other values—such as privacy, personal freedom, artistic fulfillment, or even something specific like the right to employ others for personal gain—which might (or might not) also merit attention. And we can imagine that our favored values could come into conflict with one or more of these other values in certain contexts—for example, more solidarity might reduce privacy, or more self-management might reduce quality of outputs—in which case someone could argue that one of our values should be somewhat sacrificed to attain conflicting desirable ends.

The only effective way to assess these complicating possibilities is with more specificity. We must judge the merits of specific economic institutions or whole economic types. Our judgments about economic components and whole economies will reveal the particular valuations that we favor, and readers can decide for themselves whether our conclusions are worthy or not. To start, we will utilize as guiding values solidarity, diversity, equity, self-management, and efficiently meeting needs and developing capacities.

3
Judging Economies

All who are not lunatics are agreed about certain things. That it is better to be alive than dead, better to be adequately fed than starved, better to be free than a slave. Many people desire those things only for themselves and their friends; they are quite content that their enemies should suffer. These people can be refuted by science: Humankind has become so much one family that we cannot insure our own prosperity except by insuring that of everyone else. If you wish to be happy yourself, you must resign yourself to seeing others also happy.
— Bertrand Russell

[Capitalism] is not a success. It is not intelligent, it is not beautiful, it is not just, it is not virtuous—and it doesn't deliver the goods. In short, we dislike it, and we are beginning to despise it. But when we wonder what to put in its place, we are extremely perplexed.
— John Maynard Keynes

Four economic institutions are commonplace in currently favored economic systems: private ownership of the means of production, hierarchical corporate divisions of labor, central planning, and markets. It makes sense to assess each in their own right. Having done so, evaluating types of economies will be easy.

Private Ownership

Private ownership of the means of production exists when private individuals own the buildings, equipment, tools, technologies, land, and/or resources with which we produce goods and services. Private ownership is relevant to how we evaluate an economy in three senses. By virtue of owning particular items owners decide how they are used, largely rule over their disposition, and accrue income from putting those items to work and claiming all revenues above and beyond costs.

The implications of employing private property for remuneration and decision-making are therefore pretty straightforward. Private property imposes what we earlier called norm one (rewarding property) as a dominant component of income distribution. Likewise, private property affords owners disproportionate say over decisions that involve the disposition of their property even if other people are greatly affected. Thus, when a capitalist employing many people decides to move a firm to a new locale, the impact can devastate the employees fired or the town left behind, yet neither the discarded employees nor the gutted town have significant say in the decision. Likewise, in having dominant say over how a workplace is organized and utilized the owner has vastly disproportionate influence over decisions affecting how workers spend their days.

The implications of private ownership for solidarity are largely derivative. By separating those who own means of production from those who don't, private property generates opposition. The owner tries to extract maximum labor from the workforce as cheaply as possible to generate as much saleable product at as little cost as possible, thereby maximizing profits while also working to maintain the conditions that allow owners to appropriate profits. The non-owner (worker) tries to increase her wage as much as possible and to have as desirable a work day as possible, while increasing her power to demand more and better her economic life. The worker therefore prefers to work less than the owner desires, under better conditions, and with more pay. The opposed motivations of workers and owners create conflict that obstruct solidarity.

Diversity is modestly affected by private ownership. By dividing people into owners and workers, private ownership creates a great difference between the two classes but also creates homogenizing pressure inside those classes.

Corporate Divisions of Labor

Producing any particular product or service requires various tasks. A hierarchical division of labor is one that apportions these various tasks into separate jobs graded hierarchically relative to one another. Some sets of tasks combine into jobs that have more quality of life and/or empowerment effects. Other sets of tasks combine together into jobs that have less of those same attributes. The jobs therefore form a hierarchy with respect to quality of life effects and the power that jobs accord to workers, as well as associated remuneration and status. This hierarchy marks the difference between being an all-purpose gopher, a custodian, an assembler, a foreman, a manager, an engineer, a vice president, or a CEO.

In any workplace, we can examine the pleasure or pain a job entails, the tensions it imposes, its sociality or isolation, its danger or sense of accomplishment, the pay it warrants, and the implications it has for empowering people vis-à-vis their own situations or the situations of others. If we find that some jobs have many more of the preferred features and some many fewer, then the workplace has what we call a corporate division of labor. On the other hand, if we can't line up an economy's jobs in a pyramid of their desirability or empowerment implications, then the workplace doesn't have a corporate division of labor.

So how do we judge the corporate division of labor as a means to getting economic functions accomplished? As with all institutions, we must examine the implications of this choice for solidarity, diversity, equity, and self-management.

We will start with the most obvious aspect: if you have a corporate division of labor in which a few workers have excellent conditions and empowering circumstances, many fall well below that, and most workers have essentially no power at all, you will obviously not see all actors influencing decisions in proportion to the degree they are affected by them. For one thing, a corporate division of labor nearly always entails that actors have differential voting say over outcomes. Those at the top generally have more "votes" than those at the bottom (in fact, those at the top most often have all the formal voting rights with none for those at the bottom). But even if everyone has one vote in every major decision regardless of their job, nonetheless, with a corporate division of labor, each person's specific circumstances will empower her or him differently. This will in turn ensure that despite everyone having equal formal say, for want of information, time, skills, and disposition, those with less empowering work will be less able to arrive at or manifest their views and those enjoying jobs that convey more information, confidence, and decision-making skills will dominate debate and choice. Formal democracy doesn't guarantee real democracy. The wills of empowered workers trump the wills of disempowered workers because the empowered workers set agendas and easily override uninformed preferences, and most likely monopolize votes as well. The wills of disempowered workers are unlikely even to be heard, much less implemented.

To see how this follows from dividing labor as indicated, imagine that overnight it is decided to hold formally democratic votes on various policies in a typical corporate workplace. The jobs in that workplace, however, are to remain as we currently know them. The managers, CEOs, engineers, custodians, shipping clerks, and assembly workers are all going to vote on large policies that provide the overarching norms for their daily activities—but in their daily activity they are going to do just as they have done before, with the same autonomy or lack of it, the same empowering work or lack of it, and so on. Despite the one-person-one-vote majority rules approach to the biggest decisions, we can predict that in the process of developing options to vote on and then arguing on their behalf, only the views of the employees with access to knowledge of the workplace and with relevant decision-making skills will come to the fore. They will set agendas. They will pontificate ponderously or compellingly, alone. Their desires will overwhelmingly dominate proposals, discussion, debate, and choice. The hierarchical distribution of empowering circumstances conferring to only a few actors informed opinions and decision-making information, skills, and confidence, will obstruct participation of all actors in voting. Corporate divisions of labor will ensure that a few would give orders and most obey, and these are not conditions conducive to all participating equally. With corporate organization, that is, formal democracy becomes not just a facade on top of unequal conception and debate, but an annoyance that wastes time and energy. If you are low in the hierarchy, why should you attend meetings and vote when your attendance and vote have little to no impact since real decisions are largely made before you ever arrive on the scene? Why should those who do impact outcomes put up with the participation of the uninformed and risk having to waste time trying to convince them which options to pursue? Hierarchical work organization empowers a few and gives those few every incentive to replace formally democratic rules with their own explicit domination of every facet of decision-making. Corporate divisions of labor do not advance and in fact overwhelmingly obstruct self-management.

What implications do corporate divisions of labor have for solidarity? The differential division of circumstances and power between you and me is obviously not conducive to empathy between us. If we make these differences systematic, with, say, 20 percent monopolizing the best and most empowering conditions of work, and 80 percent largely or exclusively doing what they are told—solidarity between those who rule and those who are ruled dies a quick but painful death. Worse, suppose, as is generally the case, that once there is a corporate division of labor it is elaborated into a broad and pervasive class division. Those above a certain cut-off in the empowerment hierarchy are in one class, which largely defines and controls its own circumstances and the circumstances of others below, and those who are below that cut-off are in another class, which obeys orders and gets what its members can eke out. The manners, lifestyles, dress, habits, and even language of the two classes come into opposition. The one class monopolizes information, training, knowledge, and the associated status and perquisites of expression and performance, plus all the income it can grab for itself via its inflated bargaining power. The other class, excluded from training and saddled with deadening activity, drags along behind with marginal bargaining power and income, either bent in submission, or, if aroused to its plight, angry and rebellious. The coordinator class looks down on workers as instruments with which to get jobs done. It engages workers paternally, seeing them as needing guidance and oversight and as lacking the finer human qualities that justify both autonomous input and also the higher incomes needed to support more expensive tastes. Workers in reply look up at coordinators as well-educated and knowledgeable—which in fact they generally are—but also as arrogant, elitist snobs lacking human sentiment and solidarity. Workers may wrongly accept that the empowerment and capacity differentials between themselves and coordinators are due to innate differences, and may thus bemoan their own sad—though seemingly inevitable—lot, while hating, but succumbing to, the coordinators' arrogance. Or they may realize that the differentials in talents, knowledge, and confidence derive mostly from widely different circumstances in home life and schooling and of course in the division of labor that literally imposes hierarchical outcomes regardless of people's actual potentials and capacities. In any event, as they may realize, such differences in no way justify differentials in income and power. But in either case, or in any more conflicted and ambivalent mix of perceptions, solidarity is impeded by such a class division, and hostility and supervision grow in its place.

What about equity? If we have a hierarchy of empowerment, we can confidently predict that those above will use their differential power to skew income to their own material advantage. Why? Imagine that some folks have better conditions and more control because of a hierarchical division of labor. Will those folks then decide that they deserve more income for being more trained, more informed, and for having more responsibility, as well as to feed their more refined tastes and desires? Or will they decide that the exhausted and less educated workers enduring worse conditions deserve more income for their greater sacrifice?

The reason hierarchical divisions of labor obstruct material equity is that the only way for those who are higher to see that those who are lower in the hierarchy deserve more pay would be to feel that those lower are sacrificing greatly due to their worse conditions and lesser empowerment. But if I am on top and actively agree that those below are suffering, then to retain self-respect I will have to wonder if I am unfair for being on top. The way for me to instead feel good about being above others is to tell myself that I belong above them and that they belong below. I arrive at the conclusion that those who are disempowered are suited only to obey. They are comfortable and properly utilized when they are being obedient. They would be fish out of water and make a mess of economic outcomes if they were forced to bear more responsibility. We who are on top are comfortable and properly utilized in our higher station despite our having to shoulder tremendous responsibilities. We belong here and society needs us here, and both to be comfortable and to be able to act on all this responsibility as well as so we can better enjoy the finer things in life that our refined tastes desire, we need extra income. The others won't miss it, so let's give it to ourselves, of course. That's the logic that translates predictably persisting differentials in power into parallel differentials in income.

What about diversity? On the one hand, by forcing people into classes and pressuring conformity within and confrontation between classes, hierarchical divisions of labor reduce diversity within classes and impose harmful differences between them, neither of which is a positive attribute. But if we go further and look at jobs themselves, the case is starker. If jobs are created by combining a set of tasks that are internally similar to one another in their quality of life and empowerment effects, we can reasonably predict that most jobs will be less diverse in their attributes than if jobs are created by combining a set of diverse (but compatible) tasks so that the overall quality of life and empowerment impact of the package is average. It therefore doesn't take extensive analysis to figure out whether a hierarchical division of labor will yield greater workday diversity than a non-hierarchical one. For about 80 percent of the workforce, the difference is between having a job that has only rote tasks and having a job with some rote but some conceptual tasks, or between having a job that has only tedious tasks and having one that has some tedious but also some engaging tasks.

Can we summarize this brief survey? Are hierarchical production relations consistent with the goals of a participatory, equitable, economy? Clearly they are not, for reasons obvious to most workers but nonetheless obscure to many economists. If someone's work is mechanical and mindless it will diminish her or his self-esteem, confidence, and self-management skills. On the other hand, if someone's work is exciting and challenging, it will enhance her or his ability to analyze and evaluate economic alternatives. Hierarchical work leaves different imprints on personalities. For those at the top, it yields an inquisitive, expansive outlook. For those at the bottom, it leaves an aggrieved and self-deprecating outlook, or induces anger. People's confidence or self-doubts and their intelligence or ignorance all derive, in part, from the kind of economic activities they daily undertake. Under hierarchical arrangements, many capable citizens enter industry only to exert little influence and do exclusively boring work. Those few who advance to more fulfilling and commanding jobs generally have freer workdays and greater "thinking" time than those who remain at the bottom. Each promotion increases immediate power and also the beneficiary's skill and information advantages to bring to future competitions. Not only will this lead to disparate opportunities for participation, but corporate production relations will generate remuneration as well. People who occupy favored positions in pro- duction hierarchies will appropriate more pleasant work conditions and greater consumption opportunities than those afforded their subordinates. And this will be the case whether the hierarchy is based on differential ownership or on differential access to information and decision-making opportunities, or on both.

Central Planning

Central planning is a conceptually simple solution to the problem of economic allocation. Within this system, a group of planners accumulates massive information in various ways, massages it, imposes some broad values on it, and emerges with a list of instructions for producers and prices for consumers. They then send this out to the rest of society to implement.

In short, the planning system gathers data and sets economic priorities that planners then use to determine how best to achieve society's goals with society's limited productive resources. The system consists of a relatively small group of planners in a central planning apparatus communicating with managers in enterprises. The planners decide what to produce, where workers should work, what income levels consumers will have, and by determining prices also what they can consume. The information goes from planners to managers and on to workers. This can all occur with less or more input allowed to the broad public, and while central planning is a non-market system, highly truncated markets can certainly be used to distribute goods to consumers once they are produced, to gather data, or even to assign particular workers to particular enterprises. But the broader decisions of how much of each product to produce, how many workers of different skills should work where, and how much they should be paid, are all determined overwhelmingly by the central plan, even when limited markets exist to assist lesser determinations.

Many advocates of centrally planned public-enterprise economies such as the old Soviet Union viewed their goal as a classless economy and saw central planning as an approach to allocation consistent with eliminating classes. Everyone in such a system will be workers and consumers, they argued. All workers and consumers will be on an equal footing because none will own the means of production. The nightmare of private appropriation of scarce social resources along with the inequity, alienation, and inefficiency fostered by the accumulation of profits by narrow elites is replaced, their prognosis continues, by a rational use of productive resources to best achieve society's economic goals. In this view, central planners and managers knowledgeably translate workers' and consumers' desires about consumption and about work into the most efficient possible assignment of productive assets. In reality, of course, this is not what occurred in the Soviet Union, Eastern Europe, China, Cuba, or anywhere else that the system has been deployed, nor is it what we would predict from modeling the system's institutions. Instead, in history and in our predictions, classes emerge even in the least corrupt and least authoritarian centrally planned economies. Moreover, this is not due solely to non-democratic political influences nor to betrayals by corrupt leaders, but is instead an intrinsic outcome of central planning.

That is, instead of having a capitalist ruling class, in centrally planned economies we see a coordinator class of planners and managers inexorably becoming the ruling class. The idea that the coordinators who monopolize positions of decision-making influence are simply there to carry out the will of workers and consumers is a doublespeak myth, of course. Instead it is workers who labor at the behest of the coordinator class of planners, managers, and other empowered economic actors. The coordinators consume more than ordinary workers, work under more pleasant conditions, and make all the important economic decisions—whether at the broad planning level or as managers in separate firms. Ordinary workers are alienated from decision-making and have inferior work conditions and consumption opportunities. This is not to say that all workers are equally exploited or alienated in all centrally planned systems, or that all workers are more exploited in any centrally planned economy, however enlightened, than in any capitalist system, however barbaric. But even at its best, central planning is plagued by class division, exploitation, oppression, and alienation.

How well does central planning do its allocative job? Do its operations result in undue waste, miscommunication, gluts, short-ages, and so on? The answer is well known and a bit different than publicly assumed. Central planning cannot be efficient unless central planners know the quantities of available resources and equipment, know the ratios in which production units can combine inputs to yield desired outputs, are informed of the relative social worth of final goods, have sufficient computing facilities to carry out quantitative manipulations, and can impose incentives that will induce managers and workers to carry out their assigned tasks.

But, if we generously grant these assumptions—which is no less reasonable than granting the assumptions economists typically make about markets—then we must agree that central planners could, in fact, calculate an efficient production plan and then choose intelligently from a variety of options to decide how to assign workers to jobs and how to distribute goods to consumers. In such circumstances, that is, central planners can successfully solve a giant, economy-wide problem of how to maximize the social value of final output by calculating how much of each product to produce via each technique that can be used to make the product. The planners choose from among all the production plans that satisfy the various constraints operating in their economy the one plan that yields the greatest value of final output as judged by the planners' valuations of the worth of products. The assumptions above guarantee that the planners will calculate an optimal plan and will be able to get the "optimal plan" they calculate carried out.

But even if central planning can theoretically function this smoothly and effectively, will it facilitate each actor having appropriate proportionate decision-making influence, or will it place excessive power in a few hands and diminished power in everyone else's? In all versions of central planning:

1 The famous "down/up down/up" process is down-go-questions, up-come-answers; down-go-orders, up-comes-obedience.

2   Qualitative information that is essential to evaluating human outcomes is never generated, much less disseminated.

3   Elite conceptual workers—the central planners and plant managers who we call coordinators—monopolize the technical information required for decision-making.

4   The only management left to individual production units is to "manage" to fulfill the central planners' targets using inputs allotted them by the central planners.

In other words, central planners gather information, calculate a plan, and issue "marching orders" to production units. The relationship between the central planning agency and the production units is authoritative rather than democratic, and exclusive rather than participatory. Moreover, since each unit is subordinate to the planning board and any superior agent will always seek effective means for holding subordinates accountable, methods of surveillance and verification will be employed to minimize malfeasant lying and shirking. To these ends, central planners appoint and then reward and punish managers according to the performance of their units rather than establishing procedures that give power to rambunctious workers' councils. Since it is senseless to punish managers for the behavior of workers over whom they have no control, central planners grant managers dictatorial powers over their workers. What begins as a totalitarian relationship between the central planning agency and production units ends up extending to managers a dictatorial say over workers. Not only do workers have no say over what they produce and what inputs they work with because central planners make allocative decisions outside the workplace, workers have little say over how they use inputs to meet their output quotas because plant managers make these decisions unilaterally. Real world central planning therefore prevents workers from deciding how to use their laboring capacities because its logic requires pervasive hierarchy.

Even if we assume the planners have all the information they need; that the social values of final goods are determined by a completely democratic voting procedure among consumers; that the planners forswear all opportunity to bias the social values guiding planning in favor of their own interests; that the planners accurately calculate the optimal plan; and that workers carry out the plan to the letter of their instructions (a very long and utterly implausible list of "ifs")—nonetheless, even in this highly unreal, best-case scenario, central planning would still fail to deliver self-management for three reasons:

1) Since the central planners monopolize all the quantitative information generated in the planning process, workers and consumers lack access to quantitative information about the relationship between different primary resources and final goods in the economy. And since very little qualitative information is generated in central planning about the human aspects of different work and consumption processes, workers and consumers lack information about the situations of other workers and consumers. But this means workers and consumers in centrally planned economies do not have the information required to engage in intelligent and responsible self-management. How can people sensibly decide what to produce and consume without knowing how their choice will affect others—even if they were allowed to do so?

2) Regarding valuation of outputs, central planning could let every consumer "vote" say 10,000 points, indicating his or her relative preferences for different final goods and services. But even this fair and democratic consumer voting procedure would deny self-management for workers. Once votes were tallied and used to formulate the planers' objective function, even the best central planning would translate those preferences into specific work plans for each and every production unit. But that means every consumer/worker would have had the exact same decision-making input (10,000 votes) as every other consumer/worker over every facet of what to produce and how to produce it in every single workplace. Even assuming this structure could ever be harnessed to yield workable and sensible outcomes, which it could not, it would fail to provide self-management for workers because it would not give workers input into production decisions according to how much they are affected by them. Your opinion about what to produce and how to produce it should count more towards what goes on in your own workplace than the opinion of someone who is less affected by what happens in your workplace—just as their opinion should count more than yours about their workplace. But the best that central planning can conceivably do (a goal that it never remotely attains due to devolution into class division) is to give everyone equal input in all economic decisions via a democratic determination of the plan's objective function. Central planning is therefore ill-suited to providing actors influence in accord with the differential impacts that different decisions have on different workers and consumers.

3) Finally, as we have discussed at greater length in other contexts, in any economy individuals rationally orient their preferences toward opportunities that will be relatively plentiful and away from those that will be relatively scarce. We know that orienting ourselves to want what we cannot have or cannot afford yields little satisfaction, while orienting ourselves to want what we can have and can afford can yield more. Thus our preferences are not fixed and we influence them by our actions and choices. If a bias arises in the expected future supply of particular roles or goods so that some are under-priced and others are overpriced, people will orient their development accordingly. If I can get commodity X at a price below what it ought to sell at, and can get commodity Y only at an inflated price above what it ought to sell at, I am going to feel a real incentive to change my preferences from Y toward X to benefit from this mispricing. On average, over a whole population, tastes will drift as a result. In the case of central planning, the bias against providing self-managed work opportunities keeps people from developing (systematically) desires and capacities for self-management, and instead promotes steadily greater apathy among the workforce. That is, the apathy of its workers often noted by those who studied the Soviet and Eastern European centrally planned economies was not genetic, of course, but a logical result of the bias against self-managed work opportunities in those societies, as well as a result of political alienation. But this apathy would develop even in the best case of central planning, much less in real world versions. Why should a worker in a centrally planned economy develop a keen interest in what she will produce or how she will produce it, or develop a powerful desire to influence such decisions? It is better not to care. (The parallel to the disinterest in participating in political democracy by those without means to influence agendas is obvious.)

Now what about solidarity, equity, and diversity? We need not spend excessive time on these. With a class division between workers and coordinators (including central planners, local managers, and other actors who share their relative monopoly on decision-making options and access to information), solidarity is clearly less than it would be with classlessness. With planners and managers in position to reward themselves excessively and possessing a world view that sees themselves as "conceptual" and "in charge" and that sees society's workers as "needing to be cared for," we can predict with great confidence a growing gap in income, perks, and conditions. So there is no equity.

Diversity is subtler, and can increase or decrease in this model depending on many variables, though, in practice (as all the jokes about "communist robotic regimentation" convey), our expectation is not positive. All in all, not surprisingly central planning is an allocation system that obstructs the values we favor including equity of circumstance and income, solidarity, self-management, and diversity.

Markets

"Markets" is a term denoting allocation via competitive buying and selling at prices determined by the competitive offerings of the buyers and sellers. A market is therefore not merely the food store or the mall, but the entire entwined allocation system of buyers and sellers each acting to further their own interests by selling dear and buying cheap.

Equity

Markets undeniably often permit buyers and sellers to interact conveniently for mutual benefit. In fact, taking into account only their own immediate circumstances, market exchanges nearly always benefit both buyer and seller. But unfortunately, immediate convenience and relative short-run benefit for both buyer and seller do not imply immediate equity or efficiency, much less a positive social interaction over extended periods. In these wider dimensions market exchange aggravates inequities, generates grossly under-estimated inefficiencies, and disastrously distorts human relations. To judge markets regarding equity we need some shared framework of beliefs about how markets affect people's attributes and people's attributes in turn affect the operations of markets. We propose the following:

> Proposition 1: People have different abilities to benefit others and different abilities to secure a favorable share of the benefits from exchange. We are not all alike in these (or any) respects.

> Proposition 2: Very few, if any, of the many abilities people may have to benefit others or to secure benefits for themselves bestow a rightful moral claim to benefit more or exercise more decision-making authority than those of lesser ability.

> Proposition 3: Market exchanges permit those with greater abilities to benefit more and exercise greater economic power than do those with lesser abilities. These inequities occur even with fully informed exchanges in perfectly competitive markets, much less in markets as we know them in real economies with advertising, unequal bargaining power, etc.

If these propositions are true, then clearly markets cannot provide a morally justified allocation of income and will therefore fail to uphold the values we arrived at in the last chapter. But are the propositions true—and moreover, are they true not merely in existing historical circumstances for existing and arguably contingent market arrangements, but true intrinsically and unavoidably for all market economies due to the very nature of market exchange?

The first part of p one is that people have different abilities to benefit others. This is self-evident. Mozart obviously had greater ability to please music lovers than his "rival" Salieri. Michael Jordan had greater ability to please basketball fans than other NBA players. A skilled brain surgeon has greater ability to benefit her patients than a garbage collector to benefit his "clients" (except when New York City is in day twenty of a sanitation workers' strike). In short, people are born with unequal "talents" for benefitting others, and differences in education and training or even just location can instill in people different abilities to benefit others even even when they do not have significant genetic differences.

We should note, however, that as evident as proposition one is, there are nonetheless people who reject it, at least emotionally. They presumably feel that once one admits such differences one is on an inexorable slide toward justifying economic inequality. Their opposition to economic inequality is so great it causes them to deny that genetic and training differences exist in a prophylactic move to prevent what they deem inevitably correlated inequality before the fact. They think that to assert that people have differential talents and abilities is "elitist."

However, two problems with this attitude arise: (1) To deny the existence of different abilities is obviously out of touch with reality. Imagine a society that refused to give glasses to people with poor eyesight or gave lower incomes to people with poor eyesight. Some might respond to this obvious injustice by denying that people's genetically determined attributes were different. But this would be silly. Wishing it so doesn't make it so, and anyway, there's no reason why social or economic inequality is a necessary consequence of inequality in people's eyesight. What needs to be challenged is not the fact that people differ in their eyesight, but the social practice that rewards people differently based on their eyesight.

But (2), imagine that there were no differences in talents, abilities, etc.—what a boring world it would be if each and every person had the same talents, no one was exceptional in any respect, and each was able to develop capabilities only just like those that everyone else had already developed. Sometimes aspirations for equality lead justice-advocates down strange intellectual paths. In any event, other than for well-motivated people who worry about its implications and who will in any event be freed from these feelings by the rest of our arguments, the first part of proposition one is not controversial, so we move on.

The second part of proposition one is that when operating in the context of markets, people will have different abilities to secure a favorable share of the benefits of exchanges. This is equally self-evident, but less often noted.

Different abilities to secure a greater share of benefits from competitive exchange can result, for example, from differences in people's abilities to withstand failure to reach an agreement. A single mother with a sick child and no other means of securing health insurance is at a disadvantage negotiating with a large corporate employer compared to someone with many options who can hold out for better terms, even if the two have identical skills. A peasant with no savings is at a disadvantage negotiating a loan for seed and food with a rural moneylender compared to a corporation able to withstand delays.

Different abilities to benefit from competitive exchange can also result from more accurate predictions about uncertain consequences or from differential knowledge of the terms of exchange (which in turn could stem from genetic differences in this particular "talent" or differences in training or, more often, from different access to relevant information).

Or differences could stem from personality traits that make some more willing or able to drive a hard bargain than others, or to abide the pains risked or, more often, the pains imposed on others. The truism that in our society nice guys finish last attests to this last point. If you cannot abide hurting others or at least ignoring the hurt endured by others, in a competitive context you are at a severe disadvantage when it comes to your own self-advancement.

Differences in social values could (and do) prevent some people from seeking maximum advantage at the expense of others, even as they encourage others to do so. Different opportunities and/or willingness to disobey the golden rule to do unto others as you would have them do unto you and to instead obey the rule of the marketplace, to do others in before they do you in, make for different abilities to garner benefits in the context of competition.

And unfortunately, competition—the famous harmonizer of the private and public interest—by systematically weeding out the less devious and aggressive actors, enforces lowest common denominator consciousness regarding willingness to invert the golden rule. So, in the ways listed above and others that could be enunciated as well, the second half of proposition one also proves true. And once it is clearly stated, about this there is virtually no dissent. After all, a large part of contemporary economic activity involves precisely trying to get ahead by utilizing such differences.

As compared to proposition one, the issue addressed in proposition two is more philosophical and complex, but luckily already navigated in the last chapter. What reasons for differential compensation are morally compelling and what reasons carry no moral weight? Our earlier discussion of values established that only acts under our control and not owing to luck and circumstance provide moral justification for income differentials, which makes proposition two true, with associated controversies having been dealt with in the last chapter.

You do this and I do that so that the total of what we both do is greater than if, instead, we reversed it and I did that and you did this. Who gets the gain? Proposition three points out that those with greater abilities to capture the benefits of market exchange will obviously capture a greater share of the efficiency gains from a division of labor in a market economy. And any student of the laws of supply and demand knows that the greater the benefit a commodity affords a buyer, the higher the price a seller will receive, other things being equal. So those with greater ability to benefit others will also benefit to a greater extent than those less able to benefit others.

Two actors or agents meet in a market exchange. This occurs over and over, with partners changing, rotating, and otherwise varying in an unpredictable pattern. Those who can benefit others better can demand more in return; those who can accrue more of the benefits that exchanges make available can accrue more in return. Since both these differentials among those playing the roles of buyer and seller exist, differential outcomes arise. Since having greater wealth confers further advantage, the differentials steadily enlarge. In time, therefore, there emerge people who make substantially more and people who make substantially less. More formally put, taken together propositions one, two, and three spell out the case that market economies will subvert equity whether combined with private or public enterprise:

1 People have different abilities to benefit others and to capture the efficiency gains from market exchanges.

2 As established last chapter, neither greater innate nor learned ability either to benefit others or to capture benefit for oneself earns the more able any moral right to a greater share of the benefits of economic cooperation. Only greater effort or sacrifice merits greater reward. But in fact ...

3 Markets will permit those with greater abilities of either kind to reap greater economic rewards than those of lesser abilities will receive, even when those with greater abilities exert less effort and sacrifice. (And any effort to offset this with tax policies will subvert the proclaimed efficiency of markets.)

More simply put, in a market economy the big strong cane cutter gets more income than the small weak one regardless of how long and how hard they work. The doctor working in a plush setting with comfortable and fulfilling circumstances earns more than the assembly worker working in a horrible din, risking life and limb, and enduring boredom and denigration, regardless of how long and how hard each works. To earn more due to generating more valuable output despite contributing less effort and enduring less sacrifice goes against the values that we settled on last chapter but is a defining feature of market remuneration. Is this there is for our critique, or are there additional equity problems?

First, it is instructive to note that even if rewarding according to the social value of contribution were regarded as fair, which our values deny, market valuations of workers' contributions systematically diverge from an accurate measure of their true social contribution for two reasons:

1 In market systems we vote with our wallets. The market weighs people's desires in accord with the income they muster behind their preferences. Therefore the value of

contributions in the marketplace is determined not only by people's relative needs and desires but by the distribution of income enabling actors to manifest those needs and desires. Thus, as measured in the marketplace the contribution of a plastic surgeon reconstructing noses in Hollywood will be greater than the value of the contribution of a family practitioner saving lives in a poor, rural county in Oklahoma —even though the family practitioner's work is of much greater social benefit by any reasonable measure. The starlets have more money to express their desires for better looks than the farmers have to keep alive. If you pay more, it will cause what you pay for to be "valued" more highly. An inequitable distribution of income therefore will cause market valuations of producers' outputs to diverge from accurate measures of those outputs' implications for social well-being. Plastic surgery trumps saving malnourished children not because reversing malnourishment is less valuable then cosmetic surgery, but because Hollywood stars have more cash to express their preferences than do those who suffer starvation. It follows, then, that even those who urge remunerating according to output shouldn't be market advocates, because markets don't measure the value of outputs in tune with the outputs' true social benefits.

2 Moreover, markets only incorporate in their valuations the wills of immediate buyers and sellers. The preferences of the auto consumer and the auto dealer are well accounted for (assuming we ignore income differentials distorting the weights they are accorded) when the former buys a car from the latter, but others in society who are neither buying nor selling the car but who breathe the auto pollution the car generates, have no say at all in the transaction. The price of a car negotiated by buyer and seller doesn't reflect the impact of the car's pollution on the broader populace since the broader populace isn't involved in the direct transaction and their views on the matter are never "polled." Sometimes such broader impact is positive—a person becomes enlightened by buying a book and in turn benefits others. The positive benefits to others did not affect the initial purchase price. Sometimes broader impacts are negative: a person drinks excessively and eventually spouses and friends and the broader society suffer lost productivity,

increased costs of health care, and the horrors of abuse and drunken driving. The negative by-products did not impact the initial purchase. The point of this is that the market over-values some goods by not accounting for their negative "external" effects beyond direct buyers and sellers, and undervalues others by not accounting for their positive "external" effects beyond direct buyers and sellers. This mis-valuation of transactions that have implications beyond immediate buyers and sellers implies in turn that those who produce goods or services with negative unaccounted effects will have the value of their contributions over-valued in market economies, while others who produce goods or services with positive unaccounted effects will have the value of their contributions undervalued. So again, even those who believe in remuneration according to output (rather than according to effort and sacrifice, as we favor) ought to disavow markets, since even the freest markets don't properly measure social costs and benefits. They remunerate according to contribution, but they mis-measure contribution in systematic and socially harmful ways.

Using markets to reward contribution to output is more or less as if we believed that people ought to be paid for how much they weigh, and we then adopted an elaborate system to find this out, but the system that we chose for the task involved a scale with additional bags of sand added to one side or the other, thus increasing the weight of some and not others. Obviously the whole weight norm in the first place is immoral, as we believe remunerating for output is. But, in addition, if one does advocate the weight norm, it would make no sense for anyone to also advocate a set of institutions that in fact systematically misrepresent it—unless, of course, there were other things about that system one greatly liked and the rhetoric about the weight norm was mere window dressing that one didn't take seriously.

   To return to our own standards, it is very important to note that the problem of some people receiving higher wages and salaries than others who make greater ·personal sacrifices cannot be corrected in market economies without creating a great deal of inefficiency. The issue is both intrinsic to markets and also intractable under their sway. Even at their very best, in market transactions, labor is paid what is called its "marginal revenue product"—the valuation of its contribution to output—which, as we have seen, can differ significantly from a true valuation of output, much less from effort expended. But suppose we realize the injustice of this basis for remuneration and decide to correct it by keeping markets otherwise unchanged while legislatively substituting "effort wages" (i.e. *just* wages) for "marginal revenue product (*unjust*) wages." Can't that ameliorate this particular problem? We keep markets, generally, but we correct market wages. What is there to dislike? To a degree this would ameliorate one problem, yes, but it would also lead to inefficient uses of scarce labor resources, thereby offsetting any gains made.

The point is this: while our morals lead us to want to remunerate labor according to effort and sacrifice and not the true value of labor's output, on the other side of the allocative coin, we want to use the true value of output in deciding how much labor should be apportioned to different tasks. For example, you do not want to value something more and thus put more resources into it merely because it takes more effort to produce. Instead, you only want to produce more of something if the product's worth to people actually warrants it. So suppose we pay labor according to effort and sacrifice in an otherwise market driven economy. As a result the markets will operate as though the value of the product of work is measured in large part by the effort and sacrifice that was expended in its production, but this in turn reduces attention to the impact of the product on recipients. In other words, while we do not want to pay the surgeon according to the value of the surgery to society for moral reasons having to do with what we believe people should earn, we also do not want to say that the value of the surgery should be determined solely by effort and sacrifice involved in it. Instead, the value of the surgery depends largely on the benefits it bestows. A good allocation system has to remunerate in accordance with our preferred values of effort and sacrifice, of course, but it also has to allocate in light of full true social costs and benefits. Since in a market system labor costs form a substantial portion of total production costs of most goods and services, if wages are forcibly made just, with markets this would distort the valuation of the products of that labor, in turn causing the entire cost structure and price system of the economy to deviate substantially from reflecting true costs and benefits.

The adapted system would then have products valued according to what was being paid to labor for its effort and sacrifice but not according to the amount that the products are desired by their consumers. To use the terminology of economists: in a market system with effort-governed wages, goods made directly or indirectly by labor whose effort wages were higher than their marginal revenue product would sell at prices higher than their real costs, while goods made directly or indirectly by labor whose effort wages were lower than their marginal revenue product would sell at prices lower than their real costs. Since prices in a market economy help to determine not only what laborers get paid but also how much of what items are produced, any attempt to make wages more equitable while retaining market exchange must cause a systematic misuse of scarce productive resources.

More of some items and less of others will be produced than proper valuations of their social benefits and costs would dictate. In other words, if left to their own devices, market economies distribute the burdens and benefits of social labor unfairly because workers are rewarded according to the market value of their contributions rather than according to their effort or personal sacrifice. But if we correct this problem by enforcing wages that are better correlated to actual effort and sacrifice, then the adapted market economy will misvalue products and misallocate productive resources even more than otherwise.

In addition, why would the economically advantaged in any market economy not translate their advantages in resources and leisure into disproportionate political power with which to defend market wage rates against critics? Why would they not use their disproportionate political power to obstruct attempts to correct wage and salary inequities? Of course, the answer is the advantaged *would* take both these paths, and very effectively, as we have seen throughout history.

Moreover, people naturally tend to rationalize their behavior so as to function effectively and respect themselves in the process. The logic of the labor market is: he or she who contributes more gets more. When people participate in the labor market, in order to get ahead they must defend their right to a wage on the basis of their output. The logic of redistributing income to attain more equitable wages, however, runs counter to rewarding output. So participation in markets (with or without private ownership) not only does not lead people to see the moral logic of redistribution, it inclines them to favor the argument that everyone gets what they contributed, so redistribution is unfair. Participation in markets empowers those who oppose redistributive schemes and intellectually and psychologically impedes those who would benefit from them.

In conclusion, while of course the degree of inequity is far greater in private enterprise economies wherein people can accumulate ownership of means of production and a flow of profits from that property, income inequalities due to unequal human talents and abilities, though smaller, are inequitable for the same reason. When payment is based on the value of contribution to output, unavoidable unequal distribution of human or non-human talents, abilities, and tools will lead to morally unjustifiable differences in economic benefits. Moreover, whereas it is theoretically possible to equalize ownership of non-human assets (like training or tools) through their redistribution, it is not possible to do so in the case of unequal human assets (innate talents, size, etc.). The only conceivable way to eliminate "doctor versus garbage collector" inequities of the sort discussed last chapter is to base benefits on something other than contribution to output and this is not possible in any kind of market economy.

Solidarity

Disgust with the commercialization of human relationships is as old as commerce itself. The spread of markets in eighteenth century England led the Irish-born British political philosopher Edmund Burke to reflect:

> The age of chivalry is gone. The age of sophists, economists, and calculators is upon us; and the glory of Europe is extinguished forever.

Likewise, the British historian Thomas Carlyle warned in 1847:

> Never on this Earth, was the relation of man to man long carried on by cash-payment alone. If, at any time, a philosophy of laissez-faire, competition and supply-and-demand start up as the exponent of human relations, expect that it will end soon.

And of course through all his critiques of capitalism, Karl Marx complained that markets gradually turn everything into a commodity corroding social values and undermining community:

> [With the spread of markets] there came a time when everything that people had considered as inalienable became an object of exchange, of traffic, and could be alienated. This is the time when the very things which till then had been communicated, but never exchanged, given, but never sold, acquired, but never bought—virtue, love, conviction, knowledge, conscience, etc.—

when everything, in short passed into commerce. It is the time of
general corruption, of universal venality [....] It has left
remaining no other nexus between man and man other than
naked self-interest and callous cash payment.

Like all social institutions, markets provide incentives that promote
some kinds of behavior and discourage others. Markets minimize
the transaction costs of some forms of economic interaction,
especially those that are personal and involve private agents,
thereby facilitating them, but markets do nothing to reduce the
transaction costs and thereby facilitate other forms of interaction,
especially those that are public and involve collective implications.

Even beyond simple inefficiencies, if the forms of interaction that
are encouraged are mean-spirited and hostile and the forms of
interaction that are discouraged are respectful and empathetic, the
negative effects on human relations will be profound.

In effect, advocates of markets say to us: "You cannot cooperatively and self-consciously coordinate your economic activities
sensibly, so don't even try. You cannot orchestrate a group of
inter-related tasks efficiently in light of people's shared human
needs, so don't even try. You cannot come to equitable agreements
among yourselves, so don't even try. Just thank your lucky stars
that even such a socially challenged species as yourselves can still
benefit from a division of labor thanks to the miracle of the market
system wherein you can function as greedy, non-cooperating,
competitive, isolated atoms, but still get social results. Markets are
a no-confidence vote on the social capacities of the human species."

But if that daily message were not sufficient discouragement,
markets mobilize our creative capacities and energies largely by
arranging for other people to threaten our livelihoods and by bribing
us with the lure of luxury beyond what others can have and beyond
what we know we deserve. They feed the worst forms of
individualism and egoism. And to top off their anti-social agenda,
markets munificently reward those who are the most cut-throat and
adept at taking advantage of their fellow citizens, and penalize
those who insist on pursuing the golden rule. Of course, we are told
we can personally benefit in a market system by providing service to
others. But we also know that we can generally benefit a lot more
easily by tricking others. Mutual concern, empathy, and solidarity
have little or no usefulness in market economies, so they atrophy.

Why do markets impede solidarity? For workers to compre-
hensively evaluate their work they would have to know the human

and social as well as the material factors that go into the inputs they use plus the human and social consequences their outputs make possible. But the only information markets provide, with or without private property, are the prices of the commodities people exchange. Even if these prices accurately reflected all the human and social factors lurking behind economic transactions, which they most certainly don't, producers and consumers would still not be able to adjust their activities in light of a self-conscious understanding of their relations with other producers or consumers because they would lack the qualitative data to do so, and they would still have to compete. It follows that markets do not provide the qualitative data necessary for producers to judge how their activities affect consumers, or vice versa. The absence of information about the concrete effects of my activities on others leaves me little choice but to consult my own situation exclusively. The fact that marks pit buyers against sellers—the one trying to buy cheap and the other to sell dear—means the absence of information causes no aggravation. Rather, all economic actors are forced to be anti-social and lack the means to do otherwise, in any event.

That is, the lack of concrete qualitative information and the obscuring of social ties and connections in market economies make cooperation difficult, while competitive pressures make cooperation irrational. Neither buyers nor sellers can afford to respect the situation of the other. Not only is relevant information unavailable, solidarity is self-defeating. Polluters must try to hide their transgressions, since paying a pollution tax or modernizing their equipment would lower their profits. Even if one producer in an industry does not behave egocentrically, others will. If altruists persist in socially responsible behavior they will ultimately be driven out of business for their trouble, with egoists rising to prominent positions. Market competition squashes solidarity regardless of encompassing ownership relations.

But rather than further pursue our rejection of markets on grounds of their implications for human relations, it may be more compelling to hear the US-based economist Sam Bowles, a left advocate of market allocation, eloquently explain this failure of markets:

> Markets not only allocate resources and distribute income; they also shape our culture, foster or thwart desirable forms of human development, and support a well-defined structure of power. Markets are as much political and cultural institutions as they are economic. For this reason, the standard efficiency analysis is

insufficient to tell us when and where markets should allocate goods and services and where other institutions should be used. Even if market allocations did yield [economically efficient] results, and even if the resulting income distribution was thought to be fair (two very big "ifs"), the market would still fail if it supported an undemocratic structure of power or if it rewarded greed, opportunism, political passivity, and indifference toward others. The central idea here is that our evaluation of markets—and with it the concept of market failure-must be expanded to include the effects of markets on both the structure of power and the process of human development ....

As anthropologists have long stressed, how we regulate our exchanges and coordinate our disparate economic activities influences what kind of people we become. Markets may be considered to be social settings that foster specific types of personal development and penalize others. The beauty of the market, some would say, is precisely this: It works well even if people are indifferent toward one another. And it does not require complex communication or even trust among its participants. But that is also the problem. The economy—its markets, workplaces and other sites—is a gigantic school. Its rewards encourage the development of particular skills and attitudes while other potentials lay fallow or atrophy. We learn to function in these environments, and in so doing become someone we might not have become in a different setting. By economizing on valuable traits—feelings of solidarity with others, the ability to empathize, the capacity for complex communication and collective decision-making, for example—markets are said to cope with the scarcity of these worthy traits. But in the long run markets contribute to their erosion and even disappearance. What looks like a hardheaded adaptation to the infirmity of human nature may in fact be part of the problem.

In short, markets pit buyers against sellers creating an environment that is almost precisely the opposite of what any reasonable person would associate with solidarity. In each market transaction one party gains more only if the other party gains less. What ought to be the case—economic actors sharing in benefits and costs and moving forward or back in unison with the interest of each actor furthering the enhancement of other actors—is turned topsy-turvy, to the point where each actor's interest is opposed to that of all others. As Bowles explains, even against our better natures, this literally instructs us, molds us, and cajoles us into being unsympathetic egoists of the worst sort.

Self-Management

Confusing the cause of free markets with that of democracy is typical of modern commentary, but astounding given the overwhelming evidence that market systems have disenfranchised larger and larger segments of the world's body politic. First, markets undermine rather than promote the kinds of human traits critical to the democratic process. As Bowles, who is, remember, an advocate of markets, explains:

> If democratic governance is a value, it seems reasonable to favor institutions that foster the development of people likely to support democratic institutions and able to function effectively in a democratic environment. Among the traits most students of the subject consider essential are the ability to process and communicate complex information, to make collective decisions, and the capacity to feel empathy and solidarity with others. As we have seen, markets may provide a hostile environment for the cultivation of these traits. Feelings of solidarity are more likely to flourish where economic relationships are ongoing and personal, rather than fleeting and anonymous; and where a concern for the needs of others is an integral part of the institutions governing economic life. The complex decision-making and information processing skills required of the modern democratic citizen are not likely to be fostered in either markets or in workplaces that run from the top down.

Second, markets empower those with greater ability to extract rewards at the expense of those "less able" to do so. By concentrating economic and therefore political power in the hands of a few, markets work to the comparative advantage of the more "able," and therefore, of those who are likely to be more powerful in the first place. If the more powerful party succeeds in appropriating more than 50 percent of the benefits of an exchange, as will generally occur, the exchange further disempowers the less powerful party and further empowers the more powerful party. In the next round of exchange, the deck is stacked a little more, and so on, ultimately leading to wide disparities.

Those who deceive themselves (and others) that markets nurture democracy ignore the simple truth that markets tend to aggravate disparities in economic power. Advocates focus on the fact that the spread of markets can undermine traditional elites. This is certainly true, but it does not prove that power will be more evenly spread and democracy enhanced. If new and more powerful obstacles replace old obstacles to economic democracy and participation, we are not moving forward, or at most are barely doing so. If the boards of directors of multinational corporations and banks, the free market policemen at the World Bank and the IMF, and the adjudication commissions for international treaties like NAFTA and MAI are more effectively insulated from popular pressure than their predecessors were, the cause of democracy is obviously not served, even though some old obstacles have been pushed aside.

But there is more to be said. Markets have class implications just as central planning does. Consider a workplace in a market economy: even without private ownership and profit-seeking for owners, the firm must compete for market share and reduce costs and raise revenues in pursuit of surpluses to invest. If it fails in the competition for surpluses relative to other firms in its industry, it will lack funds to invest and will steadily decline in assets and eventually go out of business. Therefore survival in a market system, even in the absence of private ownership, requires pursuit of surplus. A key component of pursuing profit or surplus is reducing labor costs and extracting more work from those employed. But this is not uncontested. Workers, of course, all other things being equal, prefer the opposite goal: higher wages and better conditions.

So imagine a workplace in a market economy. Typically, there is a broad corporate division of labor between conceptual workers making decisions and overseeing and disciplining the workforce, and rote workers carrying out orders given to them by their superiors. Given the remuneration scheme of markets, the employees with empowering work and decision-making prerogatives will earn more and enjoy better conditions than those who merely carry out orders. More, because of this disparity, the empowered group will be in position to largely implement its own schemes and defend its position to do so, also seeing themselves as worthy to do so. These people do not opt to reduce their own incomes or worsen their own work conditions (though in an economy with capitalists, the capitalists may try to do this to them) in order to reduce workplace costs. Instead, they force the rote workers to accept lower wages and worse conditions.

Now imagine that this same workplace has removed such divisions of labor. By whatever means, all workers earn according to effort and sacrifice and enjoy equally empowering and fulfilling work conditions. By the rules of the workplace they may share equally in sensible, informed decision-making. However, their workplace exists in a market, and as a result they must compete with other firms or go bankrupt.

In this context, assuming that they reject bankruptcy, they have two broad choices: they can opt to reduce their own wages, worsen their own work conditions, and speed up their own levels of work, which is a very alienating approach that they are not very emotionally or psychologically equipped to undertake. Or, they can hire managers to carry out these cost-cutting and output enlarging policies while insulating the managers from feeling the policies' adverse effects by giving the managers better conditions, higher wages, etc. In practice, very predictably, the latter is what occurs. Even ignoring their remunerative implications, markets therefore have a built-in pressure to organize a work force into two groups: a large majority that obeys and a small minority that makes decisions, with the latter enjoying greater income, power, and protection from the adverse effects of the cost-cutting decisions they will impose on others.

In other words, the information, incentive, and role characteristics of market systems subvert the rationale for workers to take initiative in workplace decisions even if they have the legal right to do so. For example, worker's councils in the old Yugoslavia had the right to meet and make decisions over all aspects of their economic activities, but why should they? Market competition created an environment in which decision-makers had no choice but to maximize the bottom line. Any human effects that did not bear on costs and revenues had to be ignored or else risk competitive failure. Workers' councils motivated by qualitative human considerations would ultimately fail, thus putting out of work the very people the councils were intended to empower. Since competitive pressures have adverse effects on workplace satisfaction, it is perfectly sensible for workers' councils in market environments to hire others to make the decisions for them. The pattern is simple: first, worker attention to and desire for self-management erodes. Next, workers hire managers who in turn hire engineers and administrators to transform job roles according to the dictates of market competition. Even in the absence of private ownership, a process that begins with workers choosing to delegate technical and alienating decisions to experts who are insulated from the negative effects of those decisions, ends up by increasing the fragmentation of work, bloating managerial prerogatives, and substituting manager's goals—or, perhaps more accurately, market goals—for those of workers. It is not long before a burgeoning managerial class of "coordinators" begins to increase the proportion of the surplus earmarked for themselves and to search for ways to preserve their own power.

Even beyond generating income inequalities, which would be more than bad enough, by creating a class division and elevating the conceptual workers whom we call coordinators to positions dominating workers who do the more rote and obedient tasks, markets empower some folks disproportionately at the expense of others, and create conditions that permit these coordinators to parlay their power into grabbing still more income for themselves. Obviously all this creates opposed interests and destroys solidarity.

Efficiency

Increasing the value of goods and services produced and decreasing the unpleasantness of what we have to do to get them are two ways producers can increase profits in a market economy. Competitive pressures drive producers to do both, a situation which is sometimes desirable, as, for example, when it leads to innovations in methods of production. But generally undesirable is the maneuvering to appropriate a greater share of the goods and services produced by externalizing costs such as pollution, and competitive market pressures drive producers to pursue this route to greater profitability just as assiduously as any other. The problem is that, while the first kind of behavior often serves the social interest as well as the private interests of producers, the second kind of behavior does not. When buyers or sellers promote their private interests by avoiding responsibility for costs of their actions and pushing them onto those who are not party to the market exchange, as with generating pollution and not cleaning it up, their behavior introduces a misallocation of productive resources and a consequent decrease in the overall value of goods and services produced.

The positive side of market incentives has received great attention and admiration, starting with Adam Smith who used the term "invisible hand" to characterize it. He meant, of course, that competitive pressures to profit induce many efficiency increasing choices, such as employing more productive technologies and guiding actors to seek more productive and less expensive options. The darker side of market incentives has been neglected and underestimated. Two modern exceptions are Ralph d'Arge and E.K. Hunt, who coined the less famous but equally appropriate concept, "invisible foot" to describe the socially counter-productive behavior of foisting costs onto others that markets also promote.

Market advocates seldom ask: Where are firms most likely to find the easiest opportunities to expand their profits? How easy is it to increase the size or quality of the economic pie and thereby accrue more? How easy is it to reduce the time or discomfort that it takes to bake the pie, thereby accruing more? Alternatively, how easy is it to enlarge one's slice of the pie by externalizing a cost or by appropriating a benefit without payment, even if the overall size or quality of the pie declines as a result? Why should we assume that it is infinitely easier to expand one's own profits through socially productive behavior that increases the size of the pie than through socially unproductive or even counter-productive behavior that actually reduces the size of the pie? Yet this implicit assumption lies behind the view that markets are efficiency machines.

Market advocates fail to notice that the same feature of market exchanges primarily responsible for making business easy to undertake—the exclusion of all affected parties but two from a transaction—is also a major source of potential gain for the buyer and seller. When the buyer and seller of an automobile strike their mutually convenient deal, the size of the benefit they have to divide between them is greatly enlarged by externalizing the costs onto others of the acid rain produced by car production, as well as the costs of urban smog, noise pollution, traffic congestion, and greenhouse gas emissions caused by car consumption. Those who pay these costs and thereby enlarge car-maker profits and car-consumer benefits are easy marks for car sellers and buyers because they are geographically and chronologically dispersed and because the magnitude of the effect of each specific transaction on each of them is small and varies widely from person to person. Individually the mass of folks who are separately affected each have little incentive to insist on being party to the transaction. Collectively they face formidable obstacles to forming a voluntary coalition to effectively represent a large number of people, each of whom have little and different amounts at stake. Nor is the problem solved by awarding victims of external effects a property right not to be victimized without their consent. Moreover, making markets perfectly competitive or making the cost of entering a market zero (even if either were realistically possible) would not eliminate the opportunity for this kind of rent-seeking behavior.

That is, even if there were countless perfectly informed sellers and buyers in every market, even if the appearance of the slightest differences in average profit rates in different industries induced instantaneous self-correcting entries and exits of firms, and even if every economic participant were equally powerful and therefore equally powerless—that is, even if we fully embraced the utterly unreal fantasies of market enthusiasts—as long as there were numerous external parties with small but unequal interests in market transactions, those external parties would face much greater obstacles to a full and effective representation of their collective interest than the obstacles faced by the buyer and seller in the exchange. And it is this unavoidable inequality in their ability to represent their own interests that makes external parties easy prey to rent-seeking behavior on the part of buyers and sellers.

Moreover, even if we could organize a market economy wherein every participant were as powerful as every other and no one ever faced a less powerful opponent in a market exchange—another ridiculous fiction—this would still not change the fact that each of us has small interests at stake in many transactions in which we are neither buyer or seller. Yet the sum total interest of all these external parties can be considerable compared to the interests of the two who are presumably the most affected—the buyer and seller. It is the difficulty of representing the collective interests of those with lesser individual interests that creates an unavoidable inequality in power, which, in turn, gives rise to the opportunity for individually profitable but socially counter-productive rent-seeking on the part of buyers and sellers.

But of course the real world bears little resemblance to a hypothetical game where it is impossible to increase one's market power so that there is no reason to try. Instead, in the real world it is just as rational to pursue ways to increase one's power vis-à-vis other buyers or sellers as it is to search for ways to increase the size or quality of the economic pie or reduce the time or discomfort necessary to bake it. In the real world there are consumers with little information, time, or means to defend their interests. There are small innovative firms for giants like IBM and Microsoft to buy up instead of tackling the hard work of innovation themselves. There are common property resources whose productivity can be appropriated at little or no cost to the beneficiary as they are over-exploited at the expense of future generations. And there is a government run by politicians whose careers rely mainly on their ability to raise campaign money, begging to be plied for corporate welfare programs financed at taxpayer expense.

In short, in a realistic world of unequal economic power the most effective profit maximizing strategy is often to maneuver at the expense of those with less economic power so as to re-slice the pie (even while shrinking it) rather than to work to expand the pie. And of course, the same prevails internationally as US-based economist Robert Lekachman points out with eloquent restraint:

> Children and economists may think that the men at the head of our great corporations spend their time thinking about new ways to please the customers or improve the efficiency of their factories and offices. What they actually concentrate on is enlisting their government to protect their foreign and domestic interests.

In any case, leftist advocates of markets concede that externalities lead to inefficient allocations and that non-competitive market structures and disequilibrating forces add additional sources of inefficiencies. And they also concede that efficiency requires policies designed to internalize external effects, curb monopolistic practices, and ameliorate market disequilibria. But there are also many significant failings of markets that market admirers do not concede, and their sum total importance is undeniable.

1 External effects are the rule rather than the exception.

As E. K. Hunt explained:

> The Achilles heel of welfare economics is its treatment of externalities ....When reference is made to externalities, one usually takes as a typical example an upwind factory that emits large quantities of sulfur oxides and particulate matter inducing rising probabilities of emphysema, lung cancer, and other respiratory diseases to residents downwind, or a strip-mining operation that leaves an irreparable aesthetic scar on the countryside. The fact is, however, that most of the millions of acts of production and consumption in which we daily engage involve externalities. In a market economy any action of one individual or enterprise which induces pleasure or pain to any other individual or enterprise constitutes an externality. Since the vast majority of productive and consumptive acts are social, i.e., to some degree they involve more than one person, it follows that they will involve externalities. Our table manners in a restaurant, the general appearance of our house, our yard or our person, our personal hygiene, the route we pick for a joy ride, the time of day we mow our lawn, or nearly any one of the thousands of ordinary daily acts, all affect, to some degree, the pleasures or happiness of others. The fact is externalities are totally pervasive.

2 There are no convenient or reliable procedures in market economies for estimating the magnitude of external effects.

This means that accurate correctives, or what economists call "Pigouvian" taxes, after the British economist Arthur Pigou (1877-1959), are hard to calculate even in an isolated market. Any hope of accurately estimating external effects in market economies lies with actors' willingness to accept damage surveys which have well-known biases and discrepancies that can be exploited by special interests. And the fact that estimates derived from willingness to accept damage surveys are commonly four times as high as estimates derived from willingness to pay surveys is hardly comforting, when, in theory, they should be roughly equal. Suffice to say, this problem is another thorn in the side of markets.

3 Because they are unevenly dispersed throughout the industrial matrix, the task of correcting for external effects is even more daunting.

In the real world, where private interests and power take precedence over economic efficiency, the would-be beneficiaries of accurate corrective taxes are usually dispersed and powerless compared to those who would have to pay such taxes. This makes it unlikely that full correctives would be enacted—even if they could be accurately calculated.

4 Because consumer preferences are at least partially affected by the economy—the technical term for which is that they are endogenous—the degree of misallocation that results from predictable under-correction for external effects will increase, or "snowball" over time.

As noted earlier, people are affected by their economic conditions and activities and they will learn to adjust their preferences to the biases created by external effects in the market price system. Consumers will increase their preference and demand for goods whose production and/or consumption entails negative external effects but whose market prices fail to reflect these costs and are therefore too low; and will decrease their preference and demand for goods whose production and/or consumption entails positive external effects but whose market prices fail to reflect these benefits and are therefore too high. In short, we adjust ourselves to benefit from what we see to be systematic bargains and to avoid what we see to be systematic scams. While this adjustment is individually rational to take advantage of market biases, it is socially irrational and inefficient since it leads to greater demand for the goods that the market already wrongly overproduces, and lowers demand for the goods the market already under produces. Morever, because the effects of this phenomenon are cumulative and self-enforcing, over time the degree of inefficiency in the economy will grow.

The upshot of these points is that the invisible foot operates on a par with the invisible hand. The degree of allocative inefficiency due to external effects is significant. Hope for "Pigouvian" correctives is a pipe dream. Relative prices predictably diverge ever more widely from accurate measures of full social costs and benefits as consumers adjust their endogenous preferences to individually benefit from inevitable market biases. In sum, convenient deals with mutual benefits for buyer and seller should not be confused with economic efficiency. When some kinds of preferences are consistently under-represented because of transaction cost and free rider problems (wherein folks get the benefit of public goods without paying for them), when some resources are consistently over-exploited because they are common rather than private property, when consumers adjust their preferences to biases in the price system, and when profits or surpluses come as often from greater power as greater contribution, theory predicts free market exchange will result in a misallocation of resources. And when markets are less than perfect (which they always are), and fail to reach equilibrium instantaneously (which they always do), the results will be that much worse.

While markets are currently widely praised, perhaps before moving on we should point out that we are not markets' only detractors. Consider the US Nobel Prize-winning economist Robert Solow's observations that:

> Few markets can ever have been as competitive as those that flourished in Britain in the first half of the nineteenth century, when infants became deformed as they toiled their way to an early death in the pits and mills of the Black Country. And there is no lack of examples today to confirm the fact also that well-functioning markets have no innate tendency to promote excellence in any form. They offer no resistance to forces making for a descent into cultural barbarity or moral depravity.

Or US Nobel Prize economist James Tobin's observation that:

> The only sure result [of free market Reaganomics] ... are redistribution of income, wealth, and power—from government to private enterprises, from workers to capitalists, and from poor to rich.

Or US novelist Edward Bellamy's (1850-1898) observation that:

According to our ideas, buying and selling is essentially anti-social in all its tendencies. It is an education in self-seeking at the expense of others, and no society whose citizens are trained in such a school can possibly rise above a very low grade of civilization.

Or, arch marketeer US Nobel Prize-winning economist Milton Friedman's recent observation that:

The greatest problem facing our country is the breaking down into two classes, those who have and those who have not. The growing differences between the incomes of the skilled and the less skilled, the educated and the uneducated, pose a very real danger. If that widening rift continues, we're going to be in terrible trouble. The idea of having a class of people who never communicate with their neighbors—those very neighbors who assume the responsibility for providing their basic needs—is extremely unpleasant and discouraging. And it cannot last. We'll have a civil war. We really cannot remain a democratic, open society that is divided into two classes. In the long run, that's the greatest single danger.

A summary of our findings regarding market inefficiencies is that the cybernetic, incentive, and allocative properties of markets involve a pervasive bias against discovering, expressing, and developing needs that require social rather than individual activity for fulfillment. Markets do not provide concrete information about how people's decisions affect the life prospects of others or vice versa. They do not even provide accurate summaries of the social benefits and costs associated with what people decide to do since markets mis-evaluate external effects—and external effects are the rule rather than the exception. Actual market allocations under supply social goods and activities and over supply individual goods and activities. They establish incentives for individuals to wean themselves of needs that require socially coordinated intercourse and accentuate needs that can be met individually. Moreover, markets reward competitive behavior and penalize cooperative behavior.

In sum, markets not only erode solidarity, they also systematically mis-charge purchasers so that over time, preferences that are individually rational for people to develop combine with biases inherent in market allocations to yield outcomes increasingly further from those that would have maximized human fulfillment. And to top it off, markets generate gross economic inequality, severely distorted decision-making influence, and class division and rule. In the end, the fears of "utopian" critics who decry the socially alienating effects of markets prove more to the point than the assurances of so-called "scientific" economists that markets are ideal allocation institutions. Regarding markets, abolitionism is an appropriate attitude.

Capitalism

Capitalism employs private ownership and markets. It remunerates property, power, and output, and, as a result, has produced some of the widest disparities of income and wealth found in human history. The division of labor within capitalism is hierarchical. Capitalists rule workers while coordinators occupy the terrain between labor and capital, partly administering on behalf of capitalists and partly trying to enlarge their own interests at the expense of both capitalists above and workers below.

Within this broad rubric there is certainly variation. Workers may or may not have unions and other forms of organization to aid in manifesting their preferences—and the same can be true for the coordinator class that may have amassed greater or lesser means of accruing wealth and power unto itself at the expense of either capitalists or workers. At its most oppressive, there is the cut-throat capitalism of robber barons with gigantic, unrestrained corporate power dominating all social choices and options. At its least oppressive, there is an ameliorated system of capitalism called social democracy in which laborers and consumers have considerable local and state power and use it to ward off the worst outcomes of markets and private ownership.

In any case, the basic model called capitalism because of its intrinsic tendencies of private ownership of means of production, hierarchical corporate divisions of labor, and competitive markets, not only doesn't facilitate solidarity, diversity, equity, and participatory self-management, it violates each of these values producing virtually the exact opposite. As the tremendously influential British Nobel economist John Maynard Keynes (1883-1946) put it:

> [Capitalism] is not a success. It is not intelligent, it is not beautiful, it is not just, it is not virtuous—and it doesn't deliver the goods. In short, we dislike it, and we are beginning to despise it. But when we wonder what to put in its place, we are extremely perplexed.

Reducing that perplexity occupies much of this book.

Market Socialism

Market socialism is the widely used name for a system that utilizes markets, a hierarchical or corporate division of labor, remuneration according to output, and either social, public, or state ownership of means of production.

Market socialism, in our view, improves on capitalism by eliminating private ownership and thus the capitalist class. But in market socialism we see, instead, that the coordinator class rises in stature and power, utilizing its relative monopoly on intellectual labor and on decision-making bearing on their own work and the work of their subordinates to attain a ruling position. Capitalists are gone and thus the most significant factor leading to income differential is gone, but there is still class division and class rule. There is still the alienation, misallocation, and immoral bases for remuneration intrinsic to markets, and there is still a division of labor that relegates most actors to greater tedium than warranted, reserving for a relative few greater power and reward.

One can imagine a range of variations in such economies, of course. The balance of power between coordinators and workers could shift. If workers accrued more power, they could enact structural reforms to ameliorate the ills of markets, reallocate wealth, etc. If coordinators accrued more power, they could enact the reverse. The system's internal market dynamics promote the latter. Courageous struggle promotes the former.

Clearly, however, whatever gains over capitalism have been achieved in attaining market socialism, market socialism still is not an economy that by its intrinsic operations promotes solidarity, equity, diversity, and participatory self-management while also accomplishing economic functions efficiently. Instead, all the intrinsic ills of markets—particularly, hierarchical workplace divisions, remuneration according to output and bargaining power, distortion of personality and motives, and mispricing of goods and services, etc.—persist, while only the aggravating presence of private capital is transcended.

Is this economic system aptly called socialism? If we call it "socialism," then the word can't simultaneously mean rule by workers over their own labors, because that is certainly absent in this system. If we do not call this system "socialism," then we fly in the face of popular labels and of the name for their aim chosen by the advocates of the system. The deciding factor in this tension for me, after some years of ambivalence, is that too many perfectly reasonable people associate the label "socialism" with this model and with associated centrally planned models to make trying to disentangle the label from the systems worthwhile. It seems to be more instructive and productive

1   to make clear that these systems are class-divided and coordinator-ruled,

2   to make clear how a preferred system differs from them, and

3   to leave behind the label socialism as a positive descriptor of what we desire so as to avoid guilt by association and related confusions.

And that's why the economy featured in this book is called "participatory economics."

Centrally Planned Socialism

Centrally planned socialism replaces the market allocation of market socialism with central planning. Having discussed this allocation institution we know that the result will be quite mixed. Depending on how the central planning apparatus arrives at data, and the harshness of its regime, we will have more or less authoritarianism and more or less means for planners and other intellectual workers in the coordinator class to propel their own interests over and above the interests of workers.

But however the chips fall regarding the exact balance of power and the institutional forms of a centrally planned economy, the continuation of hierarchical divisions of labor and remuneration according to power, and the imposition of even more starkly authoritarian command and associated personality structures guarantee that such a system will not deliver solidarity, diversity, equity, and participatory self-management. It will be "socialist" only by self-designation and popular usage. Nonetheless, the system will deny those doing the labor and consuming the outputs proper say in the decisions that affect their lives and proper remuneration for their efforts and sacrifices.

Green Bioregionalism

Green bioregionalism is a system whose characteristics are quite vague. Many green activists quite reasonably reject capitalism, markets, and authoritarianism—much as we do in this book and for rather similar reasons. Somehow, however, their additional perfectly reasonable and essential idea that an economy and society should attain ecological sustainability leads some of them—and this is where a strange jump occurs—to a notion that local material self-sufficiency is a primary virtue.

Sustainability is certainly unobjectionable. What is the alternative, after all? Is there anyone who would argue that we should organize ourselves to promote dissolution of our societies due to depletion of their means of existence? Surely everyone of all persuasions has to agree that ecological sustainability is desirable, the alternative being suicide. But then what does self-sufficiency mean? Or bioregionalism?

For some of its advocates bioregionalism seems to mean that in any sensibly demarcated region, economic and social activities should respect the biological and ecological character of the region, consistent with creating a sustainable and fulfilling existence. That seems fair enough and is obviously desirable. But for other advocates bioregionalism seems to mean that each bioregion should only undertake activities that are made possible by the resources and ecological attributes it contains. Its economy must use what resources are directly available in the region, and not depend on inputs from other regions. This seems, in contrast to the earlier sensible formulation, quite misguided.

First, what is ecological about separating each region from all others? The core concept of ecology is arguably interconnection and mutual dependence. For this reason, it is hard to understand why some greens, otherwise so attuned to ecological logic and values, think there is a virtue—much less an ecological imperative—in creating self-sufficient rather than mutually dependent relations among regions. Second, some regions naturally have more plentiful resources and desirable ecologies for humans than others, and no single region can offer all the benefits that can be generated by sensible attention to balanced utilization and sharing of resources from all regions. So why should we eliminate the benefits of sharing ecological bounty across all borders? We cannot find any reason to forego such benefits unless one argues that mutual interaction intrinsically breeds ecological devastation. But why should that be if we use means of mutual interaction that are ecologically sensitive (and rule out markets)?

What has all this got to do with green bioregionalism? Well, for us it is hard to evaluate it as an economic system without raising these points because to evaluate it as an economy we have to specify its component economic institutions. Some greens advocate a localized community economy, with small work units and no major allocation institutions other than direct interpersonal barter. They often seem to favor equitable roles and incomes, including no hierarchies in decision-making influence or job quality. However, they provide no explanation of how to accomplish these desirable aims. Instead, there is an implicit presumption that such admirable results would flow inexorably from the logic of small size and self-sufficiency. Yet this belief has neither historical nor logical basis. Indeed, in contrast, the only thing that necessarily flows from bioregionalist self-sufficient aspirations and small size is a needless dissolution of social ties, a harsh inequality of resources, and a self-negating rejection of economies of scale.

When green bioregionalists react to such criticisms, they say: "Oh sure, of course, we don't mean that people in the desert have to suffer compared to people in areas with great climates and plentiful resources. Who would favor such unfairness in life?" But then when asked how the bounty of the latter finds its way, in part, into the hands of the former, they have no answer ... and in our view the green bioregionalist now confronts an economic decision. Do I want markets, or do I want central planning, or do I want some other allocation mechanism to mediate this transfer? It is our view that if they opt for either of the first two allocative means they will wind up with either market or centrally planned socialism/coordinatorism. Their vision will incorporate class division and class rule and will lose the qualities they aspired to, including proper attention to the ecology in relation to human well-being and the capacity to sensibly relate to broader ecological dictates having to do with the rights of other species—as well as rejection of hierarchy in work conditions, assertion of mutual empowerment, and attainment of equitable distribution of circumstances and incomes. On the other hand, if Bioregionalists wish to retain all these values and to also facilitate the diverse ecological realities of countless regions, then they will have to adopt a suitable economic vision for those goals—which is not accomplished by favoring an a priori dissolution of inter-connectedness or prioritization of self-sufficiency.

The final point we would like to make about bioregionalism is the even more extreme one that ubiquitous smallness and self-sufficiency are not only not in every case necessary or sufficient for a good economy, but that taken by themselves they are not even always ecological values or values of any desirable sort at all.

To say that an economy should prioritize small structures, or assemble itself into regions subsisting without benefit of interaction, opts for such choices even when they are contrary to worthy values and themselves convey nothing positive. It would be sensible for greens to demand that a good economy should take proper account of the full ecological implications of economic choices, and should help people make choices in light of these implications. It would make sense to demand that an economy permit sensible choices of scale in light of ecological and social implications, not prejudging one way or the other. When dealing with workplaces, living units, industries, and pretty much every type of institution and social structure, sometimes larger is better, sometimes smaller, whether ecologically, or to achieve face to face relations, or for many other reasons. Similarly, it would make sense to demand that an economy not dissolve relations of mutual benefit and support among regions or exaggerate their potentials either, but, instead, allow ecologically proper and materially just and beneficial flows from region to region. Sometimes it makes sense for resources, goods, and services to flow freely even over large distances, sometimes not. The point is that an economy should not make such choices a priori, but provide workers and consumers the needed information and appropriate decision-making influence to collectively arrive at desirable choices, as conditions and opportunities arise.

We have come to the end of this chapter and to the end of part one of this book and have arrived at the positive questions that motivate the rest of our exploration. Can we specify a new type of economy that facilitates solidarity, diversity, equity, and self-management, and that gets desirable economic functions done without imposing costs that offset its benefits in ways that we find too onerous?

If yes, then we have a new economic vision we can truly celebrate. If no, then we either keep trying or we will have to choose from among the horribly flawed models we have already discussed— forcing ourselves to settle for the one we find least evil.

Having shown that existing economic options impede the values we hold dear, we desire a new and better vision. Espousing good values, as in earlier chapters, is a part of going forward. But a serious alternative vision must delineate new institutions with different properties than those we now endure. These new institutions should accomplish production, allocation, and consumption at least as well as institutions found in capitalism, market socialism, centrally planned socialism, and bioregionalism. But the new institutions should not induce class divisions nor produce the rule of one class by another. And they should enhance rather than obstruct equity, diversity, solidarity, and self-management. To accomplish these ends we are going to propose a system called participatory economics.

A New Vision

Participatory economics, or "parecon" for short, has as its central institutional and organizational components:

- social rather than private ownership

- nested worker and consumer councils and balanced job complexes rather than corporate workplace organization

- remuneration for effort and sacrifice rather than for property, power, or output

- participatory planning rather than markets or central planning

- and participatory self-management rather than class rule.

Taken together the above structures define participatory economics as a separate and new economic model—one that we believe meets our norms for a good economy.

From our earlier discussion of economics, various economic institutions, and various economic systems, we already know that in a desirable economy each worker and consumer should have equal access to information regarding the full social effects of proposed actions on themselves and throughout the economy. They should influence decisions in proportion as the decisions affect them. They should share one another's successes and suffer one another's hardships so that the daily functions of economic life enhance rather than destroy solidarity. A good economy's incentives, information, and circumstances should foster empathy and mutual concern. A good economy's economic activity should diversify opportunities and paths people can choose, rather than homogenizing them. A good economy's workers should be justly remunerated for their labors in accord with the actual effort and sacrifice they expend on behalf of the social product, or, if they cannot work, in accord with social averages and special needs. A good economy's division of labor should respect and advance people's diverse preferences at the same time that it promotes solidarity and facilitates self-management. Class divisions should not be produced, either by ownership or different circumstances of production or consumption. All in all, a good economy should accomplish central economic functions and meet people's needs and develop their potentials in accord with our highlighted values and without ill effects on other values we also hold dear.

In Part II, therefore, we will describe participatory economics, focusing on its defining institutions and their implications for workers and consumers. In the concluding parts three and four of the book we will explore daily life circumstances in parecon and address criticisms of parecon.

Describing an entire economic system one step at a time is a bit problematic: half a suspension bridge is worthless; the same holds for half an economic system. The new meaning and viability of each part of a good economy can only be fully evident when we take into account its interactions with the new economy's other parts. So as you read the rest of this book, please keep in mind that we will occasionally, and of necessity, allude to features that will not be fully described until later. Each chapter in the coming section will only partly explain the full meaning and implications of what is introduced. Full clarity comes only when we can situate each new structure in proper relation with all other new features. Please finish all the chapters and see the mutually dependent implications of all component parts before you fully judge any one of them.

Part II:
Participatory Economic Vision

There is no reason to accept the doctrines crafted to sustain power and privilege, or to believe that we are constrained by mysterious and unknown social laws. These are simply decisions made within institutions that are subject to human will and that must face the test of legitimacy. And if they do not meet the test, they can be replaced by other institutions that are more free and more just, as has happened often in the past.
— Noam Chomsky

If you think you are too small to make a difference, try sleeping in a closed room with a mosquito.
—African Proverb

Sometimes anti-capitalist economic vision offers markets or central planning plus public or state ownership. Not here. Sometimes anti-capitalist vision is a very broad and general presentation of inspiring values and aims, basically a collection of exalted adjectives, with little institutional substance. You will not find that here, either. The next five chapters deal with social ownership of productive assets, self-managing worker and consumer councils, balanced job complexes, remuneration for effort and sacrifice, and participatory planning—the five defining components of participatory economics. Two chapters then offer a summary of the parecon model and evaluate it.

4

Ownership

An apt and true reply was given to Alexander the Great by a pirate who had been seized. For when that king had asked the man what he meant by keeping hostile possession of the sea, he answered with bold pride. "What thou meanest by seizing the whole earth; but because I do it with a petty ship, I am called a robber, whilst thou who dost it with a great fleet art styled emperor.
— St. Augustine

There has to be a shortest and simplest chapter in every book. This is ours. Alone among chapters in this section it consists almost entirely of negation rather than positive envisioning. It is also trivially simple but nonetheless essential.

In every economy there are tools, workplaces, resources and other means of production with which we combine our efforts to produce new items for consumption. Historically, having a few members of society own these means of production, decide on their use, and dispose over the output and revenues they generate has meant that this privileged group has always had more wealth, more income, and more economic power than others in society. There are owners and non-owners. The non-owners may as a group have further categories of differentiation, but this does not complicate the current issue. By separating ownership from non-ownership of the means of production, society places some of its members on top and other below. Our commitment to equity, solidarity, diversity, proper distribution of influence, and classlessness precludes all this. So what is our alternative?

There are two issues:

- No one should have disproportionate say due to having a different relationship to owning means of production than anyone else.

- No one should have excessive income, nor for that matter, should anyone receive anything other than remuneration according to effort and sacrifice, or, if unable to work, according to need. Never should anyone's income be correlated to their owning means of production.

There is a simple logical step we can take to accomplish both these aims most quickly and easily. We simply remove ownership of the means of production from the economic picture. We can think of this as deciding that no one owns the means of production. Or we can think of it as deciding that everyone owns a fractional share of every single item of means of production equivalent to what every other person owns of that item. Or we can think of it as deciding that society owns all the means of production but that it has no say over any of the means of production nor any claim on their output on that account.

In short, we simply remove ownership of the means of production as an economic consideration. Property in the form of means of production becomes a non-thing. It has no bearing in a participatory economy. No one has any ownership of means of production that accrues to him or her any rights, any responsibilities, any wealth, or any income different from what the rest of the economy warrants for him or her. No one has wealth, income, or economic influence different than what anyone else has due to having different ownership of means of production. It is not just that ownership of the means of production changes hands from what we now know. It doesn't move from one set of actors to some other set. In a participatory economy ownership of the means of production no longer even exists as a concept. It is banished, and with it goes the category "capitalist." No one is distinguishable from anyone else by having different ownership of means of production. There is no separate concept of such ownership, and therefore no class of owners, and therefore no capitalists—nor is there any sector of folks acting as agents for others in administering means of production through the state. The whole idea and dynamic are gone.

Of course, this is not a full economic description of an alternative to private ownership, by any means. We cannot just negate and remove and call what remains something new. It is one needed step in arriving at something new, but not the total picture. Means of production are no longer owned in a participatory economy, but we still have to worry about the allocation of means of production to different production processes and about dispensation over the use of means of production. It is just that we have to do this having removed ownership from the equation, and we thus have to come up with an alternative to some people having deeds to this or that factory, assembly line, coal mine, and so on. As to how we accomplish this, that comes to light in the next few chapters.

5

Councils

The only possible alternative to being the oppressed or the oppressor is voluntary cooperation for the greatest good of all.
— Errico Malatesta

Economics is conducted by and for workers and consumers. Workers create the social product. Consumers enjoy the social product. In these two roles, mediated by allocation, people conduct economic life.

To do their jobs responsibly, workers ought to consider what they would like to contribute to the social product, both by their own efforts and in association with those they work with. They ought to address how to combine their efforts and the resources and tools they access to generate worthy outputs that other people will benefit from. They ought to be directly in touch with the dynamics of production and with its implications for themselves and others. And they ought to weigh their direct understanding of their production situation and preferences about it against their choices' implications for those who consume their product.

To enjoy output responsibly, in contrast, consumers ought to consider what they would like to have from the social product, either as individuals or in collective association with their family, neighbors, or others. They ought to address what to ask for to advance their lives as best they can in tune with the effects their choices will have on the people producing their outputs. They should directly assess their own desires and the conditions under which they live. They should closely consider the likely implications for their personal development of the various possible consumption choices they might make. They should weigh the implications of benefits of their consumption activities against the adverse effects those activities may have on those who will do the required work.

Coming chapters address very closely how workers and consumers receive the information they need, what incentives they have for their choices, and what income they get to use for their consumption. But here we address the prior question, in what local structures are workers and consumers organized?

Historically, in times of economic upheaval, it has been very common for workers and consumers to organize themselves into collective bodies for the purpose of influencing economic outcomes. These bodies have most often been called workers' and consumers' councils, and we adopt that name as well to describe the vehicles through which people in a participatory economy manifest their economic preferences and in which they determine and carry out most of their daily economic activities.

Workers' Councils

Every participatory economic workplace is governed by a workers' council in which each worker has the same overall decision making rights and responsibilities as every other. When necessary, smaller councils are organized for work teams, units, and small divisions. Larger councils are organized for divisions, whole workplaces, and industries.

Given a workplace's overall agenda, how the people in a work group organize themselves affects almost exclusively themselves— so they function as a unit vis-à-vis that decision. And the same happens at diverse levels, from teams and projects though units and divisions up to larger councils for whole workplaces, industries, and even for workers as a whole. Different-sized councils address different issues in accord with the norm that decision-making input should be proportionate to the impact of decisions on those who make them.

Council decisions are sometimes one-worker-one-vote majority rule, but in cases where that system would yield equal input for all council members in making decisions that actually have very unequal impact on each of them, councils employ different procedures with different degrees of consensus required for resolution, different actors participating, and so on. By leaving decisions that overwhelmingly affect a subset of workers overwhelmingly to only those workers and their councils, by assigning most initiative in decisions to those most affected by those decisions, and by weighing or otherwise organizing voting procedures to reflect the differential impacts of voting outcomes on those who will be affected by the decisions, workers' councils collectively fashion their own best approximations to self-management (a point we shall deal with in more detail as we proceed).

Of course neither conceiving nor agreeing on the most appropriate participation and voting system, much less on decisions themselves, will be free of dispute within actual workers' councils. Nor will any single approach to arriving at conclusions be universally applicable. To understand what workers do in their councils, what incentives and motives they have, what information they use, and what decisions they undertake, requires that we have a better understanding of diverse other institutions of participatory economics, and so must wait a few chapters. But the key point here is that in a situation where each worker has an interest in self-management, and no worker has disproportionate power, it is not unreasonable to assert that workers' councils will actuate decision-making structures and ways to delegate responsibility that accord with self-management rather than with unjust hierarchies of power. Or, we should better say, it is reasonable to think this will be so, assuming that other facets of the economy don't impose other norms, such as those that would be imposed by a hierarchical division of labor or markets—but instead also further this desirable aim.

Consumers' Councils

As with workers, the principal means of organizing consumers in a parecon is consumer councils. Each individual, family, or other social unit would comprise the smallest such councils and also belong to its larger neighborhood consumption council. Each neighborhood council would belong in turn to a federation of neighborhood councils the size of a city ward or a rural county. Each ward council would belong to a city consumption council (or perhaps a borough and then a city council), and each city and county council would belong to a state council, and each state council would belong to the national council (or maybe to a regional and then to the national council). This nested federation of democratic councils would organize consumption, just as the nested federation of democratic workers' councils organizes production.

Participatory economies incorporate this nesting of different consumers' councils to accommodate the fact that different kinds of consumption affect different groups of people in different ways. The color of my shirt concerns me and my most intimate acquaintances. The shrubbery on my block concerns all who live on the block, though perhaps some more than others. The quality of play equipment in a park affects all in the neighborhood. The number of volumes in the library and teachers in the high school primarily affect all in a ward. The frequency and punctuality of buses and subways affect primarily all in a city. The disposition of waste affects all states in a major watershed. "Real" national security affects all citizens in a country, and protection of the ozone layer affects all humanity—which means that my choice of deodorant, unlike my choice of shirt color, directly and primarily concerns more than just me and my intimates.

Failure to arrange for all those affected by consumption activities to participate in choosing them not only implies an absence of self-management, but, if the preferences of some are disregarded, also a loss of efficiency in meeting needs and developing potentials. It is to accommodate the full range of consumption activities, from the most private to the most public, that we organize different "levels" of consumption councils. As to how consumers get necessary information about product availability and indeed influence the choice of what is made available, and as to how they then make their own choices, with what budget, and in what ways—for both individual and collective consumption—we must wait until we have described more of the overall structure. But what we can say now is that once we recognize that consumption activity, like production activity, is largely social, we must insist that consumption decision-making, like production decision-making, be participatory and equitable. In that event it is reasonable to conclude that consumption councils will be one valuable component in the mix that accomplishes that aim.

Consensus?

As we prepare this book, in mid-2002, many economic activists are deeply committed to "consensus decision-making." They rightfully celebrate its lack of hierarchy, its mutual respect, and its openness. Critics of consensus decision-making, however, claim it is horribly inefficient in many venues and can be abused because it gives too much power to single actors who can prevent consensus from being attained. Actually, the use of consensus as a tool of left dissent and ensuing debate is not new. These emerged—or more accurately re-emerged—approximately thirty-five years ago in the early New Left, and then had a large boost during the anti-nuclear activism of the 1980s, and now again at the turn of this new century.

Participatory economics does not institutionally prejudge what procedures should be used for decisions made in workplace or consumer councils. It does not say you have to use majority rule or consensus or any other particular procedure. It could be that in a real parecon, workers and consumers opt for consensus decision-making all the time, much of the time, or rarely. That is a choice for them. What parecon prescribes is that people should ensure, as best they are able without investing excessive time and energy, that each actor has an impact on outcomes in proportion to how much he or she is affected.

As potential participants in a participatory economy, however, do we ourselves think it would make sense for workers and consumers to conduct all their decisions via consensus? No. We think consensus makes very good sense for some decisions, but not for others. There are two key but quite different aspects to consensus decision-making that bear on this perspective. One is about process. The other is about formal power.

The process of consensus decision-making, circa 2002, emphasizes respect for all parties and the use of diverse methods of information preparation and dissemination and subsequent discussion and exchange to ensure that each person's input is appropriately accessed and addressed. It is important to realize, however, that techniques for how information is gathered and addressed are one thing, and for how power is allotted are another. That is, the same methods of being sure that information gets out, preferences are expressed, issues are addressed, etc., as are used in contemporary consensus decision-making can be utilized when decisions are being made by one-person-one-vote majority rule, or by one-person-one-vote two-thirds needed for a positive outcome, or by other norms. Indeed, it would probably simplify debate about these matters if we had two concepts or names: one for the method of mutual discussion and information exchange, we could call this participatory preparation, and one for requiring unanimous consent, which we could call consensus.

At any rate, the second component of contemporary consensus decision-making is that for a decision to be settled, all must agree with it or at least refrain from blocking it. Each actor has a veto they can employ. The theory is that people (whether individually or in groups) will not veto options unless the impact of the choice on them is so great that they ought to have the right to block it. In other words, the implicit and sometimes explicit logic of consensus decision-making is that it permits each person to determine, relative to the others, the degree to which they are affected, and to then submit or withhold their expressions of opposition in accord with their best estimate of their own situation relative to the reported preferences and situation of others. If one actor or a group together among the people making a decision is sufficiently affected that they believe their rejection of the decision should dominate the outcome, then he, she, or they will oppose or block it. If they do not like it, but they do not think they should dominate the choice, then they will abstain or otherwise avoid blocking it. In this sense, when used as intended by actors who are attuned and respectful of one another, consensus decision-making works perfectly. Only individuals or subgroups that dislike an outcome and would be in sum sufficiently affected by it to warrant dominating the outcome, will opt to impede decisions. Working thusly, when consensus decision-making fails, imperfections derive not from having established an inflexible and inappropriate procedure for making decisions, but due to mis-estimates of each other's feelings or the impact felt, or to abuses of the unfolding process by individuals in the group. So the question becomes, how likely are we to have good interaction and outcomes rather than problematic ones, and are the prospects for the latter low enough, in all contexts, to warrant using consensus all the time? Or do the prospects differ for different situations and decisions, so that in some cases using other approaches will be more likely to yield the best results with the least hassle?

Consider hiring a new worker for a small workplace, or adding one to a small work team. Suppose we collectively assess this type of recurring decision in our workplace and decide that in light of who we are, the time we have for this type of decision, our general situations relative to decisions of this type, etc., this is a situation where the impact on each person of a choice to hire someone that they don't like is huge, whereas the impact of hiring someone they do like on any actor is much less. Everyone has to work in close proximity with a new person day in and day out, and if anyone really doesn't like him or her, that will potentially be a far more serious problem for that person than it is a plus that everyone else favors the hire.

So in our workers' councils, we decide that for each new hire to our small workplace where everyone works in close proximity and knows one another well, everyone involved is entitled to a veto. The voting guideline might be that you need three quarters to approve someone for that person to be hired, but that anyone who is strongly enough opposed can block any proposed hire no matter how many others favor it. The voting rules aren't reworked for every new hiring situation, but nor do they imply a universal rule that applies to all other types of decision. Instead, this is a pre-agreed rule specifically about hiring decisions.

And note, it is chosen because it makes life easier, not harder, in that it approximates most closely what we generally think will be appropriate input for each person involved and thereby reduces the complexity of arriving at the desired result once we begin our deliberations. The person who is highly upset over a new hire doesn't have to convince everyone of the validity of her concern and get them to vote her way as well. She is concerned, period. She doesn't have to explain why. She gets a veto because being strongly opposed to hiring trumps favoring hiring. There is no need for everyone to engage in fancy mutual calculations to decide if they have the right to trump, though of course, as with any procedure, we can include diverse methods for communicating feelings, etc.

But suppose we had instead adopted a one-person one-vote majority rule approach to hiring decisions. Now the person who feels her life would be made miserable by the new person's entry must convince a majority of others to respect her strong feelings and vote her way. If she fails, her strong feelings will not have their appropriate impact on the final decision.

Something interesting characterizes the above comparison. In this particular type of decision, it turns out that the consensus approach (not the communications methods but the voting system itself) can yield proper results even with less mutual empathy and less communication of preferences and compromise than simple majority rule voting would entail. In this case it is the one-person one-vote approach that would fail to yield the appropriate influence for each actor, unless, due to an extensive process of discussion, the actors mediated very constructively on behalf of one another.

The lesson is clear. Good process is always good to have, of course, though one can spend more time on communication and mutual exploration than warranted by a decision's importance. But different decision procedures will put more or less weight on having a perfect process and will arrive at better or worse representations of the proportionate will of the actors involved more or less quickly and more or less easily. Some might achieve proportionate say almost automatically as compared to others achieving it only with great difficulty and due to very precise jockeying by each actor in light of knowledge of the others' views and willingness to bend toward their stronger preferences. The irony is, if consensus advocates want to say that consensus is good because it forces actors to mediate their choices in accord with their mutual assessments of one another rather than merely consulting their own preferences, then they should in fact opt for one-person-one-vote majority rule, not consensus, for a decision like hiring. The second irony is, this would precisely reverse the type of logic that we think a council should employ in choosing decision procedures.

In our view the upshot is that the processes we settle on to prepare for, debate, and finally make decisions should be chosen to maximize an appropriate level of give and take, exploration, and mutual understanding, as well as appropriate influence for the importance of the decision and the time available. Communication should not be coerced by choosing a procedure that will fail miserably if communication falls short of optimal forcing people to spend more time deliberating than another procedure would require. In other words, the voting procedure used in decisions should approximate as closely as we can arrange to directly facilitating proportionate say, so that if the supporting process doesn't work perfectly the procedure is least distorted by the communicative inadequacies.

Those who favor using consensus all the time presumably feel, instead, that we should opt for the approach that so demands good process that we must expend great effort in having good process all the time, or we will get horrible results. For that matter, the folks who advocate ubiquitous use of one-person-one-vote majority rule are presumably saying something like, let's have a middle of the road orientation. But why should we have any single orientation at all? Sometimes one procedure is better, other times a different one is better. Why prejudge the choice universally, as compared to settling it differently, if appropriate, for each different venue?

The differences between always favoring consensus or favoring one-person-one-vote majority rule or some other option, or favoring different procedures for different situations, are not simple to see, experience shows. So let's consider a different kind of decision, to clarify a bit more.

Let's say we have to make choices about investment options in a workplace. We might imagine workers in a workers' council considering a consensus approach for this type of decision but opting against it, because in application it would be cumbersome and any errors could easily lead to harmful outcomes. For investment, non consensus procedures would be easier to enact and less likely to diverge from optimal choices due to errors or bad faith by anyone involved.

For example, suppose there is a proposal to put in a new heating system. After discussion there needs to be a decision. With a consensus approach anyone can block a choice for any reason, but if you are considering doing so, how do you know whether you have the moral right, given the scale of the decision's relative impact on you, to block it or not? In the context of the debate you have to decide yourself if it is warranted for you to veto a choice given the intensity of your feelings and those of others. With a relatively few trusting people and enough time, and with thorough information flow, consensus may be optimal, but without these features working nearly perfectly, using consensus for this type of decision is asking for trouble.

With that in mind, workers might decide it is better to prejudge that in cases of investment choices they should opt for the abstract approach that each worker gets a vote and majority rules, but also allow any strongly dissenting minority to put off a decision for further discussion, at least twice. The point is, the workers might decide that something other than consensus (which allows for individual veto) comes closer to correct apportionment of influence and for that reason leaves the actors less difficulty in choosing to moderate or to strongly express their preferences to attain proper proportionate input for all.

Now, nothing is perfect. So (to make the point graphically), suppose there is a worker who will die if the temperature goes down to 68 degrees but is fine at 70 and above. Obviously, with consensus he will have no problem manifesting his intense preference even if the mutual exchange of information is faulty. In the one-person-one-vote majority rule approach, for the decision to come out properly the debate (or perhaps overarching rules about disabilities) needs to to give that person his extra due. But the view of a group opting for majority rule for investment decisions is that the degree of sensitivity required for the chosen approach when deciding investments and the harm that errors due to poor process will most often be less than the degree of sensitivity required and the harm that would arise from errors were the algorithm for investment decisions consensus.

The point of all this is to see that decision-making procedures and communication methods are flexible and not goals in and of themselves. They are a means to the desired end of proportionate, informed, participatory, and efficient influence. It follows that we should be principled about the goals, but not about the means.

Something that emerges from this is that in all modes of decision-making, if everyone operates ideally after a full exchange of relevant information and feelings, they will reach ideal decisions. Perfect process plus perfect people plus any decision-making system at all yields perfect decisions.

Consider the case of decision-making by a single leader. The leader hears everybody, calculates all impacts and preferences perfectly, and decides the perfect outcome, incorporating into her choice each actor's will in proportion to how they will be affected by the outcome. In a one-person-one-vote majority rule framework everyone has access to the same information and is able to freely express themselves, then modulate their vote so that the sum of all yeas and nays is appropriate. Or, of course, this same thing occurs in a consensus framework, with each person coordinating their choice to advocate or to block an outcome in light of impact on self and on others.

In other words, in any setup, if all the actors are able as a result of a free exchange of information and feelings to determine perfectly accurately their own relevant input and that of all other actors, and then in hearing the preferences of the others, if each actor decides accurately and justly whether those in the overall yea camp should carry the day and if yes maintains their yeas and if not rescinds them, all choices will come out ideally and unanimously, regardless of the voting procedure used.

In this sense, assuming our norm of self-management, in any system the abstract situation is identical. That is, those involved have to assess feelings, preferences, and information, and then decide what to do to collectively reflect every actor's cumulative will in accord with the norm that decision-making input should be in proportion as one is impacted. In all cases, with perfect process and choice, final dissent or assent is not solely a singular decision based on one's own feelings but depends on whether those assenting or dissenting see their joint appropriate influence level as warranting their choice. If so, they persist in it. If not they retire from it.

So is it just convention that determines which system we use for settling outcomes, the only important consideration being the process of exchange of information, feelings, and preferences, and the willingness of actors to support and respect one another's depth of feeling and opinion in pursuit of proper proportionate influence for each? No. Instead, in the real world it makes sense to prejudge certain types of decisions and decide that they would best be handled with certain decision-making processes, and not to rely on continually reassessing each, or, even worse, on using some fixed approach for everything. Why?

The primary reasons for preferring a flexible approach are:

1   It is desirable to come as close as one can to determining in advance how best to give each person involved in a decision appropriate impact on it, so that the need for each actor to bend their expressed vote in light not only of their own preferences but the preferences others have is minimized and the entire process is simplified. And it is also a truism that no one can know my interests as well as I do—unless I'm a child or deranged.

2   It is desirable to minimize the extent to which any actor can inappropriately distort decisions from ideal proportionate say whether whether this is due to honest mistakes, preset biases, or even dishonest manipulations.

We do not always opt for having a perfect communication process plus the smartest and most perceptive person present making the final decision unilaterally, or for a randomly chosen person doing so—and surely no consensus advocate would favor this. But why not? It involves as good a pre-vote process as we can muster. And if we say that by such processes everyone always arrives at perfect estimates of their own and all other people's proper input, then everyone is in position to make the right decision. So why not let anyone do it? Well, we do not do that for four very good reasons.

1   It is not true that everyone is always going to accurately know everyone else's situation perfectly, nor that they could, and obstacles can be a matter of benign lack of under-standing or less benign self-interest and bias.

2   Even if people did know everyone else's desires and the relative impact of all options under consideration, it is not true that everyone will always behave honorably.

3   By having the ultimate decision made by one person, whether he or she is randomly chosen or otherwise, there is no record of dissent from the decision. We just have the ultimate yea or nay. We have no lasting feeling for or permanent record that we can consult of the existence of a minority and its views, and there is no tendency to empower the minority to try other alternatives or even to remember

that the minority exists, should difficulties with the decision emerge down the road.

4 In practice, we know unilateral decision-making would devolve into steadily reduced participation and a divergence from real self-management.

But this rejection of one person making the final decision by fiat tells us that different approaches have different merits for different situations, which is why parecon does not prejudge how decisions should be made, but only the broad norm or goal regarding self-managing input and participation.

We like to think advocates of consensus favor it precisely because if there has to be only one method elevated above all others they are seeking the method that will at least in modest-sized groups most promote participation and permit the emergence of appropriate influence. Our response to this is that there doesn't have to be only one approach, and there shouldn't be.

So the bottom line for this chapter, however complex the diverse cases and their specific logic can turn out to be, is simple. To facilitate and organize worker and consumer decision-making in keeping with the goal of self-management, parecon incorporates councils at diverse levels, from the smallest work team or family to the largest industry or state, and beyond. The actors involved need appropriate information and need to be properly confident, empowered, and skilled. They should utilize decision-making procedures and communication methods in their councils as they see fit, adapting these as best they can to the time and hassle involved and to the possibilities for error and abuse, and seeking to attain appropriately informed decision-making influence in proportion to the degree each person is affected by decision-making outcomes.

6

Job Complexes

As it happens, there are no columns in standard double-entry book-keeping to
keep track of satisfaction and demoralization. There is no credit entry for
feelings of self-worth and confidence, no debit column for feelings of
uselessness and worthlessness. There are no monthly, quarterly, or even
annual statements of pride and no closing statement of bankruptcy when the
worker finally comes to feel that after all he couldn't do anything else, and
doesn't deserve anything better.
— Barbara Garson

We have established that workplaces should be organized and run
by workers' councils and that these councils will also be the vehicle
through which workers manifest their preferences regarding how
long they wish to work, what they wish to produce, what tools and
methods they wish to use, and so on. We have said that workers in
their councils at various levels from small teams to whole industries
will have appropriate say. But, there is a wrinkle to work out. What
does it mean to suggest that an assembly worker toiling at a
repetitive task all day, a financial executive overseeing workplace
information and budgeting, and a manager overseeing the activities
of dozens of rote workers, should have equal say in the activities of
the company for which they all work?

Not all tasks are equally desirable, and even in a formally
democratic council, if some workers do only rote tasks that numb
their minds and bodies, and other workers do engaging and
empowering tasks that not only brighten their spirits and
attentiveness, but also provide them with information critical to
intelligent decision-making, saying that the two should have equal
impact on decisions denies reality. Democratic councils help create
conditions that enable participation and give people appropriate
impact over decisions, but something more is needed to equalize
daily work assignments vis-à-vis the impact people's work
experience has on their capacity to participate and render informed
judgments. If some workers have consistently greater information
and responsibility in their jobs, they will dominate workplace
decisions and in that sense become a ruling "coordinator class," even
though they operate in democratic councils and have no special
ownership of the workplace.

Parecon's antidote to corporate divisions of labor imposing class division is that if you work at a particularly unpleasant and disempowering task for some time each day or week, then for some other time you should work at more pleasant and empowering tasks. Overall, people should not do either rote and unpleasant work or conceptual and empowering work all the time. We should each instead have a balanced mix of tasks.

This does not say that every person must perform every task in every workplace. The same person need not work as a doctor, an engineer, and a literary critic, much less work at every imaginable task throughout an economy. Those who assemble cars today need not assemble computers tomorrow, much less every imaginable product. Nor should everyone who works in a hospital perform brain surgery as well as every other hospital function. The aim is not to eliminate divisions of labor, but to ensure that over some reasonable time frame people should have responsibility for some sensible sequence of tasks for which they are adequately trained and such that no one enjoys consistent advantages in terms of the empowerment effects of their work.

We do not mean that we have doctors who occasionally clean bed pains, nor secretaries who every so often attend a seminar. Parading through the ghetto does not yield scars and slinking through a country club does not confer status. Short-term stints in alternative circumstances—whether slumming or admiring—do not rectify long-term inequities in basic responsibilities. We do mean, instead, that everyone has a set of tasks that together compose his or her job such that the overall implications of that whole set of tasks are on average like the overall implications for empowerment of all other jobs.

Further, for those doing only elite work in one workplace to do only rote work in another would not challenge the hierarchical organization of work in either one. We need to balance job complexes for desirability and empowerment in each and every workplace, as well as guarantee that workers have a combination of tasks that balance across workplaces. This and only this provides a division of labor that gives all workers an equal chance of participating in and benefitting from workplace decision-making. This and only this establishes a division of labor which does not produce a class division between permanent order-givers and order-takers.

Since disparate empowerment at work inexorably destroys participatory potentials and creates class differences, while differences in quality of life at work could be justly offset by appropriate remuneration, we will focus more on empowerment for the rest of this chapter. In practice, there probably is not much difference since balancing empowerment likely takes us a long way toward balancing quality of life, and in any event, broader issues will resurface as we proceed in other chapters.

To start, almost everyone is aware that typical jobs in familiar corporate contexts combine tasks with the same qualitative characteristics so that each worker has a homogenous job complex and most people do one level of task. In contrast, seeking appropriate empowerment, a participatory economy offers balanced job complexes where everyone typically does many levels of tasks. Each parecon worker has a particular bundle of diverse responsibilities, and each person's bundle prepares him or her to participate as an equal to everyone else in democratic workplace decision-making.

This might be a good time to point out that in part III of this book we include considerable daily life detail, including describing hypothetical workplaces and consumer units, to illustrate the nuts and bolts of possible implementations of participatory economics. Even more description is available online at www.parecon.org. In this chapter, it is only the essential abstract character of the matter that we highlight.

At any rate, we hope the idea is starting to crystalize. With a typical capitalist approach to defining jobs we can imagine someone listing all possible tasks to be done in a workplace. We can then imagine someone giving each task a rank of 1 to 20, with higher being more empowering and lower being more deadening and stultifying. So in this experiment we have hundreds or perhaps even thousands of stripped-down tasks from which we create actual jobs. No single task is enough to constitute a whole job. Some jobs may take only a few tasks, some many. When the corporate approach is adopted, each defined job is a bundle of tasks, but each task in that bundle has very nearly the same rating as all the others. As a result, the corporate job bundle may come up with a 1, a 7, a 15, or a 20 as its average empowerment rating. The average could be any number on the scale, but the job itself will be comprised of a fairly homogenized bundle of tasks all rated about the same. In other words the job will be pegged to a position in a 1 to 20 hierarchy and all its component tasks will be at that rank or just a bit above or below. Rose gets mostly 5s, some 4s and 6s. Robert gets mostly 17s, some 16s and 18s.

Now suppose we switch to the participatory economic workplace. There are quite a few differences in tasks due to the transition to a new type of economy, for reasons to be discovered as we proceed, but still it is a long list. The tasks are of course still differentiated in terms of their empowerment effects, just as in the capitalist economy and we again rank each one of them from 1 to 20 (though there are fewer at the low end than before). However their combination into parecon jobs changes dramatically. Instead of combing a bunch of 6s into a 6 job, and a bunch of 18s into an 18 job, every job is now a combination of tasks of varied levels such that each job in the workplace has the same average grade. Maybe the workplace is a coal mine and the average is 4 or maybe it is a factory and the average is 7 or it is a school and the average is 11 or it is a research center and the average is 14. Whatever the average for the unit is, everyone who works there has a job whose combination of tasks yields the same average. In the coal mine, where the average is 4, jobs may have tasks that are all rated 4, or maybe a job has some 7s, 4s and 2s but it averages to 4. In the research plant someone may have all 14s, or maybe a 4 and 5, a bunch of 13s, 14, and 15s, and a 19 or 20. The point is that every worker has a job. Every job has many tasks. The tasks are suited to the worker and vice versa, so the tasks combine into a sensible agenda of responsibilities. The average empowerment impact of the sum of tasks in any job in any workplace is the same as the average empowerment for all other jobs in that workplace. When the workers come together in their workers' councils, whether for work-teams, units, divisions, or the whole workplace, there is no subset of workers whose conditions have prepared them better and left them more energetic or provided them greater relevant information or skills relative to everyone else, such that they will predictably dominate debate and outcomes. The preparation for participation owing to involvement in the daily life of the workplace is essentially equalized. Of course, in real circumstances the procedures of job balancing are not precisely as we describe above but involve a steady meshing and merging of tasks into jobs, with workers grading the overall combinations and bringing these into accord with each other by tweaking the combinations far more fluidly than parceling out all tasks as if from some gigantic menu. But the graphic image conveys the relevant reality.

Now, whether having balanced job complexes is efficient or not, whether it can get economic functions completed with a high level of competence or not, and whether it is compatible with the other institutions of a participatory economy or not, are all matters that have to wait until we have provided a more complete picture of the overall system. But what should be clear already is if it turns out to be preferred and desirable, there is no law of nature or of "job definitions" that precludes doing as we have suggested to a reasonably high degree of attainment of the end sought. Of course it cannot be perfect. There is no perfect grading of tasks, no perfect meshing of graded tasks into balanced jobs, and thus no perfect balancing. This is a social dynamic enacted by human beings in complex circumstances. But short of perfection, we can easily balance job complexes in each workplace quite well, tweaking the results over time to get an ever more just allocation. Still, even recognizing that we could achieve this, and even assuming efficiency and compatibility with the rest of the economy (to be addressed later), there is a problem.

We should add a clarification to avoid a possible confusion. Balancing empowerment across jobs is not the same as balancing the amount or type of intellect required for that job. That is, if you do some highly abstract theoretical physics that only two other people on Earth can understand, your activity is not necessarily immensely more empowering than my helping decide how we can best build automobiles or when the chef at a restaurant decides how to best cook a meal. If it were simply a question of intellect, then arguably no amount of balancing is going to get me and Hawking equalized. Thinking about unified fields requires too much intellect to balance. But when we are talking about empowerment, there are empowering tasks in all kinds of workplaces, including those that involve figuring out how to best do other jobs, how to best satisfy consumers, how to plan for the future, etc., and thinking about elementary particles or cosmic black holes actually is not all that socially empowering.

In balancing job complexes within each workplace for equal empowerment, the goal was to prevent the organization and assignment of tasks from preparing some workers better than others to participate in decision-making at that workplace. But balancing job complexes *within* workplaces does not guarantee that work life will be equally empowering *across* workplaces. One workplace could average out at 7, another at 14, to use the hypothetical example from earlier, or at 3 and 18, for that matter. In such cases, those in the more empowering industries would be far better able to manifest their preferences throughout the broader economy. Indeed, over time, they could further polarize workplaces in the economy, with a subset of workplaces housing all the most empowering jobs and with the least empowering work ghettoized off into (huge) disempowering and menial workplaces—with the former of course overseeing and ruling the latter. Since this is obviously not our aim, we deduce that establishing conditions for a truly participatory and equitable economy requires cross workplace balancing in addition to balancing within each workplace.

The only way to balance for desirability and empowerment (or even for either alone) across workplaces is to have people spend time outside their primary workplace offsetting advantages or disadvantages that its average may have compared to the overall societal average. If you work in a coal mine that is a 4, and society is a 7, you get to work considerable time outside the mines in another venue, raising your average to 7. If you work in a research facility that is a 13 in a society whose average is a 7, you would have to work outside that facility a considerable chunk of each week at rather onerous tasks to get down to the overall average of 7. How does a participatory economy calibrate these balances? For that matter, how do people wind up working in a particular workplace in the first place?

Though the full answer requires a full picture of a participatory economy, including its means of allocation, we cannot reasonably go any further regarding job complexes without providing at least some clarification. In a participatory economy, everyone will naturally have the right to apply for work wherever they choose, and every workers' council will have the right to add any members they wish (using appropriate decision-making methods, of course). We have no choice but to wait until after describing participatory allocation to analyze when and why workers' councils would wish to add or release members, but for now it is sufficient to know that once the economy has a work agenda for the coming period, each workers' council may have a list of openings for which anyone can freely apply. So any worker could apply for any opening and move to a new workers' council that wants them should they prefer it to their present council.

In this respect, parecon job changing is superficially like changing jobs in a typical capitalist economy. But while the situation *looks* a bit like a traditional labor market, it is ultimately quite different. First, in a traditional labor market, people generally change employment to win higher pay or to enjoy working conditions generally considered more desirable, not solely conditions they themselves prefer. But since a parecon balances job complexes across as well as within workplaces, and since it remunerates effort and sacrifice (as we will soon describe), people will be unable to attain these traditional goals by changing workplaces. Instead, everyone already will have average job quality and income conditions, and thus also an instance of the best available income and job conditions. On the other hand, if a person would prefer a different group of workmates, or working at a different combination of tasks due to his or her personal priorities and interests, of course she or he might have a very good reason to apply for a new job, perhaps even at a new workplace. However, to the extent that job complexes are balanced and pay is for effort and sacrifice only, personal reasons will be the only motives to move. Conversely, people's freedom to move to other workplaces will provide a check on the effectiveness of balancing job complexes across workplaces. Higher pay will not be available by changing jobs, nor will objectively better work conditions, since pay and conditions will be balanced.

Just as workers must balance jobs internally in each workplace through a flexible rating process (whose exact character would vary from workplace to workplace), so will delegates of workers from different councils and industries develop a flexible rating process to balance across workplaces. As one plausible solution, there could be "job complex committees" both within each workplace and for the economy as a whole. The internal committees would be responsible for proposing ways to combine tasks and assign work times to achieve balanced work complexes within workplaces. The economy-wide committees arrange positions for workers in less desirable and less empowering primary workplaces some time in more desirable and more empowering environments, and vice versa. Within a workplace, it would become clear that more fine-tuning of job assignments was required when more and more or fewer and fewer members of a workers' council apply for one job or another. Similarly, the need for better balancing of conditions and job complexes across workplaces becomes evident the same way; that is, through excessive (or minimal) applications to switch to one workplace or another.

It should be clear that creating perfectly balanced job complexes is theoretically possible. But can it be done in real life situations? Of course not. We are not talking about pure geometry nor even the engineering of plastics. We are talking about people and social arrangements. But the point is, it can be done quite well, with deviations and errors being only deviations and errors, not systematic biases. Over time errors will not multiply or snowball, but will instead be corrected. And most important, the entire process is democratic. There is no elite that bends everyone else to their will and each person winds up in circumstances collectively agreed upon by procedures respecting their appropriate input. If we combine our best effort at creating balanced job complexes with well-designed democratic councils, we attain a venue favorable to non-hierarchical production relations that will promote equity and participation and will facilitate appropriate voting patterns. Still, you may reasonably wonder, in practical real world situations, could workers really rate and combine tasks to define balanced job complexes within and across workplaces even reasonably well, much less very well as we suggest?

Provided we understand that we are talking about a social process that never attains perfection, but that does fulfill workers' own sense of balance, the answer is surely yes.

The idea is that workers within each workplace would engage in a collective evaluation of their own circumstances. As a participatory economy emerged from a capitalist or a market or centrally planned socialist past, naturally there would be a lengthy discussion and debate about the characteristics of different tasks. But once the first approximation of balanced complexes within a workplace had been established, regular adjustments would be relatively simple. For example, if the introduction of a new technology changed the human impact of some tasks, thereby throwing old complexes out of balance, workers would simply move some responsibilities within and across affected complexes to re-establish desirable balance, or they might change the time spent at different tasks in affected complexes, to attain that new balance.

The new balance need not and could not be perfect, just as the old one wasn't, nor would the adjustments be instantaneous, nor would everyone be likely to agree completely with every result of a democratic determination of combinations. And of course individual preferences that deviate from one's workmates preferences would determine who would choose to apply for which balanced job complex. If I am less bothered by noise but more bothered by dust, I will prefer a complex whose rote component is attending noisy machinery rather than a complex with a sweeping detail. You may have opposite inclinations.

In practice, balancing between workplaces would be a bit more complicated. How would arrangements be made for workers to have responsibilities in more than one workplace? Over time, balancing across workplaces would be determined partly through a growing familiarity with the social relations of production, partly as a result of evaluations by specific committees whose job includes rating complexes in different plants and industries, and partly as a result of the pattern of movement of workers. That all this is possible within some acceptable range of error and of dissent ought to be obvious. Those wanting to see a more detailed description of the specific division of tasks into jobs in and across some hypothetical workplaces will have that chance in part III of this book, and can do so at the parecon website (www.parecon.org), as well.

Basically, participatory economic job complexes would be organized so that every individual would be regularly involved in both conception and execution tasks, with comparable empowerment and quality of life circumstances for all. The precision of the balance would depend on many factors, and would improve over time. At any rate, no individual would ever permanently occupy positions that would present him or her unusual opportunities to accumulate influence or knowledge. Every individual would be welcomed to occupy positions that guaranteed him or her an appropriate amount of empowering tasks. In essence, the human costs and benefits of work would be equitably distributed. Corporate organization would be relegated to the dustbin of history, with council organization and balanced job complexes taking its place. The question that remains, of course, is whether—in concert with other essential innovations of a participatory economy—employing balanced job complexes would have as much positive impact for solidarity, equity, diversity, and self-management as we seek, whether this would permit effective utilization of talents and resources to produce desired outputs, and also whether it would have other undesirable effects that mitigated these virtues. We address these questions in upcoming chapters.

7

Remuneration

In a society of an hundred thousand families, there will perhaps be one hundred who don't labour at all, and who yet, either by violence, or by the more orderly oppression of law, employ a greater part of the labour of society than any other ten thousand in it. The division of what remains, too ... is by no means made in proportion to the labour of each individual. On the contrary those who labour most get least. The opulent merchant, who spends a great part of his time in luxury ... enjoys a much greater proportion of the profits ... than all the Clerks and Accountants who do the business. These last, again, enjoying a great deal of leisure, and suffering scarce any other hardship besides the confinement of attendance, enjoy a much greater share of the produce, than three times an equal number of artisans, who, under their direction, labour much more severely ..... The artisan again, tho' he works generally under cover, protected from the injuries of the weather ... and assisted by the convenience of innumerable machines, enjoys a much greater share than the poor labourer who has the soil and the seasons to struggle with, and, who while he affords the materials for supplying the luxury of all the other members of the common wealth, and bears, as it were, upon his shoulders the whole fabric of human society, seems himself to be buried out of sight in the lowest foundations of the building.
— Adam Smith

How can a rational being be ennobled by anything that is not obtained by its own exertion?
— Mary Wollstonecraft

What claim should each worker have on consumption goods, based on their involvement in the economy? Earlier we discussed the logic and morality of different approaches to defining and pursuing equity, and arrived at the conclusion that if people are able to work they should be remunerated for the effort or sacrifice they expend in contributing to the social product, and if they are not able to work they should be remunerated at some appropriate level based on social averages and special needs. Everyone might also enjoy certain basic guaranteed provisions—health care and education, for example—depending on what the society democratically determines it can afford.

This orientation establishes that no one should have claims on output on the basis of owning some means of production. No one should have claims on output on the basis of bargaining power. No one should have claims on output on the basis that they put a larger sum into the social product than others by using some special genetic endowment or talent or size, or due to having some highly productive learned skill, better tools, or more productive work-mates, or because they happen to produce things that are more highly valued. Rather, each worker should have a claim on output in proportion to the relative magnitude of the effort or sacrifice that they expend in their socially useful work.

There is another angle from which we can see this. Why, if we believe in equality, don't we give everybody one car, one tennis racquet, seven plums, thirteen books (one by Jacqueline Suzanne, one by Chomsky, etc.), and two green shirts? The answer, of course, is that being equally deserving does not mean that people have the same preferences. We want people to have the freedom to follow diverse preferences, but equality does imply that people shouldn't draw more from the public supply than anyone else. Okay, so what if I prefer leisure time to an extra shirt? Shouldn't I be allowed to take my "benefits" partly in extra time? Of course. Therefore, rewarding according to effort is another way of saying that we are all rewarded equally, but that some will choose shirts, some movies, some leisure or less stressful or onerous time at work, and some saving for next year.

But are we sure what all this means? And, once sure, do we have any idea how it can occur? Though we did address the meaning of the aim when we highlighted our new values earlier, given how controversial the approach is, it will not hurt to recapitulate its logic here. We will then move on to the issue of implementation.

The Logic of Remunerative Justice

Private enterprise market (capitalist) economies distribute con-sumption opportunities according to personal contribution to social output plus the contribution of property owned, with large allowance, in practice, for the impact of bargaining power. Public enterprise market economies (market socialist or what we call "market coordinatorist" economies) distribute consumption oppor-tunities according to personal contribution only, having removed ownership of productive property from the equation, but with allowance, again, for the impact of bargaining power.

We claim these approaches are inequitable in that they reward people for what does not deserve reward (such as a deed in one's pocket, advantageous circumstances, or special genetic endow-ment); mis-reward people for things that do deserve reward if they are onerous (such as training and education); and do not properly reward people for what they have control over, are responsible for, and do merit compensation for—that is, the pain and loss they undergo while contributing to the social product. Contrary to these familiar norms of remuneration, we propose that desirable economies ought to distribute consumption opportunities only according to effort or sacrifice.

Whereas differences in contribution to output will derive from differences in talent, training, job assignment, tools, luck, and effort, if we define effort as personal sacrifice for the sake of the social endeavor, only effort merits compensation. Of course effort can take many forms. It may be longer work hours, less pleasant work, or more intense, dangerous, or unhealthy work. It may consist of training that is less gratifying than the training experiences others undergo or than the work others do during the same period.

The implications of rewarding property as compared to output or effort are pretty much self-evident. Bill Gates prospers tomorrow whether he does anything in the form of work, and he prospers to a degree that bears no relation whatever to what he (or any thousand humans) could personally produce. But how can we more concretely understand the difference between rewarding people for their actual personal contributions to output, which is the lynchpin remunerative proposal of most non-capitalist market models, and rewarding people only for their effort/sacrifice, which is the lynchpin remunerative proposal for parecon?

By all accounts, the musician Salieri was a dedicated, hard-working, but plodding composer at the same time and in the same city as Mozart, who was a frivolous, irresponsible, genius. Assume these accounts are accurate. Assume also that both Mozart and Salieri could best serve the social interest by working as composers. If we reward output Mozart deserved to be paid thousands of times as much as Salieri. If we reward effort/sacrifice, Salieri likely deserved more pay than Mozart.

So here we have a possible test of ethical inclinations. Ignore questions of incentives (a matter we will address shortly) and assume that amount and quality of output would not vary whatever your answer is. Also realize that you can listen to whomever you want, whatever your answer is, and assume that both composers do work that is socially valued enough for them to be paid for their musical pursuits. Would you pay Mozart or Salieri more? Do you monetarily reward Mozart on top of his fantastic luck in being born genetically endowed with special talent? Or do you just pay him for effort, enjoying the fantastic bounty it provides but not materially enriching him in accord with it? Do you punish Salieri (relative to Mozart) because he has to work longer and harder to produce a creditable composition? Or do you pay him for his effort too, like everyone else, then enjoy the product—although not nearly as much as you enjoy Mozart? We confront these options and opt for remunerating effort/sacrifice, not output, for all the reasons that we have offered in prior chapters. But how?

If in a parecon we had jobs more or less like the ones that exist now, those doing the most onerous, harmful work would be highest paid; those doing the most pleasant and intrinsically uplifting work would be lowest paid—the opposite of the current condition. To achieve this goal we would have to assess each job's characteristics for the effort or sacrifice per hour expended at an average level of exertion, plus have some means of oversight to keep track of which workers are expending effort at levels above or below average.

But, a participatory economy wouldn't have jobs like now. Instead it would have balanced job complexes and if we assume balance for empowerment (which we must have, by the arguments of the last chapter) and balance for quality of life effects as well, then each worker has a job complex for their standard work week—let's say thirty-hours—that is comparable to every other worker's. How much claim on consumption does each worker then have?

Let's call the amount a worker earns for working at an average intensity for him or her at a balanced job complex for thirty hours, the base income. With everyone having balanced job complexes, each worker will earn either the base income or some higher amount due to having worked longer or more intensely, or some lower amount due to having worked fewer hours or at below average intensity. Counting the hours a person works is easy; more difficult will be measuring effort expended.

The precise methodology for doing this need not be the same from workplace to workplace. Adherence to the norm is what should be universal, not a particular specific approach to the nuts and bolts of implementation. Here is a general approach, however, that many workplaces might opt for. Imagine each worker receives a kind of "evaluation report" from their workplace that determines their income to be used for consumption expenditures. This evaluation report would indicate hours worked at a balanced job complex and intensity of work, yielding an "effort rating" in the form of a percentage multiplier. If the rating was one, the person's remuneration would be the social average. If the rating was 1.1, a tenth more, if .9, a tenth less. What explains a person getting higher or lower remuneration is having worked more or less hours or at a higher or lower intensity of effort.

But who judges these differentials, and by what form of evaluation? This would be the zone of variation from workplace to workplace. The assessment could be a highly precise numeric rating system where people are graded to two decimal places above or below average, for example. Or it might simply read "superior," "average," or "below average," with the designation meaning average income, or a tenth above or a tenth below (that having been agreed in the workplace to be the only variation permitted). Similarly, the judgment could be made by a workplace committee (all members of which, of course, have balanced job complexes) or instead by a vote of whole councils, or by whatever other means the workplace opted for. (For those wondering what prevents a whole workplace from exaggerating their effort, regrettably, the full picture of parecon, as we warned at the outset, depends on all institutions and their interactions. In this case, allocation is also an essential factor, so the question must wait for next chapter.)

One choice that might be prevalent is for a workplace to assume that everyone works at an average intensity level so that for the most part income will vary only with hours worked. The only exception to that, a workplace could decide, is by petition to the council—either by a person claiming to deserve more, or by workmates who are convinced some person deserves less, each of which would, in this model, occur only infrequently.

Another quite different choice many might make is to implement a much tighter rating system that would yield a significant number of employees getting various amounts more or less than average.

But the main point is that since circumstances and opinions will differ regarding the best and most accurate means to calibrate effort and how closely to do so, different workers' councils will likely opt for different systems. And assuming different workplaces do opt for different methods of work evaluation, workers would presumably make this one of the factors to consider in selecting a job in the first place. And, most important, however different various procedures might be, they would surely not lead to extreme income differentials, since there can only be so much variation in time worked and in intensity, even if workplaces are very accommodating of different preferences on this score.

Finally, we should clarify how a parecon will handle "free consumption." Even in contemporary economies where there is little solidarity, the public sometimes allows individuals to consume at public expense on the basis of need. Since we believe one of the merits of an equitable economy is that it creates the necessary conditions for attaining humane economic outcomes, and since we incorporate features designed to build solidarity in our allocative procedures, we expect considerable consumption on the basis of need. This will occur in two different ways.

First, particular consumption activities such as health care or public parks will be free to all. This does not mean that they have no social cost, or that they should be produced beyond the point where their social costs outweigh their social benefits. But individuals will not be expected to reduce their requests for other consumption activities because they consume more of these free goods. On the other hand, of course the average consumption per person will drop if society as a whole consumes more free goods. For example, if we produce more health care overall, we have less productive potential left for everything else. Basically, everyone pays for free goods equally (in the reduction of other output available), regardless of their direct participation in consuming the free goods. This occurs on the assumption that the benefits of the consumption are generalized, or that (with medicine, say) the costs ought to be socialized rather than penalizing those in need. What items should be on the free list is something that will have to be debated in consumer federations, but medical care is an obvious example.

Second, people will also be able to make particular requests for need-based consumption to be addressed case by case by others in the economy. Frequently, for example, individuals or collectives might propose a consumption request above the level warranted by effort ratings accompanied by an explanation of what they regard as a justifiable special need. These requests are considered by relevant consumer councils and either approved or rejected. If approved, the costs would be spread over the population of the council approving.

Note that the above discussion of remuneration only describes how parecon could remunerate in a just and equitable way. It does not provide evidence or logic that doing so will elicit desired quality and output or foster the values we favor, nor that there won't be negative side effects mitigating benefits. In this chapter, the point was only to present the option we favor. Later we shall assess it, and test it against possible concerns.

8

Allocation

Annual income twenty pounds, annual expenditure nineteen pounds and six, result happiness. Annual income twenty pounds, annual expenditures twenty pounds ought and six, result misery.
— Charles Dickens

The familiar notion of planning is that done by experts, with scientific knowledge. We have seen the results of that rational planning: tower blocks, food additives, valium—the list of horrors is endless.
— Sheila Rowbotham

In 1983 the British economist Alec Nove wrote an influential book titled *The Economics of Feasible Socialism*. He argued to a surprisingly receptive leftist audience that for economic allocation we could only choose either markets or central planning, two systems that in this volume we have already rejected. Nove summarized his argument":

> It is clear that someone (some institution) has to tell the producer about what the users require. If that someone is not the impersonal market mechanism it can only be a hierarchical superior. There are horizontal links (market), there are vertical links (hierarchy). What other dimension is there? In a complex industrial economy the interrelations between its parts can be based in principle either on freely chosen negotiated contracts (which means autonomy and a species of commodity production) or on a system of binding instructions from planning offices. There is no third way.

If Nove was right, we would have to go back and pick a lesser evil from between markets and central planning, no other option being possible. Our economic choice would then be limited to capitalism or to market or centrally planned coordinatorism, with as many features as we could impose to better the lot of citizens.

British Prime Minister and statesman William Pitt (1759-1806), an otherwise unlikely cast member of this book, noted accurately and succinctly, though in an entirely different context, that "Necessity is the argument of tyrants. It is the creed of slaves."

We never knew Alec Nove. We are confident that he was no tyrant and that he was no slave. Yet, despite its influence, it is hard to find in his book any other rationale than the argument from necessity. Nove notes that no links other than horizontal or vertical exist. But this ignores that there may be means other than markets for horizontal relations unless one assumes, by necessity, that markets are the only horizontal allocation system possible. Nove asserts that there can be no third way. Alternatives are logically impossible. But he gives no reason why this must be so other than complexity. This is precisely what Pitt means by "arguing from necessity."

Nove believes producers and consumers cannot together respectfully arrive at "instructions" that they mutually carry out without any central agency and without competition and commodity exchange, except with horrible repercussions. But why can't it happen? Or why must there be horrible repercussions?

Does Nove examine the properties that such a system might have and find them wanting in comparison to class division, alienation, and exploitation? Does he describe features that must accompany such a system and show that they have consequences we cannot abide? He does neither. Instead, the only answer Nove provides as to why cooperative allocation cannot happen is that allocation is too complex for anything other than markets or central planning to work. He offers a negative proof—an alternative to markets or central planning is impossible. Nove achieves his proof by simply stating that nothing could fulfill complex allocation needs other than markets or central planning. That is, his supporting logic is to simply state the result itself. His only evidence is to pile up indications of what no one doubts in the first place: that is, that allocation is complex and important. Nove's presentation argues only from necessity. It must be that there is no third way because it must be that there is no third way. We do not have one now, therefore we cannot have one ever. With this mindset, and this was part of Pitt's point, we would never have advanced beyond the institutions of the Pharaoh's Egypt.

As Nove's claim, repeated by many others, is operationally very important in communicating with various left audiences, let's back up a step. If a person thinks a society promoting solidarity, diversity, equity, and self-management is potentially attainable, then for him or her to say it should be morally off the agenda and therefore that people should not try to define it, explain it, and forcefully advocate for it, would be to say that humanity should stop progressing and resign itself to an economic system that falls short of desired virtues. In the US case, this would make sense only if the person actually thought it was ideal to have an economy in which one percent of the population owns the great majority of the means of production and accrues gargantuan profits as a result; in which roughly 4 percent own most of the rest of the productive assets, thereby also becoming immensely rich and powerful; and in which another 15 percent or so own some residue of productive assets and also monopolize the economic positions in society that largely decide daily economic outcomes and circumstances, thereby enjoying associated status, power, work conditions and, of course, grossly disproportionate income. It would mean that the person was satisfied with roughly 80 percent obeying orders for their whole economic lives, subordinate in their workplaces and even in much of their consumption activities, and in which many in this huge majority are downright hungry, even if alternatives were possible.

It is hard to imagine a person in full possession of his mental faculties and with a level of morality higher than a dung beetle's, who would argue that in society less solidarity is preferable to more, less equity is preferable to more, less justice and democracy are preferable to more, and less control over our lives is preferable to more. But this is what it would mean to argue that implementing participatory economics or some other system able to attain these values while also accomplishing required economic functions should be off the agenda, supposing one thought it was potentially attainable. So those who wish to take economic vision off the human agenda and who also wish to retain a shred of dignity and rationality do not generally make the argument that we shouldn't want to meet needs and develop potentials better than we do now. They instead make the argument that something about parecon, or even about any conceivable alternative economic system at all, is necessarily so adverse or so unattainable that even thinking about implementing such a system is a waste of time.

Why do so many people argue that the desire to attain a better economy should go into history's garbage bin? Why do so many people assert that no better economy is possible and that trying to attain one is a deluded pipe-dream detracting from useful pursuits? One answer is that a person could feel that a better economy would be wonderful, thus being a morally sound and sensible person, but nonetheless feel that regrettably there is no combination of institutions that could possibly bring about better outcomes. Any effort to improve economic solidarity, equity, justice, self-manage-ment, diversity, etc., would (a) fall short of our intentions, and/or (b) cause so much loss of output and/or of other desired outcomes (such as privacy, say) that the gains it did attain in equity or self-management or whatever else would be far outweighed by countervailing losses in output, privacy, etc. This is the real logic of Alec Nove's position and also of TINA—Margaret Thatcher's famous assertion that "there is no alternative"—which is better termed TINBA, for "there is no better alternative."

The first reply to TINBA is why would anyone in his or her right mind utter such a phrase gleefully? Imagine at some point in history someone yelling TINBA about slavery, or about child labor, or about overwhelming illiteracy, or about average life spans in the 20s, 30s, 40s, or 50s, or about dictatorship, and so on. Any sane and morally sound person yelling TINBA about such things would presumably do so only tearfully, and only if he or she had had his or her hopes dashed by a very powerful set of arguments and associated evidence. Why else would one erect a "do not enter" sign in front of domains that of course everyone with a shred of moral decency would like to enter? Without compelling evidence for the claim, it would be pathological on the part of those suffering the ills of slavery, child labor, overwhelming illiteracy, short life spans, dictatorship, or, in the modern instance, stupendous inequalities of economic wealth and power, or it would be grotesquely self-serving on the part of a few who benefit from such conditions, to declare that nothing better than such ills is possible and to be gleeful about it.

The second reply to those proclaiming TINBA is that there is, in fact, not only nothing compelling that supports their stance, but no argument whatsoever on behalf of TINBA other than the loud pronouncements of sectors of the populace who greedily benefit from such beliefs. There is no operational evidence or analytic argument that economic institutions which empower workers and consumers to influence decisions proportionately to how they are affected, or that reward people in accord only with their effort and sacrifice, or that disperse responsibilities in a manner which balances empowerment and quality of life, are either impossible or fraught with problems so damning that they outweigh their virtues—or even with problems at all. In fact, the situation is quite the contrary. Those who have made preliminary studies of such institutions have found them to be very promising, while the advocates of TINBA have (predictably) virtually ignored these analyses.

At a minimum, therefore, until and unless someone makes an overwhelming and unassailable case that equity, solidarity, self-management, diversity, and other desirable values unmet by current economic institutions are either (a) incapable of being delivered by different economic institutions, or (b) impossible to deliver without bringing with them horrible ills offsetting the benefits—attaining a better economy, and, more specifically, an alternative to markets and central planning, should be very much on the agenda. Still, the only definitive final refutation of Nove's academic denial of a third way or of Thatcher's emotive assertion that "there is no alternative," even when such claims are made without serious rationale, is to present an actual third way itself.

Therefore, in this chapter we describe an allocation alternative we call "decentralized participatory planning." We take you through it sequentially, from describing its methods of communicating information, to its institutional structure, to the planning steps, and finally to a typical example of planning. Our claim, to be further explored in coming chapters, is that decentralized participatory planning permits consumers' and workers' councils to participate directly in formulating a plan that would benefit everyone in a just and equitable fashion. It arrives at more accurate pricing and economic adjustment than markets and central planning can achieve, but additionally it enhances rather than obliterates solidarity, diversity, equity, and self-management.

Allocation, remember, is the process whereby an economy determines the amounts to be produced and the relative exchange rates of all inputs and outputs. It chooses from a nearly infinite list of every conceivable thing that might be produced in a year with every conceivable combination of patterns of labor and resource use, plus every conceivable apportionment of the product, the single final list of what all the various economic actors actually produce and consume. It is a gargantuan selection process. There is a massive, nearly endless set of possibilities of what the economy might do in the coming year. We settle, over the course of the year, on what the economy actually does. This process is called allocation. It is what markets accomplish by selecting via competition among buyers and sellers final outcomes embodying particular market properties. It is what central planning accomplishes by selecting via top down commands final outcomes with particular central planning properties. And it is what any "third way" will have to accomplish by selecting in its own manner final outcomes with its own particular (in our case, participatory economic) properties.

Participatory Information & Communication

What precisely do workers in a council need to know to regulate their production according to the effects on themselves, and on other workers, and consumers? And what must consumers know to formulate their consumption requests in light of their own needs as well as the needs of other consumers and workers? For informed collective self-management, the following conditions must be present:

- Participatory workers must weigh the gains from working less or using less productive though more fulfilling techniques, against the consequent loss of consumer well being. Likewise, participatory consumers must weigh the benefits of consumption requests against the sacrifices required to produce them.

- Participatory workers must distinguish an equitable workload from one that is too light or too heavy. Likewise, participatory consumers must distinguish reasonable consumption requests from ones that are excessive or overly modest.

- Everyone must know the true social costs and benefits of what they desire to consume or produce, including the quantifiable and non-quantifiable consequences of their choices.

First Communicative Tool: Prices

Allocation performs one very complicated function—providing a means to decide among options. Should certain productive assets be used to produce peanuts or prison cells, autos or shoes, in any conceivable combination of options? Likewise, given such products, what is their relative worth? How much of one should we exchange for another?

A key concept in making such choices sensibly is the "social opportunity cost" of doing any particular thing. If we produce peanuts, how much of other things will we have to give up because we have used labor, land, facilities, etc. in peanut production? Likewise, if we produce autos, what do we forego from not having produced something else that we could have? In markets, prices are an indicator of bargaining power. We feel they should more properly be an indicator of true social opportunity costs. They should tell us if we do x, how much of y could we have done instead, and therefore, do we really want to do x or would we prefer doing that much y? If an economy is functioning optimally, then it will be cognizant of the full social effects of both the production and consumption of its inputs and outputs. The full range of actual choices in the economy, the pattern of production and consumption that results from allocation, will simultaneously determine the social opportunity costs of every single choice among the totality of possibilities. It is a kind of circular or interactive relationship. The total quantities produced of shoes, autos, peanuts, and everything else and how they are apportioned will in sum determine the value of each particular item, which is its social opportunity cost. The economy will ideally produce peanuts up until the point when producing any more peanuts would entail losing some other item more valuable to society than the extra peanuts, which is to say, it will produce them up until the point when the social opportunity cost equals the benefit from the last peanut.

We are churning out pencils, as another example. When do we stop churning? Pencils are useful, but the more pencils we have, the less is the value of each new one added to the pile, at least after a point. Moreover, we certainly do not want to use up so much of our labor and resources churning out pencils that we start having to forego things more desirable to us than our growing pile of pencils— say, milk. Ideally the economy will churn out each output to a point where the benefit of the last item produced was equal to the opportunity cost of producing it. To produce another of the item would occur at the same or at a bit higher opportunity cost and would have the same or a bit less social value ... so that, by not producing that item we can use our productive capability to produce something else that benefits us more.

It is complicated, to be sure, but not incomprehensible. The hardest part is the interactivity—the fact that the decisions have to be made globally for a whole economy with each decision affecting the basis upon which all others should be made. Economists call it a general equilibrium problem.

Let's return to discussing what is needed for a good allocation system. Producers and consumers use prices as a shorthand way of discerning the relative value and cost of various choices. Prices should therefore embody accurate estimates of the full social costs and benefits of inputs and outputs—they should equal their true social opportunity cost. In a parecon, prices, or relative valuations, arise in the process of participatory planning and serve as guides to proposals and evaluations. The social character of prices—their emergence from the preferences, circumstances, wills, power, and social interactions of economic actors not only in parecon, but in all economic systems—is important to understand.

Too often theoretical economists ignore the interactive and social origin of prices and view them as quantitative measures that can be found technically by an analyst solving equations. In the literature on central planning, for example, prices will invariably be seen as emerging from a cut and dried mathematical calculation. In neoclassical literature on markets, similarly, all the prices in the economy are said to arise mathematically from plugging fixed preferences and given technologies into some complex equations. Used carefully this sort of thinking can shed light on some questions, to be sure. But used indiscriminately to comment on real economies, it can be very misleading.

The point is, real people's preferences arise in social interactions. Not only do the outcomes of the clash and jangle of different people's preferences depend on what those interactions are like, but the very preferences that people bring to their decisions and that lie at the basis of the results the economy attains depend on people's interactions as well. Our preferences are influenced by our circumstances and situations, which are in turn influenced by the nature of the economic activities we undertake.

In thinking about allocation, therefore, we should remember that for estimates of social costs and benefits to be accurate they must arise from realistic social, communicative processes. If we are to propose positive approaches for allocation, we have to come up with processes that give people no incentives to dissimulate regarding their true desires, that give people equal opportunity to manifest their feelings in determining outcomes, and that help people arrive at desires that are not perverted by their situations. It is precisely because our participatory planning process differs in many respects from the flawed communicative processes of market and centrally planned allocation that its prices are different as well.

In any case, prices are "indicative" during the participatory planning process in the sense that they represent the best current estimates of final relative valuations. As the process unfolds these estimates become steadily more accurate. Indicative prices in a parecon are also flexible in the sense that qualitative information about the actual conditions of labor and implications of consuming items provides important additional guidance. We do not use quantitative prices alone, and the mechanism of arriving at and refining quantitative prices has checks and balances. Indicative prices (measuring social opportunity costs) in a parecon derive from cooperative social consultation and compromise checked by dissemination of qualitative information and deliberative decision-making. These both ensure that quantitative indicators remain as accurate as possible and help develop workers' sensitivity to fellow workers' situations and everyone's understanding of the intricate tapestry of human relations that determines what we can and cannot consume or produce. But since to both assure accuracy and to foster solidarity we need not only set quantitative prices but also continually socially reset them in light of changing qualitative information about work lives and consumption activity, the burden of distributing information in a participatory allocation procedure is considerably greater than in a non-participatory economy which simply disregards such matters. Not only must a participatory economy generate and revise accurate quantitative measures of social costs and benefits in light of changing conditions, it must also communicate substantial qualitative information about the conditions of other people.

Second Communicative Tool: Measures of Work

As we explained earlier, job complexes would be balanced in and across workplaces. If there were plants with better than average work conditions, people employed there would spend some time doing more menial tasks elsewhere, while for plants with below average work conditions, workers would put some time into more interesting pursuits elsewhere. For an individual in a given period to work significantly more or less than the social average and not disrupt the humane balance of work, she or he need only diminish or increase her or his hours worked at all tasks in the same proportion. Then, each individual could receive from her or his workplace an indicator of average labor hours expended as an accurate indicator of work contributed. Over a sufficient period, whenever a person's indicator was high (or low) compared to the social average, the individual would have sacrificed more (or less) for the social good, and would be entitled to proportionately more (or less) remuneration in return. In parecon, job complexes would be balanced by a real social evaluation, but measures of hours plus intensity worked would serve only as guidelines for decisions since councils could grant exceptions for higher (or lower) consumption requests as conditions and needs warranted.

In short, because in participatory planning people have balanced job complexes, we will obtain a reasonable first estimate of effort expended by counting labor hours. These estimates can in turn be revised in light of effort ratings. In pursuing various routes to personal consumption flexibility, only significantly unbalancing job complexes will be prohibited. The measure of work is therefore another information component of participatory planning.

Third Communicative Tool: Qualitative Activity

To guard against people making decisions based only on an enumeration of quantitative costs or benefits which could begin to diverge from accuracy and in any event lacks texture, each actor in a parecon will also be able to access a list of all direct and indirect factors that go into producing goods, along with a description of what will be gained from consuming those goods. This means those who produce and consume particular goods must communicate to the (still to be discussed) planning process the qualitative human effects that cannot be fully conveyed by quantitative indicators. This does not entail everyone writing long essays about their work and living conditions. It does mean people will need to generate concise accounts that substitute for the fact that not everyone can personally experience every circumstance. Of course, not every worker and consumer will use all this qualitative information in every calculation. But when there are odd changes in preferences of workers or consumers that someone does not understand or wants to explore further to comprehend what is behind a particular indicative price, the qualitative information is available for a check and clarification. Moreover, by paying attention to this information, over time people will become familiar with the material, human, and social components of the products they use just as people are now familiar with the products themselves. In this way, everyone can more accurately assess the full effects of others' requests and even their broad collective motives in a way that enhances solidarity. Both producers and consumers must therefore be able to consult not only quantitative summaries of overall social costs and benefits in indicative prices, but detailed qualitative accounts as well. Only this will ensure that the human/social dimension of economic decision-making is not lost and guarantee that summary (quantitative) price data remains as accurate as possible.

Allocation Organization

In parecon, every workplace and neighborhood consumers' council will participate in the social procedure we call participatory planning. But besides workplace councils, we will also have industry councils and regional federations of workers' councils. And besides neighborhood consumers' councils, we will also have ward, city, county, and state federations of consumers' councils as well as a national consumers' council. Moreover, in addition to all these councils and federations of councils, parecon will have various "facilitation boards" or agencies that facilitate information exchange and processing for collective consumption proposals and for large-scale investment projects, workers requests for changing places of employment, and individuals and families seeking to find membership in living units and neighborhoods, among other functions. Finally, at every level of the economy there will also be facilitation boards to help units revise proposals and search out the least disruptive ways of modifying plans in response to unforeseen circumstances.

Steps of Participatory Planning

In participatory planning every actor (individual or council) at every level will propose its own activities, and, after receiving information regarding other actors' proposals, and the response of other actors to its proposal, each actor makes a new proposal.

Thus, each consumption "actor," from individuals up to large consumer federations, proposes a consumption plan. Individuals make proposals for private goods such as clothing, food, toys, etc. Neighborhood councils make proposals that include approved requests for private goods as well as the neighborhood's collective consumption requests that might include a new pool or local park. Higher-level councils and federations of councils make proposals that include approved requests from member councils as well as the federation's larger collective consumption request.

And similarly, each production "actor" proposes a production plan. Workplaces enumerate the inputs they want and the outputs they will make available. Regional and industry-wide federations aggregate proposals and keep track of excess supply and demand.

As every individual or collective worker or consumer participant negotiates through successive rounds of back and forth exchange of their proposals with all other participants, they alter their proposals to accord with the messages they receive, and the process converges. There is no center or top. There is no competition. Each actor fulfills responsibilities that bring them into greater rather than reduced solidarity with other producers and consumers.

Everyone is remunerated appropriately for effort and sacrifice. And everyone has a proportionate influence on their personal choices as well as those of larger collectives and the whole society.

Preparing First Proposals

Suppose we keep records of the production and consumption that took place in the just completed year. Then with each year we will have information about last year's plan. Suppose the prices used to calculate social costs, benefits, and income last year are also recorded. Then each year we will have a set of final prices from last year to use to begin this year's estimates. By storing last year's full plan in a central computer, access to relevant information, including indicative prices, could be made available to all actors in the planning process. Additionally, by accessing such information, each unit can easily see what its own proposals were in each round of the prior year's planning process. With all this available, how do workers' and consumers' councils plan for the coming year?

1   They first access relevant data from last year.

2   They more or less simultaneously receive information from facilitation boards estimating this year's probable changes in prices and income in light of existing knowledge of past investment decisions and changes in the labor force.

3   They also receive information from production and consumption councils regarding long-term investment projects or collective consumption proposals already agreed to in previous plans that imply continuing commitments for this year.

4   They review changes in their own proposals made during last year's planning to see how much they had to scale down their consumption desires or their plans to improve their quality of work life, and to remember their past aspirations in these regards. They also look to see what increases in average income and improvements in the quality of average work complexes are projected this year, and how these might best be taken advantage of.

5   Finally, using last year's final prices as starting indicators of social costs and benefits, they develop a proposal for the

coming year, not only enumerating what they want to consume or produce and therefore implicitly what they think society's total output should be, but also providing qualitative information about their reasons. This proposal enters the mix with all others, feedback arrives, and revisions are made, round by round, until a final version is reached.

Please note, this does not mean that individual or collective councils must specify how many units of every single product they need down to size, style, and color. Goods and services are grouped into categories accordingly to the interchangeability of the resources, intermediate goods, and labor required to make them, as well as the easily predicted variation of minor optional features. For planning purposes we need only request types of goods, even though later everyone will pick an exact size, style, and color to actually consume.

At any rate, individuals present consumption requests to neighborhood councils, which collectively approve or disapprove the requests and organize them into a total council request for individual goods for all their members along with the neighborhood collective consumption request, to become the total neighborhood consumption proposal.

Neighborhood proposals are added to consumption requests from other neighborhoods and then to full ward proposals, city proposals, and so on. Having the next higher-level council approve or contest lower level requests until they are ready to be passed on saves considerable planning time and is essential for collective implications, in any case, as we will see later.

In the same way, on the production side of the economy, a firm's iteration board provides all its workers with summaries of last year's production, including what was initially proposed, changes made during planning iterations, and what was finally approved. The board also issues its prediction of this year's requests based on extrapolations from new demographic data and last year's negotiations. Individual workers consider this information, discuss ideas for improving work life, and enter personal proposals in turn averaged into the firm's first proposal for inputs and outputs. After some number of iterations, firm proposals are discussed, negotiated, and decided as a unit rather than with each individual making his or her own proposal and these being averaged.

It should be kept in mind, as well, that preparing and communicating relevant planning information as part of planning facilitation either inside a firm or industry, or at various consumption levels, is a work task like any other, though with its own special features. In other words, facilitation work is included as part of a balanced job complex, of course. And note also that in addition to quantitative proposals for each production and consumption unit, a qualitative addendum including descriptions of changes in circumstances and conditions is also entered into the planning system. At any time, a council can access the data banks of any facilitation board and any other council. The whole process is open to all.

Proceeding from One Proposal to Another

The first proposals are in. We have all answered how much we want to work and consume in light of our own presumably overly optimistic assessments of possibilities. Do the proposals constitute a plan or must we have another round? To decide, it is only necessary to collect all proposals and compare total demand and total supply for every class of final good and service, for every intermediate good, and for every primary input. In a first iteration, where consumers propose in part a "wish list" and workers propose substantial improvements in their work lives, while some goods may be in excess supply, for most goods initial proposals will likely generate excess demand. In other words, initial proposals taken together will not equal a feasible plan. As the next step, every council receives new information indicating which goods are in excess supply or demand and by how much, and how the council's proposal compares to those of other comparable units. Facilitation boards provide new estimates of indicative prices projected to equilibrate supply and demand.

At this point, consumers reassess their requests in light of the new prices and most often "shift" their requests for goods in excess demand toward goods whose indicative prices have fallen because they were in excess supply or at least less in excess demand than others. Consumers' councils and individuals whose overall requests were higher than average would feel obliged to whittle down their requests in hopes of winning approval for their proposals. Equity and efficiency emerge simultaneously from this negotiation stage. That is, the need to win approval from other similar councils forces councils whose per capita consumption request is significantly above the social average to reduce their overall requests. But the need to reduce can be met by substituting goods whose indicative prices have fallen for those whose prices have risen. Attention focuses on the degree to which councils diverge from current and projected averages, and on whether their reasons for doing so are compelling.

Similarly, workers' councils whose ratios of social benefits of their outputs to social costs of their inputs were lower than average would come under pressure to increase either efficiency or effort, or to explain why the quantitative indicators are misleading in their particular case. Before increasing their work commitment, workers would try to substitute inputs whose indicative prices had fallen for inputs whose indicative prices had risen, and substitute outputs whose indicative prices had risen for outputs whose indicative prices had fallen.

Each round of planning, or iteration, yields a new set of proposed activities. Taken together, these proposals yield new data regarding the status of each good, the average consumption per person, and the average production "benefit cost ratio" per firm. All this allows for calculation of new price projections and new predictions for average income and work, which in turn lead to modifications in proposals, all of which recurs until excess demands are eliminated and a feasible plan is reached.

Flexible Updating

Converging and updating are related because both can take advantage of the large scale of the planning process. For example, assume we have settled on a plan for the year. Why might we need to update it during the year, and how might this be done with the least disruption?

Consumers would begin the year with a working plan including how much of different kinds of food, clothing, meals at restaurants, trips, books, records, tickets to performances, and so on they will consume. What if someone wants to substitute one item for a slightly different one? Or what if she wants to delete or add entries to what she had expected to prefer for the year? Or what if she changes her mind and wants to save or borrow more than she planned to?

Well, she belongs to a neighborhood consumers' council that in turn belongs to a ward council, a city federation, and so on. Some changes that Tony and Thalia and all the rest opt for will cancel out when taken together with changed requests from all the consumers within the neighborhood (some people going up for a particular product, other people going down for it). Other variations will cancel out at the ward level, and so on. As long as consumer adjustments cancel each other out at some consumption federation level, production plans need not change. Indeed, making adjustments without disrupting production plans will be one function of consumer federation boards.

But what happens if aggregate demand for a particular item rises (or drops)? Suppose individuals record their consumption on "credit card" computers that automatically compare the percentage of annual requests "drawn down" with the fraction of the year that has passed, taking account of predictable irregularities such as birth dates and holidays, seasonal variation and the like. This data can be processed by planning terminals that communicate projected changes to relevant industry councils that, in turn, communicate changes to particular firms. The technology would be similar to that used in contemporary computerized store inventories, where cash register sales are automatically subtracted from inventory stocks. In any case, what would then happen is that consumer federations, industry councils, and individual work units would negotiate adjustments in consumption and production, which could in turn entail adjustments in work assignments to account for changed demand. Such dialogues may lead to work diminishing in some industries and increasing in others, including possible transfers of employees, but there need be no more moving about than in other types of economies. In any case, the need for workers to change jobs or increase or diminish workloads and the ensuing impact of that on their lives would be a factor proportionately considered in the negotiations over whether and how to meet changed demands.

Notice also, since each firm's activities have implications for other firms, if planned matches between supply and demand are calculated too closely, any change in demand could disrupt the whole economy. For this reason a "taut" plan would prove unnecessarily inconvenient since it would require excessive debating and moving. To avoid this and to simplify updating, the plan agreed to should be loose enough to include some unutilized capacity for most goods. A practical knowledge of those industries most likely to be affected by non-canceling alterations would facilitate this type of preparatory slack planning and is logically no different than planning in advance for medical, disaster or other needs that individuals alone can't predict, but that we can socially gauge.

There is a related technical issue, however. During the planning period there emerges a certain array of exchange rates or prices based on planned inputs and outputs for the economy. At the end of the year, we will have had actual inputs and outputs for the whole economy. Due to changes in output of various goods from the initial plan to the final reality, final real prices will be somewhat different from planned ones. A person could have benefitted or lost, having paid the plan price but gotten items whose true value was somewhat higher or lower. A parecon could simply reassess people's overall expenditure, charging them accurately at year's end, leading to some debt or remittance compared to their initial intentions. Additionally, facilitation boards could release price estimates every few months, for those who wished to avoid any large variations by adapting choices based on new valuations. Or, a parecon could instead allow such errors to pass on the assumption that over many years they would average out to no one's undue advantage. These are low order details that will no doubt be resolved in practice, perhaps in different ways in different economies, not purely in theory. The thing to keep our eye on, instead, is the broad institutional structure of our preferred vision.

Converging On a Plan

Realistically adjusting indicative prices in light of stated preferences to balance supply and demand is more complicated in practice than in economists' theoretical models. A product in excess demand in one planning iteration could overshoot equilibrium into excess supply as workers offer to produce more and consumers offer to request less responding to indicative prices. Since each product's status affects many others, progress in one industry could disrupt equilibrium in another. Regarding market-driven economies subject to similar dynamics, theoreticians' solutions to these headaches simply assume away the troublesome phenomena. Whether the issue is market equilibrium or the convergence of iterative planning procedures, abstract mathematical remedies with names like "convexity" and "gross substitutability" are good aspirin for theoretical headaches, but assumptions that grossly distort reality are no aspirin at all for sincerely putting theory into practice.

To make the participatory planning procedure efficient, therefore, specific economies will incorporate flexible rules that facilitate convergence within a reasonable time but do not unduly bias outcomes or subvert equity. Procedures can range from simple formulas carried out by computer that take short cuts toward equilibrium, to rules designed to prevent time consuming cycles of dissent and discussion, to adjustments fashioned and implemented by workers who are experienced in facilitating convergence when particular situations arise. Devising and choosing from among these and other possibilities is a practical issue in implementing any actual participatory economy. Some considerations in a choice of methods include, for example:

1   The extent to which iteration workers could accidentally or intentionally bias outcomes.

2   The extent of reductions in the number of iterations required to reach a plan and ensuing time savings.

3   The amount of planning time saved through compartmentalizing subsets of iterations with special simplifying procedures.

4   How much less onerous to producers and consumers their calculations could be made.

One thing to make clear about participatory planning and parecon in general is that there is no single right answer to how to do most functions. As with capitalism, within a parecon various approaches to problems will be taken in different parts of the economy and different institutions. Different approaches could exist for measuring labor effort, for example, or for balancing job complexes in or across units, or for organizing councils, or regarding the trade-off between different kinds of decision-making affecting participation and apportionment of influence, or regarding tradeoffs between individual and social consumption and among different instances of the latter, and regarding methods for facilitating convergence.

The point is that a parecon is a parecon insofar as it employs pareconish remuneration, job definition, ownership, council organization, allocation, and decision-making, with the values of solidarity, equity, diversity, and self-management guiding people as they make diverse choices among different means of implementing pareconish aims.

A Typical Planning Process

Since the procedure we have described is dramatically different from traditional market and central planning allocation, it is useful to describe what a typical planning process might actually look and feel like to its participants.

The first step is for each individual to think about her or his plan for the year. Individuals know they will end up working in a balanced job complex, and can expect to consume an average consumption bundle unless their work effort is above or below normal intensity or they have special needs that dictate greater reward. The first decision each individual will make is whether they want to "save" by working longer or consuming less than average, or to "borrow" by working less or consuming more than average. Facilitation boards will provide an initial estimate of the year's likely average consumption and workloads based on the previous year's levels, on investments in equipment and training, and on adjustments made during the planning period. When you prepare your first proposal you understand that you are not only proposing a level of work contribution and consumption request for yourself, but by extrapolation you are also proposing, on average, a level for everyone else as well. To be realistic you must coordinate your work and your consumption with one another, though you need not agree with facilitation board growth estimates.

In other words, what you propose is: "I would like to work so much at my job complex and to consume so much (for that work) broken down in the following way." And this proposal would be based on last year's experience, your prediction of economic growth, and your individual saving and borrowing. Everyone able to work makes such a choice, trying to optimize their well-being given their particular preferences and within the constraint that the overall amount consumed must also be produced and that responsibilities and rewards in this endeavor will be distributed equitably.

After first proposals are collected, new indicative prices are calculated and new projections of social averages estimated. Note that it would not even be possible to precisely implement most initial production proposals since in most firms one person in a team may have proposed working more hours than another person in the same team, where their tasks are interdependent so that workers can only do their work together. Moreover, most goods will be in excess demand so the initial plan is of course infeasible on those grounds as well.

So in the next step, every individual would formulate their response. You compare your proposed workload and proposed consumption level to the average proposals of others. You might also consider more localized averages, for example for your firm or industry, and for your council or neighborhood. You consider the status of each item you ordered or proposed, not least because excess demands and supplies will be reflected in changes in indicative prices. That is, you will be faced with summaries of the statuses of goods as well as new estimates of social opportunity costs and benefits. After you consult descriptive explanations for anything that might seem odd to you, like large gaps in worker productivity or consumer choice, and after you consult with whomever you like and examine whatever data interests you, you make any desired changes and enter your second proposal.

And, once again, all these new proposals are summed and the new information is made available for the third iteration. So far there have been no rules or limits on workers' or consumers' responses. Now, however, there could be a change. (The phrase "there could be" means a particular implementation of participatory planning might opt, perhaps after experimentation and in light of experience, for what we now describe. Another implementation may use different techniques, however.) Instead of being able to change proposals in any direction by any amount, limits might be imposed. For example, consumers might be prohibited from increasing their demand for certain goods beyond some maximum percentage above projected averages for the economy. Or producers might be prohibited from lowering output proposals by more than some percentage, in this and subsequent rounds.

The point is that it is possible to impose rules limiting changes to specific ranges to keep the status of goods from varying excessively from round to round. Any particular implementation of participatory planning will settle on socially desirable and mechanically efficient rules to guide the behavior of producers and consumers in different iterations.

In the third or fourth iteration, proposals might be limited to councils instead of individuals. Consumers would meet in their local neighborhood councils and workers in their workplace councils to settle on council-wide proposals. In this stage, work proposals would go from being abstract averages to consistent plans that could be enacted if the inputs requested were made available.

Note that nothing about our procedures forces people to consume the same amounts of different goods. Individual consumers and producers can hold steady on proposals that are far from average. On the other hand, workplaces will feel pressure to work up to average benefit-cost ratios, and consumers will be pressured to keep their overall requests from exceeding average income. Indeed, at this stage, production councils that persist, with proposals that have benefit-cost ratios below their industry's average might have to petition their industry not to disband them for being dysfunctional. And, similarly, local consumers' councils with above average proposals might have to petition higher federations, including an explanation of special circumstances that justify their requests.

The fifth iteration in our hypothetical procedure might deploy still another rule to accelerate planning. This time facilitation boards would extrapolate from the previous iterations to provide five different final plans that could be reached by the iterative process. What would distinguish the five plans is that each would entail slightly different total product, work expended, average consumption, and average investment. In this version, everyone affected would then vote, as units, for one of these five feasible plans. Each plan would be a viable consistent whole. Once one of the five was chosen as the base operating plan, units could adjust their requests in subsequent iterations in conformity with the base plan until individual agreements were also reached.

The Problem of Externalities

The above discussion focuses on individuals making consumption requests and on workers and workplaces making production proposals. It explains how proposals for what producers wish to supply and for what consumers wish to demand are conveyed and contrasted, and how, in light of related information, each individual alters their proposals until a plan is reached. Embedded in the logic and structure of the discussion is how collective consumption is handled as well, but we need to clarify that a bit more.

Collective Consumption

Suppose your neighborhood would like a new swimming pool, your town wants to expand its public park, or your state wants to overhaul its public transport system. A consumer council proposes any or all of these as part of its plan. There are two aspects to consider. First, if the collective consumption is to occur, it of course has implications for what must be produced. This is no different than what holds for a whole bunch of private consumption requests taken together, and handling this is like the private consumption case, as described earlier. Second, these types of collective goods are still, ultimately, consumer goods that benefit people, and they must be both charged to consumer budgets and considered with attention to their impact on everyone they would affect, presumably the people making the order and benefitting from it.

At first glance, there would seem to be no new issues. The neighborhood council discusses the matter and decides to ask for a pool. If the proposal goes through, people in the neighborhood will be charged on their consumption budgets their fair share of the indicative price, which price in turn may alter during the plan's iterations. If the cost to be charged is too high, that is, if the neighborhood residents feel they will have to give up too much of their consumption allotment to have the pool, the neighborhood foregoes the request. If the amount they have to pay from their budgets to get the pool is acceptable to them, given their desire for the pool, they persist in their request.

So far so good, but some problems arise. Larry and Lance both live in the neighborhood. Larry is going to swim but Lance is not. Are they both charged a share, or only Larry? Suppose the pool will be used and enjoyed by folks in the surrounding towns as well. Larry and Lance's neighborhood may have proposed the pool, but if it is going to be built should not all those benefitting bear some of its cost? And what if the reverse is the case? What if the pool's effect on water delivery will adversely affect the neighborhood next door? How do people suffering repercussions from the decision to have a pool influence the decision to propose the pool to the planning process of a council they are not even in?

Or consider the same problem on a larger scale: suppose Michigan's citizens, through their councils and after due deliberations, decide to collectively request a hydroelectric dam to replace a horribly polluting series of coal-based electric generators. How do the people of Michigan decide to request this in the planning process? More, how is the dam's cost to be allocated against the consumption budgets of the people of Michigan? Do the asthmatic citizens who suffer hugely from coal-generated pollution pay more than the folks less bothered by that pollution? But more, it turns out that the pollution from the coal plants afflicted Chicago and to a lessor extent other cities in Illinois. Shouldn't those citizens who will also benefit bear some of the costs of the new dam, and, if so, how does that come about? To what degree do they pay and what impact do they have on the deliberations?

Or suppose the reverse is the case. The Michiganites are proposing some mass project which will not benefit but rather adversely affect people in Illinois. Again, how do the citizens of Illinois have their appropriate impact? Even more complicated, suppose the rest of the country enjoys clean air. Isn't there an equity issue? Why should Michiganers, even if they are most affected, foot the bill if, in fact, they were enduring worse than average air conditions in the first place? Parecon's answers to these queries are rooted in the logic of council-based organization and participatory planning understood as social deliberative processes.

* First, unlike in markets, we want decisions about goods to account for their *full* social costs and benefits. We want the indicative price of goods to reflect *all* their effects as best we are able to make that happen.

* Second, we want all people affected to proportionately influence decisions.

* Third, when a proposal is made that affects large numbers of people, it is not just that we want the initially formulated proposal decided on properly. We also want the system to permit and even to facilitate the proposal's improvement.

That is, suppose a proposal has negative external effects. In addition to properly accounting for them, why not amend the proposal to reduce them or even completely offset their impact? The participatory planning process should not only promote that all those affected decide on collective proposals, but that they be able to amend and otherwise improve such proposals. When my neighborhood requests a pool or Michigan requests a dam, very likely the people involved do not have at their disposal the full awareness and insights of people in other neighborhoods or states. We do not want to incorporate only the decision influence of those other people, but, if they are affected, also their ideas and ingenuity.

To these ends, in participatory planning, when the residents of a smaller council propose some desired collective consumption (a pool or a changed energy delivery system), the proposal has to not only gain support in their own council, but must also be delivered to more encompassing councils above. So a proposal may go from a neighborhood up to a town and then to a city, a county, and so on, and likewise it may go from a state to a region and on to a country.

If a pool is proposed in my neighborhood, or a new dam in my state, and if there will be beneficiaries beyond the area of the proposing council, then in passing up the proposal its advocates are looking for it to become a proposal of the higher level council, with the hope that all who benefit at that next higher level will also be charged for its consumption, rather than only a subset in the smaller proposing council footing the whole cost.

If we have a proposal, in contrast, which has negative impact beyond our own council's citizens, then after passing it up, broader constituencies will presumably indicate their displeasure. In this case too, the proposal is taken over by the higher level council, but this time it is likely adapted through deliberations to rectify or otherwise account for its broader negative impacts. The point is that regardless of where proposals originate, collective goods consumption proposals are eventually sponsored at the level where they have their overwhelming proportion of impact, and at that level they are massaged and refined before acceptance. Only then will the proposal be put to producers and other consumers, to assess opportunity costs, etc.

What about the apportionment of influence over these decisions, and payment for the items? In the absolute ideal case, each individual is going to influence a choice in proportion to the extent it affects him or her. Likewise, each is going to carry a share of the cost proportionate to the extent that he or she benefits.

Members of a council make decisions by means that involve both information transfer about the decision's properties and about people's reactions to it, as well as deliberations over possible refinements, etc., and via some agreed upon set of voting rules. Parecon principles say we ought to choose all these mechanisms to try to make most likely an outcome that accounts for all relevant information and effects, is appropriately influenced by all concerned, and takes time and energy commensurate to what is at stake, but no more. There is no single right answer to how to achieve all this. One person might feel that with each decision we should try as perfectly as possible to represent divergent opinions. Another person might feel that over the whole planning process there are many such decisions and if we err a little in some of them, the deviations from perfection will average out. Why not do a good job, therefore, but save the extra time required to do a nearly perfect job in the knowledge that in sum and on average, deviations in each decision will more or less be made up for by deviations in others?

There are other possible attitudes as well. But the point is that unlike in other systems where the outcomes are determined by elites with no attention to either most of the relevant information or most of the impact, or to the wills of most people affected, or to the merits of the methods utilized, in parecon all these considerations are central.

Take the case of the pool in the neighborhood. It is proposed by someone living there, is supported by others, and so is put forward as a specific proposal. Members express their reactions. The proposal clearly fits into some broad category of decisions typically decided by a particular decision-making approach, let's say majority vote by the whole neighborhood. If the proposal passes, it is is adopted along with a plan for how the bill will be charged throughout the neighborhood. The proposal then goes up to the next council level. If folks in higher councils are adversely affected, they begin to debate anew, and they may reject the proposal, or, more likely, add various amendments that would make it acceptable by reducing or eliminating its adverse implications. Debate between levels could also occur, leading to refinements as well. If the neighborhood felt that broader constituencies should help with the payment, it would pass up the pool request not as a finished proposal, but as an entreaty that the higher level council adopt it as their proposal, rather than the neighborhood having to go it alone.

What if the original vote in the neighborhood council failed? The proposers have a number of options. Those in favor could form a subgroup and join resources to propose the pool as part of their personal consumption allocations. As with other personal consumption requests, if there were harm to others, the neighborhood could intervene; but otherwise personal consumption requests that are within average consumption levels are approved. However, because these are personal consumption requests, the requesters would have to forego help with payment for the pool from others in the neighborhood. A second alternative that could be pursued if the original vote in the neighborhood council failed would be that the proposers could go to the next higher council to see if they could convince that body to fund a pool, though the opposition of the neighborhood council would be a strong count against doing so.

The situation is essentially the same for Michigan enacting a massive project that would affect people throughout the state, or also in Illinois. Each collective consumption good proposed in the planning process is addressed first to determine the appropriate council level to handle it to be sure all its significant positive and negative effects are dealt with appropriately. Next, deliberations discover the properties of the proposal and its implications for various users or bystanders, etc. Reactions are presented. Deliberations take place. Finally, decisions are made using voting rules chosen to be as suitable as possible to the case in question.

In the negotiations themselves, proposals are altered in an effort to arrive at ones that are universally desired or at least over-whelmingly accepted. Take the Michigan dam. Suppose it would displace various people. The initial proposal (we might hypothesize) could have come from a city well away from the proposed site of the dam that was seeking better energy provision and cleaner air, and that might have ignored the harsh implications the dam would have for those displaced. As the proposal goes up through the ascending council levels, the local people who would be displaced gain knowledge of it and join the deliberations. Given the huge impact on them, they would play a powerful role, being given a chance to make known their horror at the idea. The proposal is changed to include reimbursing people from the dam region, providing them new houses in locales of their choosing, up to and including recon-structing their town, all as part of the cost of the dam.

The point of all this is that goods with substantial collective impact are handled by social deliberations that arrive at choices that try to appropriately incorporate the wills of the people affected, to massage and modify proposals so they become optimal, and to apportion payment for them in accordance with the benefits they bestow, and when need be, to correct for negative implications or make restitution for them.

Is it all accomplished perfectly? Not always. Are there disputes or mistakes? Of course. These are fallible social processes. But in contrast to markets and centrally planning, problematic outcomes arise due to ignorance or to errors, not due to systematic failings that always elevate some groups and make others subordinate, that incorporate only limited information, and that employ author-itarian procedures. Moreover, the above description of how participatory planning deals with collective goods and externalities reveals that the planning process has additional implications for individual consumption beyond those earlier explicitly described.

Individual Consumption

Consider a cigarette smoker. In the best possible world, the price of cigarettes (assuming they are not outlawed) should reflect not only the usual matters of the labor and other ingredients that go into cigarette production, but also their impact on those smoking them and on the health system that cares for those who become ill, and their impact on those in the vicinity of smokers, and on the health system that cares for them. How does the price of cigarettes get set in a parecon? How well does it accord with the best possible world? Who pays the costs and enjoys the benefits?

The adverse impact of smoking on health, society might decide, should be paid for by the smoker. Health care would be free, but why should everyone in society foot the bill for health care that arises due to predictable, avoidable choices? On the other hand, what about sports injuries or even pregnancy—are these comparable? There are issues, obviously, about what aspects of a good's implications are the responsibility of its users, and what aspects are properly a part of society's responsibilities. There is no need to explore all dimensions of all variants for all goods here. What is important about parecon is the institutions that arrive at assessments in such matters.

Thus, if our particular prediction about what people would decide was appropriate, the price of cigarettes would include a component fee to cover the costs of health care for medical problems that arise from smoking cigarettes. The cost would be high. But what about second-hand smoke? Cigarettes are, in this respect, a collective good. If a local council proposes, in sum, to consume a total volume of cigarettes—5,000 cartons, say—if their consumption was entirely unregulated, the adverse impact from second-hand smoke would be significant. Councils at many levels, wanting a healthy environment, would be appalled by the overall consumption request. What happens? As with the earlier examples, councils deliberate.

The first possibility is to implement restrictions that would reduce ill effects, such as no smoking zones. A second options is to charge fees that cover the costs of ventilation methods, and medical charges. A third possibility is to alter the product itself to reduce its ill effects. A fourth possibility is the more aggressive banning of the product entirely, on grounds that there is simply no way to reduce the ill effects sufficiently to permit its safe consumption. Perhaps there are other possibilities. The point is, as with more typically collective consumption, individual goods which yield adverse collective effects are deliberated partly on a personal level, as in each consumer saying that they want or do not want cigarettes, but also by larger councils that would consider the sum total consumption by all members and its broader implications.

One last example: consider the purchase of gasoline for an automobile. The consumer wants gas in order to travel from place to place. Let's ignore, for the moment, the obvious option of providing cleaner burning cars, better public transit, etc., assuming that these options have not yet been achieved. Consumers are in a position to request gas for their travel in light of a clear understanding of how much they desire to travel, as well as the conditions of the workers who produce and dispense gas, and the opportunity costs of foregoing other uses of the gas and of the assets used in the gas's creation. Likewise, if informed by a high indicative price and by qualitative information that gasoline burning has external pollution effects of great cost, consumers will moderate their requests accordingly (while also, we assume, clamoring for better modes of transport). The problem is, how does the impact of pollution affecting distant and diverse citizens translate into appropriately modified qualitative information and indicative prices that are conveyed to the gasoline consumer? How is it, for gas or for other similar products, that what are currently called external implications of transactions become, in a parecon, appropriately weighted factors integral to pricing and therefore also to consumers' and producers' choices?

If no one seeks clean air, there is no issue to be addressed. No economy can account for unexpressed preferences, of course. But if local, regional, or wider constituencies, through their councils, desire clean air, then the situation becomes analogous to the case of the cigarettes. Suppose the sum of the gas requests the Los Angeles council receives comes to a billion gallons of gas consumption for the coming year, or whatever number it turns out to be. The cumulative effect, if the requests are adopted, will facilitate transportation but will worsen air quality with resulting sickness and other problems. Citizens concerned about their health will, acting through their local, city, and regional councils, insist that the greater Los Angeles council include the costs of pollution in their assessment— abatement measures, medical costs, work time lost to illness, etc.— and urge stricter emission standards and other changes in the consumption choices. Again, there would be a collective deliberation because there is a collective impact, and the result is that while each gasoline consumer makes a personal choice, the implications for the broader community have an impact on that choice by pushing up the indicative cost, on the one hand, and conveying information that helps propel alterations in options, on the other hand.

Conclusion

The point of these special cases addressing collective consumption is threefold.

1 We wanted to specify the pricing and deliberative properties of participatory planning vis-à-vis public goods and what are currently called externalities, whether positive or negative.

2 We wanted to convey, again, our two-track approach to its subject matter. On the one hand, we talk about basic institutions, like balanced job complexes, remuneration for effort/sacrifice, participatory planning, and council democracy, and in doing so we lay out demanding norms and features. On the other hand, to make the meaning of these defining features clear, we also describe a more detailed context of features that are more hypothetical and could vary within particular economies and also from one economy to another, with many of the likely possibilities to be discovered and refined in the future.

3 We wanted to emphasize, again, that in a society, outcomes arise from social processes. Written descriptions tend to get cut and dried, logical, precise, math-like. But the actualities these summary accounts describe in fact involve infinite details. There is no such thing as perfect remuneration for effort/sacrifice, perfectly balanced job complexes, perfectly accurate attribution of perfectly proportionate say in decisions, nor is there one best method for all the steps associated with trying to accomplish these aims in every possible context What we have done is to construct a vision whose logic advances these aims, and whose social processes will diverge from the aims only due to ignorance or the choice to save time by settling negotiations satisfactorily rather than perfectly, but not due to some systematic incapacity or bias that always and inexorably obstructs these aims. If we compare the "ideal" participatory economic model to the "ideal" capitalist, market socialist, or centrally planned socialist model, the participatory economy maximally attains our aims where the other economies systematically violate them. If we examine not the rarified world of perfect models, but the real world of actual social processes, the case becomes stronger because the fall-off in achievement in parecon as we move from theory to the real

world is quite modest, but the fall-off in performance of the other models is huge and destructive.

We have now presented a description of a third way to accomplish economic allocation beyond markets and central planning. Most readers will probably find evident by now that implementing a parecon is possible. When we address possible criticisms of participatory economics, concerns about whether implementing it will have adverse implications for matters of efficiency, incentives, and other reasonable concerns, will be addressed further. But we should also tell professional economists reading this volume that in *The Political Economy of Participatory Economics* (Princeton University Press, 1991) and also online at www.parecon.org we provide a mathematical model demonstrating parecon's superior convergence, efficiency, and stability properties as compared to those demonstrated by similar models for market and centrally planned economies, all with the understanding that desirable allocation should produce each item until its true social opportunity cost equals its true marginal benefit to society. Parecon, in other words, attains familiar productivity and allocative aims better than old systems, and goes on to as well advance equity, solidarity, diversity and self-management, unlike old systems which trample those values.

9

Summary and Defense

I have the audacity to believe that peoples everywhere can have three meals
a day for their bodies, education and culture for their minds, and dignity,
equality, and freedom for their spirits. I believe that what self-centered men
have torn down, other-centered men can build up ... human progress is
neither automatic nor inevitable .... We are now faced with the fact that
tomorrow is today. We are confronted with the fierce urgency of NOW. In this
unfolding conundrum of life and history there is such a thing as being too late
.... this is no time for apathy or complacency. This is a time for vigorous and
positive action.
— Martin Luther King

Where are we at so far? What characterizes a participatory economy? Also, since we will not get to serious treatment of plausible
worries about a parecon until part four, and since some readers may
not be ready to jump into an assessment of its benefits before at
least having certain key problems rebutted, why isn't parecon
flawed in the variety of ways most folks initially worry about?

Workers' Councils and Balanced Job Complexes

As we have described thus far, in a parecon, democratic workers'
councils would carry out production. Everyone could freely apply for
a job and membership in the council of their choice, or form a new
workers' council with whomever they wish. Decisions within
councils would be self-managed. Appropriate information dispersal,
means of expressing preferences, and decision-making processes
would ensure as best as possible that each individual influences
outcomes proportionately to the effect of the outcomes on him or her.
To facilitate this, parecon would balance individual work
assignments for desirability and for empowerment within and
across workplace units.

To revisit this key point in more detail: every economy organizes
work tasks into what are usually called "jobs" that constitute all the
tasks a single individual will perform. In hierarchical economies
most jobs contain a number of similar, relatively undesirable and
unempowering tasks while a few jobs consist of relatively desirable
and empowering tasks. Why should some people's work lives be less

desirable than others? Doesn't taking equity seriously require balancing jobs, or work complexes, for desirability? Similarly, if we want everyone to have equal opportunity to participate in decision-making so that the *formal* right to participate translates into an *effective* right to participate, doesn't this require balancing work complexes for empowerment? If some people sweep floors all week while others review new technological options and attend planning meetings, is it realistic to think the former will all have equal opportunity to participate as the latter simply because they each have one vote in the workers' council and a chair at the decision table?

Balanced job complexes do not entail an end to specialization. Nor do they deny the need for expertise. Instead, as we have described earlier, each individual in a parecon—including specialists and experts—will do a modest number of tasks some of which will be more enjoyable and some less, and some of which will be more empowering and some less, such that over a reasonable period the overall average empowerment impact for each job will be the same as that for all other jobs.

The usual arguments against balanced job complexes are:

1 Talent is scarce and training is socially costly, therefore it is inefficient for talented people or people with training to do menial tasks.

2 Requiring everyone to participate equally in economic decisions ignores the fact that some can do a much better job than others.

In brief, previewing a more comprehensive treatment to appear later in this book, how does a pareconist reply to these objections? The "scarce talent" argument against balancing work complexes is generally overstated. If one assumes most of the work force has no socially useful, trainable talents, then the conclusion follows. If one assumes we could not have more people doing skilled tasks, it follows. But these assumptions are false. It is true that not everyone has the talent to become a brain surgeon and also that there are social costs to training brain surgeons. But it is not true that everyone who can do it is doing it. And as well, most people have some socially useful talent whose development entails some social costs. An ideally efficient economy would identify and develop everyone's most socially useful talents. If this is done, then there is a significant opportunity cost no matter who changes bedpans and the conclusion that it is grossly inefficient for brain surgeons to change them no longer follows. When Joe, who is currently a surgeon, has to also change bedpans, we may lose some of the possible output we could enjoy from Joe's training and talents—assuming he could instead do complex surgery all day long. But we do not forego the surgery entirely, of course. We just have more people who do surgery less time each. And when Sue—who now only changes bedpans goes through a process of socialization and schooling and on-the-job experience that elicits her best capabilities, we gain those best capabilities from their having been suppressed in the older model.

What is the trade? Well, before tallying, we have to also consider moving from a situation of injustice and its resulting oversight and resentment to a situation of solidarity, and take into account the impact of that change on morale and output, and also on social relations more broadly. The argument against balanced job complexes on grounds that on average in switching from our current society to the proposed one we will lose huge quantities of needed output is racist, sexist, and classist because it asserts that those displaying few talents in contemporary hierarchical corporate work arrangements actually have few talents, rather than having diverse talents that were buried by debilitating social structures and mind-numbing work. It is also myopic, or perhaps more accurately, profit-centered or productivist, in discounting the benefits of self-management, solidarity, diversity, and equity, which would all be enhanced by incorporating balanced job complexes even if society does get less output as a result from some particular Mozart or Einstein (though also very likely discovering others of comparably immense productive talent who would otherwise have subserviently swept floors forever or, for that matter, died at any early age of malnutrition).

Of course in circumstances where the consequences of decisions are complicated and not readily apparent, there is a need for expertise. But economic choice entails that we both determine and evaluate consequences. Those with expertise in a matter may well predict the consequences of a decision far more accurately than non-experts could. But those affected by a matter will know best whether they prefer one outcome to another. So, while the need for efficiency requires an important role for experts in determining complicated consequences, efficiency also requires that those who will be affected determine which consequences they prefer. And of course experts don't just decide things, they also have skills—like precise hands for doing brain surgery, so I do not want a surgeon to decide for me whether I should have surgery, but I do want the surgeon to do the cutting, not myself or another citizen.

This means if we seek to attain optimal choices, it is just as misguided to keep those affected by decisions from making them (after experts have analyzed and debated consequences) as it is to prevent experts from explaining and debating consequences of complicated choices before those affected register their desires.

Self-managed decision-making, defined as decision-making input in proportion to the degree one is affected by the outcome, does not eliminate experts but does confine experts to their proper role and keep them from usurping a role that it is neither fair, democratic, nor efficient. That it obstructs proper attentiveness to experts is not a viable critique of establishing balanced job complexes, because it does not, in fact, do so.

Consumers' Councils and
Remuneration for Effort and Sacrifice

Every individual, family, or living unit would belong to a neighborhood consumption council. Each neighborhood council would belong to a federation of neighborhood councils representing an area the size of a ward or rural county. Each ward would belong to a city consumption council, each city and county council would belong to a state council, and each state council would belong to the national consumption council. The major purpose for this nesting of consumer councils is to allow for the fact that different kinds of consumption affect different numbers of people. Failure to arrange for all those affected by consumption activities to participate in choosing them not only implies a loss of self-management, but, if the preferences of some are disregarded or misrepresented, a loss of accurate, appropriate accounting of preferences as well. One of the serious liabilities of markets is their systematic failure to allow for the expression of desires for social consumption on an equal footing with the expression of desires for private consumption. Having the different levels of federations participate on an equal footing in the participatory planning procedure prevents such a bias from occurring in a participatory economy.

Members of neighborhood councils present consumption requests accompanied by effort ratings done by their workplace peers in accord with norms established there. Using indicative prices the social burden of each proposal is calculated. While no consumption request justified by an effort rating is denied by a neighborhood consumption council without very good reason (as in, for example, a request for machine guns or large quantities of poison, etc.), neighbors could express an opinion that a request was unwise, and neighborhood councils could also approve requests on the basis of need in addition to effort. Individuals could "borrow" or "save" by consuming more or less than warranted by their effort level for the year, and anyone wishing to submit an anonymous request for collective consumption could do so.

The major questions are whether "to each according to effort" is fair, and whether this distributive maxim is consistent with efficiency.

Capitalist economies embody the distributive maxim: "to each according to the value of his or her personal contribution and the contribution of property owned." Public enterprise market economies operate according to the maxim: "to each according to the value of his or her personal contribution." In a participatory economy the only reason people would have different levels of consumption would be differences in work effort or differences in need in the event of special circumstances. By effort we mean anything that constitutes a personal sacrifice for the purpose of providing socially useful goods and services. If work complexes were truly balanced for desirability, and if everyone worked at the same intensity, then effort could be measured in terms of the number of hours worked. For variation in intensity, there is reward. In other circumstances, effort could take the form of working at a less pleasant or more dangerous job, or undergoing training that was less agreeable than the average training process.

Socialists have long argued that consumption rights derived from the ownership of productive property are unjustified. Beside the simple fact that they generate grossly unequal consumption opportunities, the usual rationale is that those who receive the extra income did little, if anything, to deserve it. They neither contributed more to the value of social production through their own labor than others, nor underwent any greater personal sacrifice than others. But in *Capitalism and Freedom*, the right-wing Nobel Prize-winning economist Milton Friedman pointed out the hypocrisy of denouncing income differentials due to differences in ownership of property while tolerating differentials due to differences in talent. "Is there any greater ethical justification for the high returns to the individual who inherits from his parents a peculiar voice for which there is a great demand than for the high returns to the individual who inherits property?" Friedman asked. Friedman, of course, was arguing in favor of both genetic and financial inheritance. But his challenge is still a legitimate one. In our view, the honest answer to Friedman's challenge is "no." Despite the historical fact that private ownership of productive property has generated considerably more economic injustice than differential talent has, there is nothing more fair about the birth lottery than the inheritance lottery. Greater personal sacrifice made in the production of socially beneficial goods and services is legitimate grounds for greater access to those goods and services. But neither ownership of property nor possession of talent that makes it possible to produce more valuable goods and services carries any moral weight, in our view.

As stated earlier, we believe this creates an ethical dilemma for those who support public enterprise market systems. If wages are determined via the market some will earn more than others who work longer and harder. But if wages are set according to effort by a dynamic overriding market wage determinations, markets will assign prices that deviate from the true social opportunity costs of goods, yielding a price system that systematically misjudges social costs and benefits (even worse than other market failures cause it to). There is no way around this dilemma in an economy with a free labor market.

In contrast, in a participatory economy, while individuals consume according to their work effort, users of scarce labor resources are accounted according to the actual value of those resources, their opportunity costs, via the mechanisms of participatory planning. This avoids the contradiction between equity and allocative efficiency intrinsic to a market economy.

But what about the common view that rewarding according to the value of one's personal contribution provides efficient incentives while rewarding according to effort does not?

Differences in the value of people's contributions arise from differences in talent, training, job placement, luck, and effort. Once we clarify that "effort" includes personal sacrifices incurred in training, the only factor influencing performance over which an individual has any control is effort. By definition, neither talent nor luck can be induced by reward. Rewarding the occupant of a job for the contribution inherent in the job itself does not enhance performance. And if training is undertaken at public rather than private expense, no reward is required to induce people to seek training. In sum, if we include a training component in our definition of effort, the only discretionary factor influencing performance is effort, and the only factor we should reward to enhance performance is effort. Not only is rewarding effort consistent with efficiency, but rewarding the combined effects of talent, training incurred at public not private expense, job placement, luck, and effort, is not.

Participatory Planning

The participants in participatory planning are the workers' councils and federations, the consumers' councils and federations, and various Iteration Facilitation Boards (IFBs). Conceptually, the planning procedure is quite simple. An IFB announces what we call "indicative prices" for all goods, resources, categories of labor, and capital. Consumers' councils and federations respond with consumption proposals taking the indicative prices of final goods and services as estimates of the social cost of providing them. Workers councils and federations respond with production proposals listing the outputs they would make available and the inputs they would need to produce them, again, taking the indicative prices as estimates of the social benefits of outputs and true opportunity costs of inputs. An IFB then calculates the excess demand or supply for each good and adjusts the indicative price for the good up, or down, in light of the excess demand or supply, and in accord with socially agreed algorithms. Using the new indicative prices, consumers and workers councils and federations revise and resubmit their proposals.

The procedure whittles overly optimistic and otherwise infeasible proposals down to a feasible plan primarily in two different ways. To achieve the approval of other consumer councils who regard their initial requests as greedy, consumers requesting more than their effort ratings warrant are forced to reduce or shift their requests to less socially costly items. To win the approval of other workers, workers' councils whose proposals have lower than average social benefit to social cost ratios are forced to increase either their efforts or their efficiency. Both workers and consumers easily access not only indicative prices which summaries the whole economic picture, but qualitative and descriptive data as well. As iterations proceed, proposals move closer to mutual feasibility and indicative prices move closer to true social opportunity costs. Since no participant in the planning procedure enjoys an advantage over others, the procedure generates equity and efficiency simultaneously. Social deliberations in councils arrive at sensible proposals for collective consumption in light of true opportunity costs including incorporating desirable refinements that reduce ill effects and expand positive effects. As to possible worries about the possibility of adverse by-products or other implications of participatory planning overriding its benefits, we will consider these in coming chapters.

Conclusion

The issue at hand is in our view quite simple: a participatory economy is built on workers and consumers councils, balanced job complexes, remuneration for effort and sacrifice, participatory planning, and self-managed decision-making. It therefore rejects private ownership of the means of production, corporate workplace organization and markets and/or central planning. In place of rule over workers by capitalists or by coordinators, parecon is an economy in which workers and consumers together cooperatively determine their economic options and benefit from them in ways fostering equity, solidarity, diversity, and self-management. Parecon is classless.

The choice that parecon poses can be summarized as follows:

1   Do we want to try and measure the value of each person's contribution to social production and allow individuals to benefit from social production in tune with that, or even with their bargaining power or property, or do we want to base any differences in consumption rights only on differences in personal sacrifices made in producing goods and services? In other words, do we want an economy that implements the norm "to each according to the value of his or her personal contribution, property, or power" or an economy that obeys the norm "to each according to his or her effort?"

2   Do we want few people to conceive and coordinate the work of many? Or do we want everyone to have the opportunity to participate in economic decisions to the degree they are affected by the outcomes of those decisions? In other words, do we want to continue to organize work according to corporate hierarchies, or do we want council democracy plus job complexes that are balanced for empowerment?

3   Do we want a structure for expressing consumer preferences that is biased in favor of individual consumption over social

consumption? Or do we want it to be as easy to register preferences for social as for individual consumption? In other words, do we want consumers to compete with each other as atomized buyers, or to cooperate in nested federations of consumer councils?

4 Do we want economic decisions to be determined by competition between groups pitted against one another for their well-being and survival? Or do we want to plan our joint endeavors democratically, equitably, and efficiently? In other words, do we want to abdicate economic decision-making to the market or do we want to embrace participatory planning?

In this book and in greater detail in *Quiet Revolution in Welfare Economics* (Princeton University Press, 1990), and also online at www.parecon.org, we have explained why markets are incompatible with equity and systematically destructive of solidarity. We have explained why market economies will continue to destroy the environment, and why a radical view of social life implies that external effects are the rule rather than the exception, which means that markets routinely misjudge social costs and benefits and misallocate scarce productive resources. And we have explained that while markets may fulfill the liberal vision of individual economic freedom to dispose of one's personal capa- bilities and property however one chooses, they are inconsistent with the radical goal of self-management for everyone.

In conclusion of this summary, we believe those who reconcile themselves to market "socialist" or other coordinatorist models do so illogically and unnecessarily. The choice is illogical because the negative experience of authoritarian planning in no way rebuts the potential of participatory planning. The choice is unnecessary because the vision of an equitable, democratic economy that promotes solidarity among its participants is as attractive and appealing as ever, and now has substance.

10

Evaluating Parecon

Works are of value only if they give rise to better ones.
— William Von Humboldt

In part I, we offered as guiding values equity, solidarity, diversity, self-management, fulfillment and development, and classlessness. We evaluated centrally important economic institutions and then also capitalism, market and centrally planned socialism/coordinatorism), and bioregionalism, and we rejected all these models as obstructing our preferred values.

Having now presented participatory economics, it is appropriate to briefly assess it as well. How does participatory economics fare vis-à-vis equity, solidarity, diversity, self-management, fulfillment and development, and classlessness? Of course, having conceived parecon with these values as our guides, it won't be that surprising that in our view it meets them with flying colors. The daunting question will be whether it has other failings that compromise these merits. That will be the subject of part IV, where we will take up the diverse criticisms people have expressed about parecon, and reply as best we are able.

Equity

What is equity, after all? As good a definition as any is that equity is a condition in which each person gets what they deserve for what they have done, and no one gets more (or less) than that. Of course, this begs the question of the meaning of "deserve."

We have already dealt with "deservedness" at such great length that almost anything said here would be severely redundant. Parecon rewards effort and sacrifice. If one thinks that doing that is just, one will favor parecon on this score. If one thinks instead that rewarding a deed to property is just, one certainly won't favor parecon as equitable. Likewise, if one thinks that rewarding output—or luck, talent, or training insofar as they contribute to output—is just, as compared to rewarding only effort/sacrifice or even in addition to rewarding effort/sacrifice, again one will not favor parecon. If one thinks rewarding power is just, of course, one won't favor parecon.

Similarly, parecon equilibrates conditions of work so that all people have equally fulfilling work lives, or, failing that, parecon compensates those with less than average conditions by rewarding them proportionately more. Again, if one favors equity as we have defined it—that people's economic income and circumstances should together be comparably desirable—and if one believes that the right index for detailed equilibration is effort/sacrifice, one will favor the parecon model.

In parecon there is no mechanism to accrue property or bargaining power and no means to use either to increase income. There is no way to translate luck of genetic endowment or of relative position into greater income. There is no way to have better circumstances and not have income reduced, or, if one has worse circumstances, to not have income enlarged. The economy only materially rewards effort and sacrifice.

It follows that if we adhere to the same equity standard with which we rejected various other economic systems earlier, parecon succeeds admirably. In a participatory economy not every person will get precisely his or her due all the time, but deviations will not be systemic, will not enrich any one sector at another sector's expense, and will occur due to errors of judgment sometimes idiosyncratic spite, but not due to system-induced differentials.

Solidarity

Solidarity implies that individuals in an economy respect one another's circumstances and well-being as part of economic life. It means that economic activity promotes social ties and empathy rather than having an antisocial effect. Participatory planning is designed to attain solidarity. Each person gains increased income only by exerting more effort than they did before or by everyone's base income increasing at once. No one can increase their income by taking a share that would otherwise go to someone else. We do not increase our income by diminishing that of others, but only in concert with others. And similarly, we improve our conditions of work if our balanced job complex improves and not otherwise. But if my average job complex improves, by definition everyone else's average improves as well. When one person gains, everyone gains.

These attributes are already so singularly different from typical capitalist dynamics as to provide an overwhelming argument for parecon. But if we look deeper, will the gloss fade? Consider trying to make a choice among various investment proposals in your workplace or in the economy as a whole. What criteria do you use to judge whether one innovation is better than another? Let's suppose you are a greedy individual with no concern for others. In that case, the answer will be that you will consider solely the impact of the innovation on your own job and income. But in a participatory economy an innovation will affect your income only via its impact on the overall social product and the average social product per person. Even to cast a greedy ballot, you have to assess the social good. People may disagree about which choice will have a better social impact, and mistakes will certainly be made, but in a parecon the mode by which we all advance is inexorably social, not antisocial.

What about job circumstances? The logic is identical. An innovation in your own workplace is not more valuable to you than an innovation elsewhere if the distant one has a better impact on average job complexes than the near one. We each gain when the overall average improves, so to seek gain we must each pay attention to the average.

The bottom line is simple and striking: in market systems if compassionate people wish to get ahead they are compelled to do antisocial things. In a parecon, even antisocial people, if they want to get ahead, must do socially positive things. The market system breeds instrumentalist, competitive attitudes that destroy solidarity even among those personally inclined to be empathetic. The participatory economic system fosters solidarity and empathy even among otherwise egocentric and antisocial people. Of course, this was a central criterion in constructing participatory economics. The final proof of parecon's worthiness will be whether parecon scores as well when we address issues that weren't firmly in mind during its conception, our focus in part IV of this book.

Diversity

Regarding diversity, there should be diverse economic options for us to choose among to enrich our lives. Additionally, we shouldn't have our choices among diverse options narrowed by some pressure independent of our own inclinations. So there should be great diversity not only in options available, but also in what different people consume or in the jobs they opt for from among available options. We should have a diversity in outcomes reflecting our diversity in preferences. Each person has many options and remains a unique individual in selecting them, making his or her own choices that reflect his or her own unique dispositions, talents, and inclinations, and not some conforming pressure from without.

For example, in a society fostering diversity, we anticipate there would be no homogenizing pressures causing large numbers of people to settle on just a few options among many, attaining similar situations not because they all have similar personal preferences, but because they all caved in to similar overriding pressures. We all drink water and that is certainly not a sign of conforming to pressure. It reveals, instead, a fundamental similarity that derives from our natures. We all wear clothes, and that too is not a mark of onerous homogenization but of benign common history and conditions. But if many of us wear a uniform not out of unbiased agreement on its aesthetic or practical appeal, but to indicate that we are like others wearing it—because to do otherwise would be to suffer a loss—there is a loss of diversity due to a homogenizing pressure. Or, if out of all possible genres of music the population divides into those who like country, those who like classical, those who like rap, and those who like rock, and if what a person likes can be predicted by attributes that have nothing to do with their actual freely developed musical tastes, but instead reflect only the impact of structurally imposed identities having literally nothing to do with music, then we can reasonably deduce that a homogenizing effect has diminished diversity and limited individual choices. Diversity is a subtle matter, but not entirely impossible to assess.

Another dimension of diversity is that in decision-making attention should be paid to the possibility for error and therefore diverse alternatives should be explored alongside preferred choices, even after a preferred option is chosen, or should at least be kept open for future exploration. This is done to preclude all actors from becoming embedded in an irreversible trajectory of choice that limits future possibilities or diminishes the quality of future outcomes. Put colloquially, we should rarely put all our eggs in one basket. So how does a parecon score in terms of diversity?

Relative to other economies, some causes of difference are removed, which could be seen by some as reducing options and therefore reducing diversity. A parecon does not have capitalists and coordinators and workers, but only economic actors. Class differentiation therefore disappears. Likewise, in a parecon, you cannot choose to hire wage slaves nor to sell yourself as a wage slave. These options too are gone. In a parecon you cannot parlay productive genetic attributes into greater income or power, another lost option. And there is a sense in which these changes may seem to some to reduce diversity since we have gone from having three classes to having none. But in our view this is like the sense in which instances of capitalism reduced diversity by removing the option to own a slave or be a king—not exactly great failings. Looking deeper, in the parecon case, it is not only a matter of removing bad options, there is also an offsetting increase in diversity. That is, if a society has classes, each actor is part of a group that has interests contrary to those in other groups. This collective confrontation, and the commonality of internal class conditions together lead to homogenization within classes even as they force competition among them. If we hold up babies in the hospital and report about them merely what class their parents are in and we then ask people to predict what tastes and preferences the baby will have later in life, under capitalism we will guess right in a remarkable proportion of cases about a remarkable number of life choices. This means that being in a class narrows the range of choice that a person winds up with. It makes some outcomes highly probable regardless of all other attributes of each baby—whether innate attributes or due to unfolding (unbiased) life experiences. In parecon, with no classes, the homogenizing effects of class membership are gone.

The scorecard for how diversity is upheld in a parecon is positive on other counts as well. Not only are class homogenization effects eliminated, but parecon self-consciously favors respect for minority positions and gives defeated views of minorities every opportunity to persist to insure against majorities making mistakes. This is built into participatory planning, by preserving past data and by the checks on indicative prices that qualitative information and the initial phases of each new round of planning provide.

In contrast, a central but rarely discussed failure of markets is that because they ignore the fact that people's preferences are affected by economic circumstances, if a population is confronted by offerings for which some prices set too high and some set too low relative to actual social costs and benefits—then in a market system preferences will bend toward the latter and away from the former. This inaccurate bending of people's true desires will in turn further propel the incorrect prices in the wrong direction, and so on, in a snowball effect. The key point is that this market phenomenon is not random. There is always a systematic mis-pricing of goods with positive or negative external effects. People in the system become increasingly individualistic due to increasingly favoring private consumption over consumption of goods with public benefits beyond what a true comparison of personal and collective benefit would warrant had there been proper initial pricing. Because market systems promote pursuit of profit, not of social well-being, there is no pressure for anyone to notice and curtail such developments. Capitalists see profits to be had producing mis-priced goods and follow that path mercilessly. People's consumption preferences become skewed in accord.

Participatory planning, in contrast, impedes such phenomena in the two ways mentioned earlier. First, it properly values items by taking into account all social and individual factors. Deviations from proper pricing derive from honest mistakes and not systematic biases built into the allocation system. Second, participatory planning re-calibrates valuations and behavior with every new planning period precisely to guard against prices snowballing away from what they should be due to past errors persisting into future periods. It synchronizes tastes and behavior consistent with independently presented preferences. The goal is social well-being and not private profits.

A participatory economy cannot, of course, guarantee perfect adherence to diversity. For one thing, it is critical that other sectors of society also promote diversity, especially a society's cultural institutions. For another thing, no system precludes all biases, much less all errors. But what we can say about parecon is that the most egregious contemporary economic pressures for conformity are removed. No more class conformity, prices snowballing away from true representation of preferences, or profit-seeking that takes advantage of any opportunity, however socially counter productive. In their place parecon elevates diversity to a central value, employs decision-making that permits and even welcomes attention to minority views, properly values economic products, recognizes economic impact on consumer and producer preferences, and self-consciously avoids irrational pricing trajectories.

It might be that affirmative action will be deemed necessary even in a parecon in order to eradicate lingering manifestations or continuing effects of racism or sexism. Parecon doesn't prejudge this, but parecon is not inconsistent with such programs, and could indeed facilitate them. Because jobs won't vary by income or empowerment, economically there won't even be a lowest-paying or least-rewarding employment for one race or gender to be consigned to. Because parecon freely disseminates qualitative economic information, racial and gender equity can be made as important a goal as society wishes.

Self-Management

How does parecon fare regarding people's degree of influence over the decisions that affect them?

Parecon decisions are made by whatever method best allows each person to affect each decision in proportion to how much the outcome of the decision affects them. Can this be done perfectly all the time? Of course not. But does parecon provide context, information, and motivations in accord with this aim? Yes, it is a defining feature.

Within a workplace there are two broad kinds of decisions. The first involves establishing plans for the unit. Should we invest in improving our workplace? How much output, produced by how many people, should be our goal? The second kind of decision involves how we accomplish each month, week, and day what we have set out to do.

Consumption decisions are similarly broad: what do I want collectively for the groups I am part of, and what do I want for myself, individually? And having received what I wanted, now what do I do with it?

Allocation, decisions are broadly about what level of work and output should be enacted, what exchange rates should exist among items, and therefore what relative amounts should be produced, who should get what income, and various choices of implementation such as those concerning facilitation boards.

So at risk of some repetition, let's briefly consider each domain in terms of its rating vis-à-vis self-management.

Production

In the workplace we have councils that vary in size from work teams to industries. This facilitates people's interactions at each level of autonomous or collective involvement. If a plant decides together on some action that delimits aims for a specific work team, decisions for how that team then accomplishes those aims may be overwhelmingly its own affair. If so, the team's council will make decisions internally adhering to the norms that guide the whole workplace. But within a whole workplace, division, or team, how does each participant make such decisions?

There is no single answer for all workplaces or even universally within each given workplace. Decisions have different spectrums of impact. For one thing, most of our work decisions affect not only our workplace and those in it, but everyone who will consume our products. Our production utilizes inputs that could have been used to produce other things that might meet other needs, so consumers need a degree of say in what goes on in production, just as producers have an impact, of course, on what consumers can opt for. Should consumers of VCRs have some degree of say even over what a peanut factory produces? Yes, because if the peanut factory makes soy nuts, chicken farmers have less soy feed, which increases beef output, which affects leather production, which reduces some plastic production, which reduces economies of scale in plastic production, which raises the price of VCRs. Mediating this complicated interrelationship of production and consumption is allocation—in our case participatory planning—and we will assess the self-management implications of such planning below. For now, assuming consumers and workers elsewhere have appropriate input into decisions in a specific workplace, what about workers in that workplace themselves?

Some decisions overwhelmingly affect only me. Some affect only you. Some affect only a specific work team and each member equally; some affect that team, but each member unequally. And there are the same variations for projects, divisions, the whole workplace, or even the whole industry. The point is, there is no single decision-making process that can universally deliver influence in proportion to impact for every person, every time. What is needed is instead what parecon delivers:

- The organization of all actors into appropriately defined subgroups.

- Giving each of these decision/work units, or production councils an appropriate amount of say.

- Decisions having been allotted in that manner to various levels of council, in turn using appropriate processes *within* councils at each level: Sometimes one-person one-vote with majority rule, sometimes two-thirds majority, sometimes each actor having a veto, in each case with suitable time given to advance preparation for decisions, to assessment and reassessment, or to minority voices holding up final choices or experimenting with parallel explorations.

All in all, we can't say that a parecon will perfectly succeed in properly allotting influence over every production decision. What we can say, however, is that there is no structural impediment to doing so and there is every possible admonition and structural pressure on behalf of doing so. For example, a parecon does not have corporate hierarchies that essentially subordinate typically 80 percent of the population to having little or no say over their work, giving about 19 percent considerable say over everyone's work, though ultimately subordinate to an all powerful top 1 percent. Parecon in contrast facilitates proportionate say, allows the redress of mistakes, and balances empowerment and income properly. It is hard to see how a system without workplace councils, balanced job complexes, and remuneration for effort and sacrifice could do better in providing participatory self-management to its workers—assuming that the workers not only have this flexible array of conditions in their own workplaces, but also have proper input into allocation decisions, which we assess below. But first, what about consumption?

Consumption

Consumption is an economic activity that has inputs and outputs and that is, in this respect, abstractly the same as production. And the decision dynamics of consumption are similar to those of production as well. Again, we have layers of councils designed to group people with shared decision-making affinity such as individuals, families, neighborhoods, and counties. Again, decisions are apportioned to these councils and within them in accord with impact on the group or individuals involved. As with production, consumers collectively establish appropriate processes for different types of decisions within the appropriate level of consumer council, having only the norm of self-management in common. The system is not perfect, but there is no systematic obstacle to everyone involved having proportionate say, and as in the production case, consumers have every incentive to seek proportionate say up to not spending too much time trying to add the last dimple of accuracy to every accounting, as against getting on with life.

In a parecon, each individual largely determines his or her own personal consumption, and the impact of each person's preferences registers in the indicative prices that contextualize all choices. Each collective has nearly sole say over what they propose to collectively consume, though if there are effects in wider constituencies, the proposal will have to be reviewed at that level as well.

There are two ways in which personal or group choices can affect others, and why, therefore, others should be able to influence the final decision. On the one hand, there is the obvious implication that if I am going to consume a bicycle, someone must produce it. My choice is not without implications for those who do the work of producing it. Likewise, if I consume it, then the inputs needed to produce it aren't available for producing some other product that someone else may have wanted.

If we assume, for the moment, that allocation proportionately accounts for the mutual impact of different production and consumption decisions, and that consumption councils likewise accurately apportion influence over the consumers' share of each such decision, what about the fact that once I get my consumption items and decide how to consume them, there could be effects on others from that as well, so that perhaps others should have had a say in whether, indeed, I got them in the first place.

Suppose I ask for not much milk or juice, but so much brandy and vodka that quite obviously I am or will become an alcoholic (or a dispensary), but even so the total volume of brandy and vodka sought by our council is fine in the view of producers. This is not a problem for producers, but my choice will likely adversely impact my family, my neighbors, and my community. The same would hold if I was about to purchase lots of firearms, say ... or an outdoor sound system appropriate for a stadium but not for my backyard that abuts many other backyards. It is good that the prices of these items reflect their broader social implications, but perhaps not good enough. These choices could all be okay from the broad standpoint of allocation writ large, yet not okay viewed more locally.

The point is, consumption has diverse external effects and those effects can be globally small and fine, yet simultaneously locally large and adverse. Some of these effects are broad and general and accommodated by the participatory planning system most broadly. The overall price of alcohol reflects its average social and health impacts, as does the overall price of products that pollute. But with some products even with proper valuation in the large, specific apportionments can still be horribly adverse due to contingent local effects. So parecon includes the provision that consumption council members can collectively assess individual consumption orders, indicating their displeasure with specific ones that have harsh negative external implications, seeking remedies that may require additional expenses, and in the extreme case even collectively precluding such options from being met, when appropriate.

In other words, a neighborhood could see a private order for huge quantities of alcohol. or guns, or for a raucous outdoor sound system, and, even though the neighborhood's citizens are not over consuming in total, and even though producers are ready to supply the products in the quantity requested, and even though the people making the orders are within their budgets, nonetheless the neighborhood could intervene and first ask for an explanation (maybe the alcohol is medicinal or for household chemistry experiments, or maybe the guns are for an abstract art display, or maybe the sound system is for parts that are going to be put to an entirely different and benign or very positive purpose), and then, if the explanations are found wanting, literally forbid these types of purchases within these collective units. This is comparable to contemporary zoning laws saying that you cannot disturb the peace, for example—but in the parecon case it is democratic and without profit-seeking, and the details are organized to reflect the recognition that those impacted by decisions should influence them proportionately. Moreover, the specific individual consumption requests and the dialog about them can be anonymous.

All in all, therefore, as with production similarly for consumption: Organization into councils facilitates appropriate levels of self-managed oversight and influence. The system urges self-managing decision processes and it provides means to continually reassess and improve them. But what about allocation? Does allocation matter to self-management? If so, why and how?

Allocation

Consider having workers' and consumers' councils plus all parecon's admonitions about attaining self-management, but on top of that employing markets for allocation. Markets would not provide proper valuations or qualitative information that would enable workers or consumers to develop and decide on agendas. Markets would compel workers and consumers to make competitive choices regardless of or even against others' interests and even their own inclinations. Markets would require firms to win market share and thereby maintain or increase their workers' incomes even at the expense of their own quality of work life. Markets would apportion influence over decisions in accordance with income levels, and income levels would deviate from a just distribution due to luck, circumstance, tools, genetic endowment, and bargaining power, and while none of these factors have much to do with how much someone is affected by a decision, yet they determine how much say each person gets. Markets only consider the impact of a decision to buy or sell on the buyer or seller (in proportion to their relative bargaining power) ignoring the impact the decision would also have on others due to production or consumption externalities. For these reasons, markets would psychologically, behaviorally, and materially subvert self-managing tendencies even of council organization.

But what about participatory planning? What level of influence does participatory planning afford each actor in each decision?

First we should note that participatory planning reverses each of the above-mentioned failings of markets. Participatory planning provides accurate valuations by properly accounting full personal and social costs and benefits and providing appropriate qualitative information for regularly re-calibrating indicative prices with qualitative data. It ensures that workers and consumers pay attention to one another's conditions and allow each to advance only in accord with the others advancing, by making sure incomes and conditions correspond to social averages. It permits workers to assess their own conditions and pay attention to these in their decision-making by having workers input their preferences via their councils and with no need to maximize anything but their own and other's well being rather than having to subvert their own interests and those of others to stay in business. It apportions income in accord with effort, and, in any event, does not force or even permit people to try to maximize profits, surplus, or even revenues. It incorporates attention to all social costs and benefits of transactions, including externalities, by means of the planning procedures, accounting modes, iteration boards, and levels of council structure.

Still, while it is good to remove these various critical impediments to sensible allocation-related decision-making, this is not the same as having positively accomplished truly democratic decision-making. Does participatory planning give producers and consumers proportionate say over each type of decision as well as possible?

There are two main issues. First, does participatory planning create a context that is consistent with or that propels people to have appropriate impact in non-allocation decision-making? Or does it differentiate among individuals such that even beyond allocation their differences adversely affect their impacts? Second, specifically regarding allocation, does each participant have input in proportion to how they are affected?

For the first point, participatory planning requires of buyers and sellers attention to decision-making in general, instills expectations that each will influence decisions and not be subordinate or domineering, draws out the personal traits commensurate to involvement, and introduces no advantages or disadvantages to any group of people that would interfere with their proper participation in non-allocation interactions.

For the second point, regarding allocation decisions, each person participates at every level—personal, group or team, unit, industry, neighborhood, county, etc.—by means of council structures that have appropriate influence at that level. Each person manifests his or her individual or collective preferences in ways identical to everyone else. Each registers desire or not—to do some production or undertake some consumption, thus affecting that production or that consumption—and does so in accordance with their own desires and without inappropriate power due to inappropriate income or workplace authority. Consider the level of production of bicycles. Each consumer influences this in accord with their desire for bicycles (how much they are affected by them) as does every other. So does each bicycle worker impact this decision in accord with how they assess their involvement, and the workers have effectively the same overall impact in the outcome as the consumers, each group in essence negotiating with the other. But what about those consuming other goods that are affected by the number of bicycles to be produced, or producing other goods needed for bicycles or replaced by them? As you can see, this is a generalized problem of intersecting implications and impacts. It is one of those cases where a mathematician can provide a very subtle and detailed analysis, requiring pages upon pages of arcane formulae demonstrating the result—or where we can arrive at it more quickly and intuitively. Which factors cause/facilitate impact? Only factors equally possessed by every actor, and which each actor will manifest up to the socially designated influence of their decision-making unit and their preferences, each with the same rights and opportunities that others have. It will not always occur perfectly, of course. But it is hard to see how one could attain the desired goal more closely, overall, and on average.

Classlessness

Parecon eliminates class division by removing economic differences that empower some actors and weaken others, that enrich some and impoverish others, or that pit some systematically against any others. The class-related innovations of parecon are that:

- First, there is no private ownership of means of production. All actors have the same ownership relations to economic assets as all others.

- Second, there is no longer corporate organizational structure. In its place balanced job complexes eliminate systematic differentiations bearing on power or income due to a division of labor. And these are fostered and nurtured by the allocation mechanisms, rather than subverted and replaced by hierarchies of command.

- And finally, third, parecon establishes remuneration according to effort and sacrifice. While some people may exert more in their labors and others less, so that people have different incomes, there is no competition for income, no exploitation of some people by others, and there is a limit, in any case, on how much more effort anyone could possibly exert and therefore earn.

In parecon there is no class of owners that occupies a level above others—no capitalists. There is no commanding class above others —no coordinators. There is no obedient class beneath others—no working class. This is the case because there is no privately held capital, no monopolization of empowering circumstances, and no group that occupies a position subordinate to others in the economy. In participatory economics, there are only people who contribute to economic output and who by virtue of doing so have a just claim on it (or who physically cannot participate but have that claim by virtue of being human), who all have the same ownership condition in the economy, who all toil at balanced job complexes, and who all therefore are economic producers and consumers, without class differentiations.

Part III
Daily Life in a Participatory Economy

The love of money as a possession—as distinguished from the love of money as a means to the enjoyments and realities of life—will be recognized for what it is, a somewhat disgusting morbidity, one of those semi-criminal, semi-pathological propensities which one hands over with a shudder to the specialists in mental disease.
— John Maynard Keynes

To provide texture and definition to the broad picture of parecon that prior chapters presented, the next three chapters describe plausible details of daily life relations in a variety of hypothetical parecon economies and institutions. We hope these chapters fill out our picture of parecon, but they don't add new general content. Some people like more abstract presentations, as in prior chapters. Some people prefer more textured and specific descriptions, as in this section. One or the other approach will be sufficient for some people, who may feel wading through both is overkill. The content in this section is adapted from an earlier book by Robin Hahnel and myself, *Looking Forward* (South End Press), that was prepared just over ten years ago. The material here has been updated for this presentation.

11

Working

Suppose that humans happen to be so constructed that they desire the opportunity for freely undertaken productive work. Suppose that they want to be free from the meddling of technocrats and commissars, bankers and tycoons, mad bombers who engage in psychological tests of will with peasants defending their homes, behavioral scientists who can't tell a pigeon from a poet, or anyone else who tries to wish freedom and dignity out of existence or beat them into oblivion.
— Noam Chomsky

We have described parecon's institutions and made a preliminary case that they are both desirable and possible. We focused on large-scale, general attributes. What would a participatory economy look like from the vantage point of people's daily lives? Of course it would change from one type of ownership, organization, remuneration, and decision-making to another. Of course it would display large-scale implications for equity, self-management, solidarity, diversity, and class structure. But what about the specific daily economic situations of workers and consumers?

Consider how workers in a book publishing enterprise define and assign tasks. (I start with publishing because my own experience of helping found and define South End Press was impacted by and in turn enriched my understanding of participatory economic workplace relations.) Publishing always involves editorial, production, and accounting work, each of these including tasks ranging from rote to conceptual and repetitive to diverse. But workers can organize and carry out these and more general maintenance tasks in different ways in different economies.

Capitalist Publishing

The criteria capitalist publishing uses to determine how to combine diverse tasks into job complexes are profitability and maintaining hierarchies of power and income. Each book is a commodity to be sold for maximum revenue and produced at minimum cost. Whether people read the book is incidental.

Capitalist budgeting maximizes profits by holding off small creditors, taking advantage of new authors who lack bargaining power, and when possible setting high prices for few offerings. Will consumers buy their how-to book or ours, their romance or ours, their 90-day diet fad or ours, are central considerations. Given society's race, class, political, and gender biases, what shibboleths must be observed? Given reviewers' attitudes, which books are likely to be discussed? Which books should we give up for dead? To be sure, many people enter the publishing field committed to promoting humane values. But the dynamics of the capitalist market require first one compromise, then another, until humane values are buried by profits.

Jobs are defined, behavior patterns enforced, pay scales determined, and pink slips and promotions dispersed all to preserve hierarchy and extract sufficient labor to keep the business profitable. Employers "respect" prior repressive attitudes of more dominant new employees. Social hierarchies born outside the firm thereby reappear inside. Most women do what is considered "women's work." Most blacks do what is considered "blacks' work." Cleaning "girls," secretaries, receptionists, typesetters, and cleaning "boys" do the most deadening work. For their above average effort and sacrifice they receive the lowest wages. Even more than other oppressive attributes, two bear special comment.

1   The broader creative powers of most workers steadily erode as most people adapt the quality of their efforts to the low level of their assignments and influence.

2   Everyone's emotional energies dissipate in efforts to rationalize and defend status and hierarchy.

The result is considerable waste of human resources, immoral denial of most workers' capacities, and reduction of the publishing function to that of producing commodities for a quick killing. (And all this typifies one of the nicest industries to work in that capitalism offers.)

Participatory Publishing: Northstart Press

Naturally, the hypothetical pareconist Northstart Press organizes jobs to accomplish tasks efficiently and at high quality. But Northstart's participatory priorities also require that all workers exercise their talents and express their wills.

Instead of selling books to make profits, Northstart's workers consider themselves successful when readers are entertained or

enlightened. Northstart workers choose among manuscript submissions by deciding whether readers will benefit sufficiently to
merit the resources, time, and energy required to publish the book
in question. No one's income is correlated to volume of sales.

Writing, editing, and design occur largely as before parecon but
we can imagine that to save trees and other resources and to reduce
onerous tasks, most books might be electrically conveyed to portable
book-size hand-held computers that have the heft, look, and feel of
traditional books but allow readers to alter the size, layout, design,
and resolution of the book's pages on their system. Only volumes of
special merit or specific orders would be printed and bound
traditionally, reducing preparation and distribution costs dramatically, protecting scarce resources, and providing consumers easy,
direct, and nearly free access to whole libraries of information.
Computer programs also facilitate easy manipulation of graphics,
charts, type style and size, and page alignment, so people can adapt
pages to their own preferences. While some of these technical
changes would occur in a capitalist future, many would not or would
be channeled less desirably, to avoid conflict with profitability and
preserve hierarchy. Whether they will occur in a parecon future will
be determined solely in light of their human and social effects on
work, consumption, libraries, bookstores, the ecology, and the
reading experience.

Many business tasks would also differ in a participatory
publishing house. Due to technological innovations, most Northstart filling of orders and tracking of inventory occurs electronically.
Large warehouses are no longer necessary. Oversupply with
subsequent shredding is eradicated. Workers who fulfill customers'
orders maintain records of how many people access different titles,
since this information is useful to authors, researchers, and
Northstart employees.

Regarding promoting and publicizing titles, participatory
publishers would help potential readers decide whether they want
to take a closer look at titles, but there would be no effort to trick
people into "buying" books they couldn't benefit from. Participatory
workers would not want to waste resources, energy, or time
producing inferior products. With this in mind, Northstart sends
informative promotional messages to people most likely to enjoy,
appreciate, or learn from new titles, but is not interested in enticing
readers who won't benefit.

Similarly, the Northstart finance/budget department oversees
scheduling within limits set by council decision-making. Financial

and budgetary work differs from familiar capitalist norms in both data handling and data dissemination because guiding values are different.

In a capitalist firm, data assembled by the finance/budget department is restricted so that only top managers and owners have access. Were non-privileged workers able to access such information, they might use it to better gauge what wages to demand or when they might best strike.

In contrast, at Northstart everyone works with any information they choose. Not only can those who work in promotion access budget data, so can those in fulfillment, and people in fulfillment and promotion can access data from each other's departments as well. It is not productive for everyone to analyze all data endlessly. But it is desirable to organize information so every actor can understand Northstart's operations and experiment with projections.

Job Complexes

What other changes might result from participatory organization? The most fundamental structural change is that each Northstart worker has a job complex that includes some editorial, some production, and some business responsibilities and encompassing roughly average positive and negative work attributes. The total array of tasks associated with producing play scripts, for example, is divided among a team so that each member has comparable tasks. Similarly, the editorial team working on novels allocates editing, working with authors, and soliciting new novels so that everyone gets to use their special talents in different ways that fulfill their particular interests, but also so that no one enjoys an unfair abundance of creative tasks or gets stuck with an excess of numbing tasks.

Instead of having head editors, proofreaders, and secretaries, each parecon editorial team has equal members who fulfill diverse responsibilities suited to their own tastes and talents. One person might do more copy-editing and another might take more notes, but conceptual work would not be allocated mainly to one set of people and rote work mainly to another.

Education in a society with a parecon would have to provide its citizens with the skills, knowledge, and experience essential to playing a creative, self-managing role in the special fields of their choice. In capitalism, in contrast, schools prepare most citizens—

the 80 percent who wind up wage slaves and not coordinators or capitalists—to endure boredom and expect to take orders.

Councils

Beyond equitable job definition, there is also a council of all Northstart workers, where each member has equal voice and vote, as well as smaller councils responsible for appropriate sub-areas such as editing and producing fiction, general nonfiction, and technical books. Still smaller overlapping councils represent each business division. A variety of teams prepares particular books or researches a particular reorganization of workplace technology, for example. In assigning special jobs, there is no need to make work the same for everybody at every moment. Equity comes on average and over reasonable spans of time, as when individuals get vacations at different times or spend months doing a time-consuming creative project and catch up on rote tasks later.

Northstart's yearly plan evolves through negotiations that occur each May. Decisions are made about how many plays, novels, and books to accept and release during the year, and about workload, materials needed, work allocation, hiring new workers, and establishing new rules and technologies. Initial proposals come from all participants in the economy, go through a number of revisions, and finally are shaped into a feasible plan, including a work plan for Northstart. Northstart budget and finance workers facilitate this iterative process at each stage by providing useful data and suggestions to all Northstart workers. No one expects everyone to have the same priorities, nor is it assumed that everyone will agree that the final plan is the best possible one. But all will agree that it was arrived at fairly, with everyone having appropriate proportional influence.

Northstart's proposals are altered from iteration to iteration by a process of give-and-take guided by information from other councils. Finance/budget workers facilitate the updating and are overseen by the whole Northstart council. Once a plan for the upcoming year is determined, work for the new period begins.

As the year progresses, most decisions are taken within particular Northstart teams and councils, though some require ratification by the whole Northstart council and others require the approval of industry or consumer councils. Decisions of different types utilize different procedures, sometimes consensus, sometimes one-person-one-vote majority rule, or two-thirds, etc. But none of this implies that every decision is equally everyone's affair. Sometimes people delegate authority and autonomy to others with whom they work. Participatory organization allows democracy without intrusiveness.

In a participatory workplace, of course, there may be males and females, homosexuals and heterosexuals, blacks, whites, Asians, and Native Americans, Catholics, Protestants, Muslims, and Jews. But Northstart employees recognize that the cultural diversity that members of different social groups bring to work should be allowed to express itself in the context of job complexes balanced for empowerment and agreeableness. To help ensure this, every month optional caucus meetings discuss whether any workplace issues affect minority group interests. Workplace caucuses have autonomous rights to challenge arrangements they believe are sexually or racially oppressive. But since the rationale for these requirements stems from theories of kinship and community relations and not from a theory of economic relations, we do not address the justification for employing such caucuses in further detail here.

Finally, notice that nothing in what we have described precludes exercising leadership. At Northstart, production leaders on particular books exert influence over team members regarding quality and pace of work necessary to get the books completed. Finance department decisions have authority regarding budgeting. People working in personnel exert leadership over disputes about job assignments. Editorial decisions determine what is published.

Similarly, not having an editor-in-chief does not mean there is no editor with final responsibility for particular titles. Rejecting a fixed hierarchy does not imply rejecting discipline, monitoring, evaluation, and accountable leadership. Moreover, even as in capitalist companies, the ultimate sanction of dismissal still exists, but with crucial differences. First, the decision is made democratically, not by individuals with ownership rights or vested authority. Second, the threat of dismissal does not endanger the employee's survival. Other employment opportunities are offered, and a person's basic consumption needs are in any event guaranteed when looking for new work. Moreover, dismissal has to be ratified by the individual's council co-workers and then, if appealed, by higher councils as well, assuming such procedures were chosen.

To get a better picture we need to describe actual workdays. So here is a typical average week at the Northstart publishing house— remembering, of course, that many of the features are optional and might be handled differently in other firms, even in the same industry.

Larry's Work Week

On Wednesday Larry helps sort mail for a few hours. He does this one morning every tenth week. On Wednesday and Friday next week, for two hours he will help with general clean-up. The following Wednesday Larry will work the front desk, Friday he will do some rote data entry work. Next month Larry has a different rotation, but he always has some rote tasks assigned on Wednesday and Friday mornings. Of course, should Larry want to trade responsibilities for a certain Wednesday or Friday to attend his child's school play or tennis tournament, for example, this would be fine. Larry's rote work is evaluated by other Northstart members responsible for intervening if unscheduled task switching interrupts orderly functions.

The council for producing drama books has six work teams and Larry's does production on Wednesday, Thursday, and Friday afternoons. Although many employees prefer working on only one production project at a time, Larry happens to like doing a variety of different tasks simultaneously so he's currently working on one drama as typesetter, one as designer, and a third as a proofreader. The design and proofing are done in teams of three, and Larry is team leader for design.

On alternate Monday afternoons, Larry's editorial council meets first in teams for an hour and then as a whole department for two more hours to address concerns about possible new titles, complaints, and suggestions. Each week Larry also reads his share of submissions. Each title that Larry reads is also read by another member of the team and, after they give a summary report, if they both agree to reject the book it is returned to its author—unless some other member wishes to hold onto the title for whatever reason. If both Larry and the other reader want others to read it, the submission is held. If they disagree, a team vote decides whether to reject the title or keep it for more serious evaluation. In other publishing houses of course other approaches might be adopted.

Each week, Larry also works on his allotment of manuscripts that have passed initial evaluation. Which manuscripts he reads depends partly on his preferences and partly on how much time he and other members have for new assignments. Ultimately, books are accepted or rejected after everyone is ready to vote. Of course there is appropriate discussion to ensure that everyone is able to air their sentiments and exert proportionate influence in the vote. Three-quarters support is needed to accept a submission, and serious attention is paid to the feelings of minorities even to the point of holding up decisions for further debate. Another very particular norm (if Northstart is small) is that any single member can veto up to two books a year, even against three-quarter support, if they feel strongly enough. This is because in a small press every book project affects each employee dramatically in that if an employee really despised a book it would be a serious hardship for him or her. The point is, various decision-making methods are utilized to balance the efficient disposition of tasks with providing participants proportionate influence taking into account the actual circumstances involved.

Once accepted, each title goes to a particular team member, who becomes its editor. Larry has responsibility for editorial work on three titles yearly.

On the Mondays that Larry doesn't have editorial meetings he sometimes attends the bi-weekly Northstart policy meeting as a representative of his editorial/production council. Each of the three editorial/production councils, the four business area councils, and any major policy work teams that happen to be functioning at the moment send representatives. Representatives serve for six meetings each year, with rotation staggered so that each council always has a representative who has attended at least the four previous meetings. At these sessions, personnel representatives report on problems, sometimes asking for help with interpersonal conflicts, and the general progress of the press's efforts is discussed and evaluated. On the Tuesday following policy meetings, editorial and business councils meet for an hour to hear reports. Special teams discuss reports whenever they can arrange time.

The rest of Larry's work concerns promotion. He is currently helping produce a new catalog, working with potential authors, and soliciting new plays. He schedules all this into his work week, along with cleaning his own office, updating his own files, and impromptu clerical tasks shared with others.

Details of Northstart's arrangement seem sensible to Larry and his workmates, but may not appeal to other publishing houses. Different workplaces could adopt longer or shorter time-lines for job assignments and meeting schedules and adapt other practices leading to less or even more varied job complexes. While basic principles must be respected in all parecon workplaces, how they are implemented changes from workplace to workplace due to different conditions and preferences.

To continue, Larry is gay and meets every fourth Thursday with other gay workers to discuss the character of editorial and business decisions and the changing patterns of daily work in light of the particular needs, tastes, and values of gay employees. Suggestions are often brought back to work teams and councils and sometimes to the whole Northstart collective. If these caucuses feel threatened by proposals otherwise supported by majorities of workers at Northstart, they may bring their complaints to outside councils for political adjudication. And of course Larry doesn't work only at Northstart. Rather, Northstart has an above average average job complex, so Larry does some rote work in the neighborhood and community where he lives to attain an overall balance. But what about workplace decision making under capitalism or in a parecon?

Decision-Making at a Capitalist Firm

How does a capitalist firm decide how much to produce, who will work at what jobs, how much work each person will do, how to alter products or introduce new ones, what investments to make in the firm, and other matters?

In a capitalist firm the lordly capitalists have ultimate authority. Those in the coordinator class have jobs that are overwhelmingly empowering and they administer and otherwise define daily operations. Workers have jobs that are overwhelmingly low-level and uncreative. They obey, or resist.

The owners are interested in profits and in maintaining the conditions that allow them to accrue profits. Markets impose these motives on them. If the firm doesn't maximize the surplus available after it sells what it produces, and if it doesn't utilize a considerable portion of its surplus to enhance its market share, not only will owners complain for want of profits, but other firms will gain technological or market-share advantages which, in the future, will cause the low profitability firm to suffer grave loses or even bankruptcy. So owners wish to reduce costs (including wages), to disempower workers so the workers do not try to battle owner's agendas or raise their wages, to increase productivity per asset, to dodge expenses for by-products such as pollution, to raise prices and increase sales regardless of the impact on those buying the products, and to invest profitably in competition with other firms. But the owners cannot oversee every aspect of workplace activity and must hire special intermediate employees who we call coordinators, who will, they hope, pass on commands or even help in formulating them.

Thus we have the coordinator class of managers, lawyers, accountants, engineers, and others who are empowered by their positions and responsible for much daily decision-making and definition of workplace structure and activity. But these coordinators turn out to have dual interests. On the one hand, as employees hired by owners, they can try to improve their incomes and conditions by carrying out the owners' agendas. On the other hand, they have the potential to advance their own careers by using their monopoly over knowledge and decision-making levers to their own advantage even in ways that are sometimes at odds with profitability, but for which owners cannot punish them because coordinators hold hostage the operations of the firm.

Then we have workers hired to carry out the will of those above. They also have dual interests. On the one hand, as employees hired by coordinators at the behest of owners, they can try to advance their incomes and conditions by pleasing their employers. On the other hand, they can utilize their numbers and organizational might, including the threat to strike, to try to increase their incomes and improve their conditions even against the interests of their employers and managers.

So what about decisions? Markets establish the context. Owners will seek profits and maintain the conditions of their dominance, including reducing the incomes and power of those below to whatever extent possible. Coordinators will to some extent obey owners in pursuing profitability, and to some extent seek to enhance their own independent power against both owners above and workers below. Workers will to some extent obey coordinators out of fear of being punished or fired, and to some extent seek to enhance their own independent power.

Thus, decisions are overwhelmingly authoritarian. Either the owners decree them, or some subset of the coordinators (managers, division heads, vice-presidents) decree them, overseen more or less by the owners above. Those most affected, the workers and consumers, have marginal if any impact, often not even knowing what decisions are being made, when, where, and to what ends. This holds for the large scale—what we should produce, in what quantity, to sell at what price, paying what wages, using what ingredients, with what pollution which we avoid responsibility for by what avenues, and so on. And it holds for the small scale—what time and for how long do workers get a lunch break, when can they go to the bathroom and for how long, and so on. The overwhelming context of decision-making is the market-enforced capitalist drive to maximize surplus, accumulate profits, and invest in enlarging market share regardless of the social benefits and costs to workers and consumers. Less operative is the coordinators' drive to enhance their own relative bargaining position by gaining ever greater control of critical information and contacts and of the workforce below, even against profitability. Opposing the defining logic of the system are workers' efforts to improve their incomes and circumstances against the obstacles of coordinators and owners above. Missing is unconflicted attention to the actual opportunities for personal fulfillment and growth that workplace processes and products could have on all concerned.

If the reader sees an analogy to a politically dictatorial system ... that is perfectly apt. In Stalinist Russia, for example, we had the inner sanctums of the ruling party and the dictator himself, then the functionaries and political operatives of the bureaucracy, then the populace. We decry this as horrific in its authoritarian subordination of the many to the few. But the capitalist workplace is quite similar—with the owner or owners, the coordinator class of empowered employees, and the subordinate working class—and the degree of regimentation in the capitalist workplace is, if anything, more severe. Not even Stalin's dictatorship thought to oversee meal times and bathroom breaks and to examine all mail and calls. There is nearly absolute disenfranchisement at the bottom of a corporation, even more than the political disenfranchisement of citizens in dictatorships. And where political subordination is enforced by the threat of incarceration, corporate subordination is enforced by the threat of impoverishment and even starvation. In both the dictatorship and the capitalist corporation there is risky pursuit of personal power in the middle—political or economic palace intrigue—and domineering authority at the top.

Decision-Making at Northstart

Every firm in a parecon makes day-to-day decisions about how to fulfill the firm's agreed responsibilities. These are made within councils with appropriate input from everyone affected. Different methods may be used for different decisions. We could spend time detailing such interactions for hypothetical cases—how a work team schedules its work, how the firm decides on hiring, and so on.

But there is one facet of decision-making more unique to parecon and probably more instructive to detail, and which in any event sets the context in which more specific and narrow choices must occur— participatory planning. What does the participatory planning process look like at Northstart publishing house?

Last Year at Northstart

When workers begin their yearly planning, first they review the prior year's plan and particularly any changes from the initial proposal. They understand that work always uses inputs, including social relations in the workplace, workers with specific skills and social characteristics, and resources, equipment, and intermediate goods. Work also generates outputs, including social relations, personalities, and skills of workers as well as products others will use. Workers' plans thus always include three lists: material and social/personal inputs; work relations, policies, motivations and logic; and material and personal/social outputs.

Then, regarding the composition of these lists, more outputs require more inputs, certain work relations choices require more inputs for given outputs, and a different mix of inputs with a fixed set of work relations may yield different outputs.

Primary outputs are computer records of books, communication of books to readers, relationships with readers, and changes in worker attributes and plant social relations. Secondary products include some bound books, waste materials, used equipment, and leftover supplies of paper and other materials. Primary inputs are workers' skills and efforts, plant social relations, utilities such as gas, water, electricity, and communication, a building, old equipment, new equipment, paper, and office supplies like light bulbs and pencils.

Inputs are broken into roughly two major categories: investment goods which allow alteration of the scale or methods of production, and normal production inputs which allow operations at a chosen scale with determined social relations. The main work related choices are to determine how work will be organized, how many hours will be expended each day, and what technologies will be employed. Any change of work relations will likely require some changes in inputs and outputs, and vice versa.

One way to envision these relations would be to graph outputs for varying combinations of inputs for each possible choice of technology and work relations. A more practical tool for analysis would be simple programs showing inputs required per outputs preferred for possible work relations. These programs would facilitate estimating workplace plans by helping workers highlight how choices affect productive possibilities.

Any Northstart worker can call up a computer screen view of such a program, enter choices for technology and work relations, and see which inputs will yield a given list of outputs, or what outputs a given list of inputs will generate. No sophisticated programming knowledge is required. The assumption that a simple program can incorporate alternative choices of social relations is not so reductionist as it may at first seem to some readers. We imply only that the program, properly prepared by iteration workers, can quickly show the best estimates of the material implications of alternative options. It could even list the qualitative features that differ from option to option, as these were determined by workers themselves and entered in the program by facilitation workers before the planning period. Of course, when people finally vote on options, the program only facilitates manipulating information. Workers' feelings about the implications of the different choices guide the decisions they make.

Next, a brief plant meeting informs everyone of national iteration facilitation board (IFB) projections of trends for the coming year, including initial projections for overall growth, incomes, and indicative prices; as well as industry IFB projections, including qualitative summaries of publishing's impact on readers last year, explanations of changes expected this year; and plant IFB proposals for changes in plant organization, technologies, or policies, including detailed descriptions of human and social implications of projected changes in material inputs and outputs.

Assuming long-term investment decisions have already been settled, in assessing last year's data and this year's projections workers begin weighing their own desires and prepare to register the social relations, technology, and input and output levels they prefer for Northstart. The first and second round of plant decision-making requires workers to choose individually, with no requirement that their selections be mutually compatible.

Northstart Innovations

Before following Northstart's planning further, however, we should note one very important aspect of settling on plant organization and technology. Each worker decides the alterations in plant operations she or he wants to request and registers related preferences for investments. The ensuing changes might, for example, diminish the output-to-input ratio to improve the quality of work life, or might change how much work she or he has to do given the demand for books. Whatever changes Northstart workers finally decide they want, they also have to get an okay from the system as a whole if they need additional inputs from outside sources.

The important thing to note is that if Northstart workers request and receive significant workplace changes that dramatically improve the quality of work life at Northstart, this benefit will eventually be shared with other workers. How much work anyone does away from his or her main workplace depends on differences between the quality of work at that main workplace and society's average. Thus, when innovations significantly decrease how burdensome work is at one plant, the result, after job balancing committees have time to assess the change, will likely be that each employee spends fewer hours at that plant and more hours elsewhere. Innovations that make Northstart a relatively more pleasurable place to work will change the time Northstart workers work there and elsewhere. So because of the principle that all workers enjoy comparable overall job responsibilities, gains accruing from Northstart investments manifest themselves in slightly improved conditions for all workers rather than in dramatically improved conditions only for Northstart employees. Therefore, workers have little reason to urge innovations in their own plants at the expense of innovations that could be enacted elsewhere with a more dramatic effect on overall quality of work life.

Traditional economists will argue that this will diminish workers' incentives to improve the quality of work life, since workers will not monopolize the gains they engineer. But this view conveniently ignores that in competitive models of capitalism, technological gains are assumed to spread instantaneously to all producers in an industry. If this were not assumed, it could not be claimed that these models yield efficient results. But when this is assumed, incentives to innovate diminish since benefits spread first to other firms in the industry, and later through lower costs of production and lower price for the industry's output, to all producers and consumers. Of course, in real capitalism, as opposed to economists' models, improvements do not spread and the benefits of innovation accrue almost exclusively to a small number of owners—certainly not to workers—and there are consequent inefficiencies. In any case, since in an equitable economy technological improvements must rebound to everyone's benefit, we consider it a virtue that in a parecon innovations in thousands of plants change the overall societal average workload and work quality norms, and that those changes in turn rebound equally to everyone's benefit.

So what does this lead to in practice? If Larry works at Northstart and a proposal for a technological change there and throughout publishing would improve the average job complex for society by one hundredth of a percent, while a proposal for the steel industry (requiring the same investment expenditure) would improve the average by two hundredths of a percent, Larry will eventually benefit more from the steel innovation than from the publishing change. Likewise, Northstart workers have a greater long-term interest in an innovation in coal mining that greatly improves that industry's quality of work than in an innovation in publishing that would require an equivalent investment but improve the quality of publishing work to a lesser degree.

Larry's tastes are therefore added to those of all other publishing workers and embodied in the evaluation of possible publishing industry alterations before any comparison with other industry proposals occurs. If Larry's views differ dramatically from the collective result, Larry will not necessarily like the final outcome. But the choice will reflect a fair balance of the tastes of all workers in both industries. Larry should vote as he likes, and if he does so, and all other workers do so as well, the collective implications noted earlier will apply. The war of each against all for who will benefit from innovations gives way to a community of shared interests. Competition is replaced by cooperation. Shortening work hours to achieve the same output anywhere eventually benefits all. Improving work life anywhere eventually benefits all. An equitable economy requires all this, but to increase individual incentives job balancing committees could calibrate the speed of adjustments to provide temporary "material incentives" to innovators. Or, alternatively, and more positively in my view, teams could be assigned whose job was to develop potential innovations. Innovations would be the "output" by which their social usefulness would be judged. The equity implications of this way to stimulate innovation—essentially assigning more resources to innovation and holding those who use them socially accountable—has desirable human repercussions. In any event, in deciding on innovations, each person chooses between proposals as they wish, but everyone has an incentive to choose what is best for the whole economy because that is what is ultimately best for all. Ironically, the claim made for markets—that pursuit of individual interests coincides with the social interest—actually holds for participatory planning. Pursuit of self-fulfillment under equitable arrangements in a socially conscious way really does yield socially optimal outcomes.

Parecon's solidarity does not derive from a presumed biological transformation of our genetic characteristics, but from the concrete implications of its social relationships. Results promoting solidarity, equity, diversity, and collective self-management are not due to a postulated suddenly beatific human nature, but arise from the structure and incentives of participatory planning. Besides linking individual and collective well being, parecon promotes sociability and the qualitative side of life denigrated by capitalism.

The First Planning Iteration: Nancy's Initial Proposal

Nancy has worked at Northstart for eight years and is predominantly concerned with science books and promotion. In preparing her initial proposal for Northstart's new year she considers three proposals for reorganization that workers who investigate innovations have proposed. While recognizing that Northstart already has an above average work complex, Nancy believes plan three would greatly improve work quality by freeing energies from distracting tasks with modest investment. She estimates that while the changes in proposal three are not as valuable as some proposed transformations in heavy industries she has heard about, proposal three would be worthwhile compared to most innovations under consideration throughout the economy.

Indeed, a projected minimum standard that proposed investment should attain in increased output or improved work conditions is part of the information the national production facilitation board would provide. Wherever workers are considering changes in work organization or new technologies, differences in inputs, outputs, and work quality would need to be assessed. Obviously, any proposal that improves work quality with no loss in outputs and no investment expense would be noncontroversial since it would improve the national work complex average at no cost. However, whenever investment is necessary to improve work complexes or increase output there must be some way to decide which investments would be sufficiently beneficial to undertake. The national production facilitation board, by estimating per capita growth and anticipated change in the average work complex, provides an initial and also regularly updated estimates of the minimal returns needed from investments to make them desirable.

All workers at Northstart have access to computers on which they can make calculations and comparisons. Returning to our example, after consulting projections, Nancy decides to develop her first proposal based on implementing investment plan three. She next decides on a level of output, in other words, how many titles to publish in the coming year. She could just accept facilitation board suggestions. Instead, however, considering data on population growth, industry IFB predictions of likely growth in numbers of titles desired and in average readership per title, and her own perceptions of people's changing tastes in reading, Nancy decides industry predictions are a bit too modest and settles on a first proposal to increase titles published by 3.5 percent rather than the IFB projected 3.3 percent, and of readers by 1.2 percent instead of the IFB projected 1.1 percent.

To translate her estimates into a full proposal for Northstart, Nancy next settles on a number of employees, hours of work per day, and effort levels at Northstart. User friendly computer programs make it easy to enter workplace proposal number three, set a number of titles and readers, and then enter choices for any two of the other variables to see what the third must be to get the job done.

It is important to note that the kinds of thinking Nancy has to do become easier with familiarity, and, in any event, the programs make the associated calculations simple. In any case, Nancy has arrived at her first round proposal for Northstart for the coming year. What about other workers? And how does a final plan arise?

The Second Planning Iteration

Not only Nancy but all workers at Northstart and throughout the economy complete their initial proposals and submit these to the "planning data bank." Individuals have made no attempt to accommodate their proposals to one another but once submitted, IFBs work on the data and prepare a report of current proposed supply and demand for all goods, changes in indicative prices based on relative degrees of excess demand or supply, a summary of current averages for consumption and production, and written descriptions of the principal causes of changes in IFB projections.

Of particular importance to Northstart workers are the current proposals for goods that appear in the Northstart budget. Therefore, these are highlighted in written reports provided to Northstart workers, as are summaries of written reports from consumers regarding books. For example, since consumers are requesting more new titles than the industry suggested producing, the industry receives a written summary of consumer commentary regarding books. Although Northstar workers and consumers automatically receive this material, they can gain access to similar data for other industries at any computer console in their plant or community.

If Nancy wishes to see a more detailed breakdown of demand by region or even by specific consumer councils, she can use the summary provided by the iteration boards as a general guide and investigate details herself, using procedures we describe shortly. In addition to getting feedback important for her planning decisions, such inquiries also give Nancy an indication of the social value of her labors and the implications of her choices for others.

Let's return to the planning process. Having noticed that paper is in over-demand and paper producers have proposed no increase in production over last year, Nancy requests the paper industry's own report explaining their proposal. Then, in response to all the information she has accessed, a new set of indicative prices, and whatever consultations and investigations she wishes to undertake, Nancy updates her first proposal. The process is the same as the first except that she now takes into account the new information. We should note, however, that in line with our particular description of this society's planning system, Nancy alters the components of her first proposal in any direction and by any amounts she chooses. The issue, of course, is whether we can expect Nancy in combination with other actors to behave in ways that will bring demand and supply into balance for all items in a reasonable time frame. We address this question in our treatment of the daily life character of allocation, still to come, since it involves the whole allocation process. But since the indicative prices of goods in excess demand will rise and of goods in excess supply will fall, and since there is social pressure to reduce the overall value of requests (and increase the overall value of output), it is not difficult to see the fundamental mechanism that drives the system toward eventual agreement between supply and demand.

The Third Planning Iteration

After Nancy and everyone else submit second proposals, IFBs again adjust indicative prices, update their own projections, send relevant summary reports to all units, and store all this information in the planning data bank. The new wrinkle is that in addition to industry IFB reports on industry proposals and averages, there are also industry IFB projections for likely final industry plans, as well as suggestions to member units regarding how they might best move toward these likely final outcomes. In instances where a unit diverges dramatically from industry averages, discussions may commence between that plant's board and IFBs to explore the reasons for the differences.

Labor reallocations to and from Northstart are now largely settled. This means that in going over new data and considering how to alter proposals for goods in over-demand or, less often, over-supply, Nancy can only alter her proposals for particular items that Northstart would use or produce by less than 50 percent if she wants to move them in the direction that equilibrates supply and demand, and by less than 25 percent if her proposed change is disequilibrating. And this rule applies as well—at least in this hypothetical rendition of a specific implementation of participatory planning—for developing proposals numbers four through six, discussed below.

Preparing her third proposal, however, also involves Nancy in many more discussions with workmates. While each Northstart worker still makes his or her own proposals for all of Northstart, unlike in earlier rounds, they now incorporate modifications arising from collective discussion. Thus, one day of meetings in work groups and departments is set aside for discussing proposals. Like many other details in this discussion, the rules for changing proposals for each new iteration and for carrying out planning within workplaces seem reasonable to us (particularly in societies in which there is considerable friction when moving resources from one use to another), but keep in mind that this is just one possible choice of procedures rather arbitrarily chosen to illustrate one plausible implementation of participatory planning.

The Fourth, Fifth, and Sixth Planning Iterations

Now, Nancy and her coworkers confront a new challenge: Their fourth proposals will be made not separately but together. The different ideas of Northstart workers must finally be combined into one consistent Northstart proposal. It isn't necessary for each individual's role in the proposal to be spelled out, since such assignments are irrelevant to the rest of the economy. But workers' councils' proposals do need to be implementable. So the same limitations on adjustments that applied for the third proposal now apply to the collective new Northstart proposal.

The formulation of the fourth proposal requires various sessions held intermittently over a full week, though it is certainly part-time work so other work also continues. Mainly, a week allows sufficient time for thinking before plant members choose a new proposal.

First members of the smallest work groups compare their individual proposals and try to accommodate them with one another. These meetings serve primarily as a warm-up for more important department and area meetings to come.

Here's how it might work. Nancy has a small group meeting on Monday of "fourth-proposal week." On Tuesday she meets with the editorial department to talk about numbers of titles and readership to try to reach agreement on these matters. On Wednesday, she has a similar meeting with the promotion department, the site of her non-editorial, non-production work. Throughout Northstart, others hold similar meetings, and the Northstart IFB summarizes and distributes each day's results. Monday's meeting is limited to an hour, but those on Tuesday and Wednesday run for an hour and a half in the morning and another hour and a half late in the day.

The editorial meeting begins with members listing the number of new Northstart titles each prefers to undertake, the readership they anticipate, and the mix of different titles they desire. Debate commences regarding the difference between initial averages of proposals and current demands and projected industry averages. Since each editorial group meets separately, the Northstart IFB reports each group's results as well as an average for them all.

The following day Nancy's promotion group starts with the overall average as a premise and suggests its own adaptations in light of promotion needs and potentials. Because all departments do this on Wednesday, there emerges a new average to be considered Thursday. Finally, a council meeting on Friday functions like a senate with members considering amendments to the average as a means of developing competing alternatives and finally voting for Northstart's proposal to submit for the fourth iteration.

One important feature of this process is the effort made to accommodate competing perspectives through compromises or experimentation. This is the time when minorities provide evidence of the virtues of their positions.

The fifth and sixth iterations would proceed like the fourth, but with each taking much less time and incorporating tighter allowed percentage changes in inputs and outputs. For each new proposal there is new information about the status of goods, average outputs, and indicative prices, all facilitating moving toward a feasible plan.

The Seventh Planning Iteration

After receiving the sixth proposals from production and consumption units, industry and national IFBs have a new task (in this hypothetical rendition of one way to enact parecon methods): they consider available data and offer five feasible plans for society to choose among. Since we will discuss IFBs more when we focus on the intricacies of allocation later, here we simply assume they do their task well and present society with five proposals. But we should mention that IFB worksheets and minutes of their meetings are available to anyone with computer access.

Obviously, the choice of five plans—like many other details of the process we are describing—could be varied without changing the underlying logic of participatory planning. There could be fewer individual iterations or more collective ones, or there could be limitations on adjustments or submission of council-wide rather than individual proposals could begin earlier or later. In a real society, such refinements would evolve in accord with particular economic, cultural, and social histories, since once citizens agree that participatory planning has potential, they will modify the system to suit themselves.

In any event, in our hypothetical scenario, after a period for discussion and thought, everyone votes for one of the five proposed plans. The votes are tallied in each council, submitted to higher level federations as sub-level totals, and tallied again, and so on, until final results are available—likely within a couple of hours.

In this rendition of procedures, the two proposals that receive the least votes on the first ballot are dropped. IFBs amend the remaining three proposals in light of the relative weight of the votes. A second ballot eliminates the least popular of the three. and then the two remaining choices are slightly amended, a final choice is made, and the chosen option becomes not the plan, but the seventh aggregated projection of the iteration process. IFBs then use this projection to calculate expected indicative prices, total economic product, growth rate, average work and consumption, and outputs for individual goods, all of which are sent to the plan data bank.

Nancy and other members of Northstart (and other economic units) now accept as benchmarks the projections for society's product and average workload, consumption allowance, and work complex quality. Further revisions adjust responsibilities within federations and units in light of the overall plan.

Northstart Efficiency

The reader may wonder:

1 Aren't Northstart workers frustrated because work is too fragmented? Is this a road to enrichment or psychosis?

2 Doesn't it take endless hours to train people for so many jobs? Is this excellence or institutionalized chaos?

3 Don't people ignore the authority of "leaders" on team A, when these same "leaders" are subordinate on team B?

4 Do one's co-workers provide enough motivation and oversight to prevent shoddy, dilatory work?

In answer to question one—doesn't fragmentation frustrate Northstart workers?—first, having many responsibilities makes work life richer and more diverse for most people and is therefore positive, not negative. Of course, tasks and schedules could be fragmented to the point of distraction, but if a group decides it has gone overboard, it has only to make the required correction. Likewise, those who like fewer types of tasks would simply opt for job complexes with more nearly average tasks.

Changing from capitalism to parecon would mean that instead of most people doing rote work and being bored most of the time, everyone will spend at least some of their work day doing interesting work. Moreover, because boring tasks will be distributed equitably, they will be more bearable. It's not that digging ditches, pushing buttons, or enduring hot conditions will become joyful merely because one does it in a good society, at one's own pace, and in teams with friends, much less because one admires some great leader or fondly remembers a long-passed revolutionary upheaval. It's only that pain can be diminished and pleasure enhanced even for rote work by overcoming unnecessarily authoritarian, alienating, unfair, and uninformed facets of work life.

Moreover, there will be every reason to automate or eliminate rote work whenever doing so will enhance productivity or diminish the human burden of work. Under capitalism automation is a crucial area of conflict between labor and capital—capitalists seek to enhance profits by automating some people's livelihood out of existence while workers try to defend their jobs to avoid becoming obsolete and unemployed. Under parecon, since everyone does a fair share of rote work, all will want to minimize it. Since everyone does some creative work, everyone will want to increase the amount to go around and no one will lose their livelihood if automation eliminates rote tasks workers disliked in the first place.

Thus, question one really comes down to what happens to people who under capitalism have responsibilities which are almost entirely interesting and empowering. Yes, in participatory workplaces such work complexes will disappear because everyone will share rote work. Elementary justice dictates this, just as elementary justice dictates that consumption opportunities greatly in excess of average consumption be eliminated. Those who have benefitted from coordinator monopolization of desirable work will resist job balancing just as capitalists who monopolize wealth will resist income balancing. Both capitalists and coordinators will advance arguments to justify their advantages but the truth in both cases is that these arguments are fanciful, self-serving rationalizations. In fact, even those who now do no rote work need not be any more fragmented by having to do some cleaning, filing, and production. For under systems in which they monopolize desirable work opportunities, these people are constantly distracted by having to always oversee others even as they regulate their own behavior in the presence of superiors. Anyway, anyone who knows anything about business in capitalism knows that upper-level workers spend much of the time they are not worrying about protocol, daydreaming, gossiping on the phone, and worrying about interoffice competitions. Beside being a waste of productive talent, compared to leisure options, this is not even a particularly enjoyable way to idle time away.

In answer to question two—doesn't it take endless hours to train people for balanced job complexes?—at Northstart training everyone to do editorial, business, and production work admittedly takes more time than training people to do just one of the three types of work. Likewise, developing skill in three areas certainly takes longer than developing skill in only one. But the mutually enforcing benefits of knowing more about each type of work, the enrichment that comes from having diverse responsibilities, and the increase in morale that accompanies understanding the whole publishing process more than offset these additional training costs.

Or, it may happen that workers in a particular workplace might prefer the savings from reduced training over the benefits of greater diversity, knowledge, and morale. In these cases, provided equitable job complexes can be arranged in which each worker has fewer differently skilled responsibilities, workers can choose that option. Our description was only one possibility, after all.

But what if doing a rote task means that Larry has less time for X and might therefore be less good at X. Say Larry edits social science books. If he did only that, he would read 50 social science books a year; but because of rote task obligations, he reads 25. He is now not as knowledgeable a social science editor as he might otherwise have been. The offsetting gain is that Sally, who now reads 25 social science books a year, when in the past she read zero, is a lot better social science editor than she was before when she was not an editor at all. Are the combined skills of Larry and Sally at least as good as Larry's alone would have been, without the change? Probably. If not, is the loss more significant than the gains made from not having to spend time defending hierarchies and related useless activities? Not likely. And if it were, would avoiding this small residue loss in productivity justify putting up with a class-divided society and all its adverse implications? In our view, of course not.

In answer to question three—won't useful, necessary lines of authority deteriorate without fixed hierarchies?—respect for a team leader need not be undercut because she is in a non-leader role on other teams. At Northstart, respect for leaders depends on the logic of particular assignments and the need for tight coordination, supervision, or scheduling, for example. Far from diminishing the credibility of legitimate leadership, eliminating fixed hierarchies will undercut many class hostilities and related impediments to efficient expression of leadership that isn't based on coercive rights.

In answer to question four—is there sufficient motivation? —the desire to earn a living, do a good job, and, when necessary, peer pressure and the desire to keep one's job, more than adequately ensure that people work hard. Of course there are disagreements and personality clashes. But surely these are more manageable once demeaning hierarchy has been eliminated. Transfers to other workplaces are likely made to resolve intractable personality clashes, which could certainly still arise. Arguments about who is doing how much work, how well, how hard, and with what degree of sympathy for coworkers, are resolved by participants, or, when necessary, through council oversight. Sometimes people are fired, but not at the whim of a "boss" or in such a way as to threaten one's income. In essence, the workday at Northstart is self-managed in the context of assessing the collective's well-being and its desires to publish desired books in an effective, efficient fashion. The only inflexible rules are those precluding methods that obstruct participation or deny equitable access of all workers to equal opportunities for fulfillment and influence.

We should mention again, however, that since the Northstart work complex has more creative and fewer distasteful qualities than the average workplace in the economy, Northstart workers have to put in some of their work time elsewhere. Some Northstart employees work in community clean-up squads. Others do rote tasks at a neighboring plant that produces computer equipment. In any event, everyone does his or her share of outside work to balance the relative advantage of working at Northstart.

Would a sensible person rather work at a capitalist or a participatory publishing house? Since we have not yet described the daily texture of allocation, we only partially understand how parecon decisions are made. But more detailed allocation-related issues aside, the quality of parecon's work should be obviously superior:

1   The hassles of hierarchies disappear.

2   The pleasures of publishing for human well-being rather than capitalist profits are significant.

3   Opportunities for personal development and camaraderie with co-workers abound.

4   No one does solely debilitating, subordinate work.

Though work at Northstart has drudgery, it is nonetheless a generally enriching means to personal development and integrity within a supportive community of co-workers.

Workplace Planning: Personal Texture

With Northstart planning we emphasized overall logic and left out details of personal discussions and the qualitative dimensions of plan formation. Suppose we now consider the hypothetical John Henry Steel Plant. Here we focus on a few examples of interchanges rather than on overall dynamics. This provides a different slant on the planning process, including the types of disagreements likely to occur. It will also help explain how workers adjust workloads and pay attention to the qualitative as well as quantitative dimensions of what they produce and use.

An Overview of John Henry Planning

As at Northstart, planning at John Henry goes through a sequence of iterations involving the evaluation of demands from other units along with attendant proposals, revisions, negotiations, and decisions. The John Henry Steel plant, as conceived here, employs thousands of workers, has a large amount of heavy specialized machinery, and has a production process that involves an average work complex well below the social average. Proposals for improving work life at John Henry are therefore high on the agenda, and John Henry workers spend more than the average number of hours doing work outside John Henry at more rewarding labors.

Because the seven planning iterations are formally the same at John Henry as at Northstart, we will not summarize them again. Moreover, since each plant embellishes its own planning procedures with whatever rules, schedules, and divisions of responsibility it chooses, John Henry has many differences from Northstart, but these idiosyncrasies are not our concern here either. Instead we want to see some of the disagreements that arise in planning.

Choosing Between Alternative Production Schemes

In the early stages of planning John Henry workers must choose from among proposals to change organization/technology. Let us look in on this process once it has come down to a choice between three alternatives.

Proposal one's main features involve acquiring some new furnace equipment and rearranging a few aspects of associated processes. Its supporters claim it will allow a two percent reduction in labor hours per ton of steel output, no significant change in material inputs, and only a modest improvement in the average work complex for the plant which is achieved by removing one dangerous and one rote task from one part of the production process.

Proposal two's advocates also claim a small reduction in labor needs and modest improvement in work complex for a similar investment. Proposal two was submitted by the record-keeping department and affects only work they do. The record-keeping team estimates a slightly greater improvement in the average work complex than proposal one offers.

Proposal three evolved through discussions among a number of divisions and involves more elaborate changes including purchases of major equipment, a substantial redefinition of tasks, and a major rescheduling of plant procedures. It requires a greater investment and alteration of social relations than either proposal one or two. Its advocates claim it will only marginally increase material inputs needed per ton of steel produced, though it will increase labor needed per ton by 3 percent. The major advantage of proposal three is that it would significantly improve the average work complex at John Henry, offering improved work conditions and increased opportunity for communication among workers.

Earlier in the planning process a number of other proposals were rejected as inferior, though some of their better features were incorporated into these three proposals. At this point there is a new plant-wide debate about the three alternatives. Since both proposals one and two reduce the social cost of inputs without sacrificing output and with only minor investments, there is little doubt other councils in the industry and economy will approve them. On the other hand, the third proposal requires substantial investment and also increases inputs per output, so while the improvement in quality of work life might warrant the change, this would have to be carefully explained to other units in the economy since the usual quantitative indicators would not immediately, in and of themselves, indicate grounds for approval.

Advocates of all three proposals have personal biases coming from energy they have invested, pride in having made a proposal, and heartfelt beliefs. This creates three factions with some overlap because some workers' complexes involve them with more than one of the departments offering options. For others the grounds for choosing are preferences and assessment of prospects.

For example, Roger calculates that with either of the first two proposals his situation is likely to change only slightly—work in the plant would be somewhat more rewarding, and consequently he would probably work a bit less outside the plant at a community day care center. The third proposal, on the other hand, would substantially improve the quality of his work at John Henry and lead to a significant reduction in pleasurable outside duties that used to be required to balance his overall work experience. In the short run, Roger expects he would personally benefit considerably, but in the long run, once job balancing committees and encompassing councils restructured job responsibilities, the benefits would be spread around.

Knowing that equity will be achieved, Roger realizes that for him personally the issue is the same as for society as a whole: which combination of proposals advances well-being via improving overall average job complexes the most? Different workers feel more or less strongly about the prospects, due to being influenced by their own circumstances and by their different assessments of implications for others. The decision-making process first involves debate and discussion leading to agreement to the adoption of particular material/qualitative descriptions as the best conjectures about the most likely effects of the three proposals. Although workers cannot know for sure how changes in relations or technology will affect them before they try them, they must make estimates or there is no way to proceed with evaluations and choices. Advocates of each proposal present and defend their claims about material and human consequences and, finally, workers vote on the three options.

Suppose option one gets the fewest votes. Plant facilitation workers then propose two options which are slightly amended versions of options two and three, and provide spreadsheets that show their anticipated implications. Discussion and debate begins anew. This time, however, a council meeting is convened and works toward resolution in open session. One group of workers proposes a compromise incorporating what seem to be the most popular elements into a single package. A vote accepts this as a better starting place for consideration than either of the facilitation proposals. A period of amending commences. At some point workers sense diminishing returns and call for a vote. Indeed, any time the majority votes for closure, meeting time can be reduced, and of course, individuals who may reach their personal saturation point with meetings earlier can absent themselves at any point, returning later to vote. So in this hypothetical possibility, we get a feeling for how choices might proceed in one particular workplace.

Though some advocates of earlier proposals will likely feel that a second-best choice has been made, everyone understands that what has been decided comes from informed democratic deliberations. Everyone congratulates the facilitation workers and proposers of the plan and goes home.

The Intricacies of "Working Overtime"

Lydia lives in a complex whose members are artistically inclined. When not working at John Henry she works with a drama group that puts on plays throughout the region. She likes this so much she spends more time doing it than she is required to in order to balance her John Henry complex, but since she considers it so much fun, she doesn't even think to claim it as extra work. If she did, however, society has presumably decided in its year's consumption plan how much theater (music, spectator sports, etc.) it wants. Like any other job, people apply for the jobs in these fields and if more people want jobs than there are openings, slots are filled based on merit, etc. And if anyone wants to participate in the activity despite not being chosen, they are free to do so, but as a hobby without remuneration. Indeed, in parecon, that is the difference between work and hobbies—the latter are outside the production plan. However, Lydia wants to get a new computer this year to help her with design and writing for the coming season. She could propose this as an investment for her drama group, but she knows it would not pass, since the need is not pressing there. Lydia also has the option to "borrow" to make the purchase herself—her Emma Goldman co-housing mates and others in the neighborhood would be happy to oblige this request, especially since her plays provide so much social well being—but Lydia is not overly pleased with committing herself to pay back a loan by consuming less in the future. She prefers to work extra hours now to earn the right to the extra consumption right away. (The astute reader may realize Lydia could petition that her play writing is socially beneficial and overtime work, but suppose that that is rejected by the drama industry.)

So Lydia puts in a proposal to the plant facilitation board requesting sufficient overtime to warrant the extra consumption. She would prefer to take less time for lunch and come in early or work later each day rather than working on her days off or evenings since that is when she works with her drama group. Once John Henry's plan is settled and the time comes to assign tasks, Lydia's proposal is considered. Confident no one will protest—Lydia works hard, has made few previous special requests, and the John Henry workers are the first to enjoy her plays—facilitation workers assign Lydia the extra time subject to approval by the council as a whole.

Matthew also requests extra work because, like last year and the year before, he wants to ask for an above-average consumption bundle. Matthew wants to do the work an extra half hour a day three times a week, for as long as needed. Facilitation workers doubt, however, that others will want to juggle their work schedules to help Matthew still again, so they ask if he'd be willing to come in Sundays to clean as his additional work. Matthew balks, and his request goes unincorporated into the facilitation board proposal of work assignments at John Henry. Although Matthew later argues his case to the council, its response is the same as the facilitation workers'. He appeals, to no effect, turns down the compromise offer to do overtime on Sundays, and decides to look for a different primary workplace. In the meantime he goes without the above-average consumption he wanted.

Evaluating and "Bartering"

During the period allowed for preparing the third proposal, Sally decides the gap is so large between what the steel industry as a whole has proposed and what consumers have initially demanded that filling the demand would require a significant increase of steel production either by placing a considerable burden on current workers, or by necessitating the transfer of many workers from other areas, with disruptive effects. Sally, like many other steel workers, decides to investigate the reasons for the high excess demand before putting in her third round proposal.

Of course, Sally is quite familiar with how John Henry steel is used. She has a good overview of the whole economy and the role steel plays. She thought the facilitation board's estimate of a three percent drop in demand for this year—given the long-term switch from steel to new high-tensile alloys—was reasonable. Therefore, when she first heard it, Sally believed the high demand must have been because some town or city was making a huge request related to a major construction project, and that town or city would modify its request quickly once they were made aware of the excess demand for steel. She didn't do any serious checking on demand, only on supply, to make sure that John Henry was keeping pace with other plants. But now she becomes interested in components of demand because they are dramatically diverging from expectations.

Sally's first step is to set aside a couple of hours one evening to use one of her work complex's main database terminals to conduct her inquiries. She begins by checking information regarding current proposals for steel supply and demand, including a comparison of current demand proposals with last year's final figures and with the facilitation boards' most recent predictions. Next, Sally looks at a breakdown of demand by industry and region to see the roots of the increase. There could have been a generalized increase in demand for all products requiring steel, but that would contradict the downward trend in steel use. Sally finds that the demand jumps were common to quite a few regions, but not all, and primarily centered in two industries.

Apparently citizens in Northern regions made unusually high demands for automobiles, while people generally were making requests for refrigerators that were at least four percent higher than anticipated. Because Sally herself had not made any such requests she wonders what reasons might be at work. With a ten percent increase in automobile requests in the Northern regions, it seems likely she could find the explanation with a few well-conceived inquiries. Thus, Sally next requests a sequence of print-outs including the average commune and per capita request for automobiles in the relevant regions as well as the national average, the average for other regions, last year's national average, the projection for this year, a summary of all changes in this year's car models, and a similar summary of changes in refrigerators.

With this information, Sally sees that new cars have innovations that make them more economical than last year's models for travel in the snow and she is annoyed that facilitation workers didn't sufficiently foresee increased demand in heavy-snow regions.

There is no corresponding improvement in refrigerators that would explain a 4 percent jump in demand. Sally checks the reasons people gave in a few representative communes and discovers an inordinate number of people claiming their refri- gerators were out of service. Further research shows that a refrigerator model introduced five years ago is now showing signs of low durability, leading to the high requests for replacements. In light of her findings, Sally recalculates her own proposals for production, scaling things up more than she had initially intended, but not quite as much as consumers sought. She feels the refrigerator need is urgent, but some of the people in the cold regions will simply have to manage without new cars. She also adds her comments to the qualitative data base.

Sally is eager to see whether facilitation board workers will come to similar conclusions in their new projections and is gratified when their explanations are released. They did perceive the same causes of high demand and elevated their projections for production of steel only a bit more than Sally had thought warranted.

Differential Productivity in "Competing" Steel Plants

One of the more interesting differences between John Henry's plan and Northstart's is that John Henry varies dramatically from the productivity norm for its industry. Publishing companies are all able to attain comparable productivity and any publisher producing below average output per unit of input has to have acceptable reasons for doing so. Some steel plants, however, have technologies neither as pleasant to work with nor as efficient as others because the yearly fall in demand for steel makes retooling all existing plants inadvisable: the new capacity would just lie idle some years down the road. Instead, selected old plants were only modestly improved in the expectation that before long the plants would be closed or converted to other uses. The few plants needed to provide the lower steel demand projected for the future were retooled extensively, but plants like John Henry were only minimally updated. Thus, during the year's planning, John Henry's old technology cannot approach the productivity of the completely retooled plants, or even the industry average.

The point, of course, is that whereas in an employee-managed market economy workers at the old plants would suffer lower incomes due to their plant's lower capabilities, in a participatory economy no such penalty would arise.

Daily Decision-Making at Jesse Owens Airport

The above discussions of Northstart and John Henry illustrate the main contours of some ways of conducting participatory planning within workplaces. Of course, as we have said before, these are not the only ways. Other plants might have other rules and methods. There is much room for variation depending on the priorities, interests, inclinations, and circumstances of any workers' council. In any case, making overall planning decisions is not the only sort of policy process required for an economy to work. Every day there are countless choices to make regarding how workers meet their production commitments. We can look at the hypothetical Jesse Owens Airport to get an idea of the dynamics.

The plan for Jesse Owens is premised on a projection of the number of customers expected to use the airport each week, which in turn affects staff size, work hours, shift arrangements, and needs for resources and intermediate goods such as fuel for planes and food for patrons. Therefore, changes in the number of people flying, or where they fly, would be the most important reasons for adjustments at Jesse Owens. In any case, having a plan for the year doesn't mean that each day won't involve critical decisions about such things as numbers of people needed at work, numbers of hours of operation, or implementation of innovations. And of course, this must all be accomplished consistently with participatory values.

Jesse Owens Airport chooses to divide into units much like those in contemporary airports—shops in terminals, building maintenance, airplane maintenance, flight scheduling, passenger meals and other services, and so on. Each unit has its own council, whose internal structures may be simple or rather complicated, including separate councils for sub-units and work teams.

At Jesse Owens, larger councils meet monthly and require only representative attendance. Meetings focus on policy and personnel questions. Day-to-day and hour-to-hour decisions are handled by relevant authorities on the spot. Nothing about participatory planning precludes having a field captain of the baggage team at "Rosa Parks Terminal," or a dining maestro in the "Goddard Lounge." Nor does anything prevent these "authorities" from making decisions about short-term scheduling or calls to bring in extra employees. What is precluded is only that such "executive functions" embody levels of authority disruptive of solidarity, variety, or collective self-management. Therefore, these positions would be held only as parts of balanced job complexes and in some cases even only temporarily, to keep some people from consistently making decisions for others to carry out.

Decisions about assignments and hiring new workers or releasing workers to other enterprises are made by personnel committees and teams. These staff members also have other assignments to balance the quality of their work complexes.

Disputes arise about irresponsibility, lack of effort, bossiness, etc. How might these be resolved? Under capitalism, at best, such disputes are handled by grievance committees with union reps committed to defending employees no matter what the facts may be, while management tries to fire strong union members, intimidate employees, and sanction workers. In coordinator economies, workers have usually been less effectively represented by unions, although firing even those who do practically nothing has been almost impossible due to the rhetoric of the movements who brought these systems into existence and the absolute prioritization of full employment. In participatory economies, in contrast, disputes between workers carrying out administrative and implementation tasks will be settled in committees of other workers who all carry out both administrative and implementation tasks themselves in their balanced job complexes. Different plants might have different procedures for hearing complaints and bringing grievances. There are many ways to handle such matters, and choices would be contoured to the particular dynamics of specific and workforces.

Hiring and Firing

But consider just one issue that would naturally arise at all workplaces on a regular basis—the hiring and firing of employees. There are many reasons for hiring and firing, including an increase or decrease in demand for a company's product, incorrigible malfeasance, or the need to replace someone who has moved on to a new job. There would therefore be self-chosen movement of people among workplaces in a parecon, just as in any non-totalitarian economy. How could this be handled?

Each workplace, we hypothesize, envisioning how they might choose to fulfill guiding participatory economic principles, has a personnel committee. Some committee members would mediate interpersonal disputes and problems with employees' personal work habits, others would process requests to change assignments within the workplace, and still others would process requests for transfers and hire new personnel. Moreover, the last function would be greatly facilitated by industry and regional Employment Facilitation Boards, or EFBs. Each workplace would communicate its expected needs for new employees and/or notice of employees wanting to leave to industry and regional EFBs, which would in turn regularly provide information back to personnel committees in workplaces. All this information would also be publicly available.

Say that Jackie wanted to leave her job at Jesse Owens Airport in Boston to move south. She would report this to her personnel committee so they would know she was thinking of leaving, and contact the appropriate EFB to find out about available jobs. Although she could go any time she liked, if she wanted to remain in airport work, then for the benefit of her workmates she might agree to leave in tandem with some other individual's transfer to Boston. Or, more flexibly, she might agree to leave whenever there was an opening she wanted to fill at a southern airport and there was a potential employee available to fill her role at Jesse Owens, whether a new worker just out of school, or a transfer from the South, or someone else.

Alternatively, if fewer employees are needed at Jesse Owens, the personnel committee would work with EFBs to come up with a list of new places they could confidently apply and organize a process whereby people could decide if they wanted to volunteer to transfer.

Involuntary transfers would sometimes be necessary in a parecon —as in all economies—but they would occur far less often than in other economic systems. A parecon would not have the type of "boom and bust" cycles that plague market economies. The need to shift employees would always arise from the need to move people from one industry or workplace to another due to shifting preferences for outputs, rather than from a need to lay off workers in general. Any general decrease in total work required would be shared by all workers in the economy as a welcomed reduction in work hours or work intensity—not confined to a few as dreaded unemployment.

Also, balanced job complexes and remuneration for effort means that much of the pain we associate with transfers would be absent in participatory economies. There is every reason to expect more people to be willing to transfer voluntarily since job quality and pay will not suffer in moving. Also, we believe the EFBs would be much more efficient in matching institutions and people than any system found in present economies. While Labor Market Boards in Sweden have been head and shoulders above employment agencies and retraining programs in the US, the EFBs would have much better information available more quickly, and in particular with much longer advance notice of changes in technologies and long-term investment intentions. In any case, involuntary transfers would never be accompanied by a loss of consumption rights or the extreme social stigma and loss of dignity so common today to unemployment. And finally, if it is socially agreed that having to switch jobs is a sacrifice, it could certainly be remunerated as such.

It is a different matter, however, if someone is fired because he or she is unwilling to work or is so antisocial that nobody wants him or her around disrupting work relations. It will not do to dodge the issue pretending these problems will never arise in participatory economies. There will always be disharmony and recalcitrance of diverse types. And there will have to be provisions for dealing with cases that are curable, and others that are not. All we can say is that many of the causes of such behavior will no longer exist in participatory economies, and that we would expect the ways chosen for dealing with the fewer remaining problems of this sort to be far more humane than in present economies.

12

Consuming

Think of the whole country as a big household, and the whole nation as a big family [....] What do we see? Half-fed, badly clothed, abominably housed children [...] and the money that should go to feed and clothe and house them being spent on bottles of scent, pearl necklaces, pet dogs, racing motor cars, January strawberries that taste like corks [...] the nation that spends money on champagne before it has provided enough milk for its babies, or gives dainty meals to Sealyham terriers and Alsatian wolf-hounds whilst the infant mortality rate shows that its children are dying by thousands from insufficient nourishment, is a badly managed, silly, vain, stupid, ignorant nation.
— George Bernard Shaw

Consumption has two facets—what we do individually and what we do collectively. Here we consider first collective and then personal consumption, trying to discern features of each in a parecon.

Collective Consumption

The Capitalist Case

How are millions of citizens of a capitalist county organized so that their different desires emerge as demands for "public" goods? Who decides? Who pays? We need to consider purchases of roads, schools, hospitals, parks, fire equipment, and social services. Yet, even this does not exhaust the list of "things" consumed collectively by members of the capitalist county we will call Jefferson Park.

For example, there is the way the county looks, largely determined by its architecture. And there is the county's ecological health, determined by pollution standards and the availability of ecologically sound goods. Thus far more goods than are usually deemed "public" comprise the county's collective consumption.

In capitalist Jefferson Park, it is officially the county government that decides on the mix of public goods and the taxes that will be levied to pay for them. But in Jefferson Park the government inevitably caters to lobbies that wield power in proportion to their wealth. Traffic lights are erected and streets re-paved in upper- and middle-class areas. Toxic wastes are dumped near the ghetto.

County government also determines the location of public and private buildings by setting zoning ordinances in response to pressure with wealth being more important than numbers of voters.

Consider hospitals: How many are in Capitalist Jefferson Park county? How are they designed? What ailments do they treat? The number of private hospitals established depends on whether they attract investors, which in turn depends on the county government's efforts to provide services. The number of public hospitals established depends on the county budget, which is in turn affected by the tax base held hostage by business. In a system where those who pay the piper call the tune, the design of any hospital and disposition of its resources will naturally reflect the tastes of its financiers. If a hospital's clientele is wealthy, then providing attractive rooms, fine care, and a maximum of amenities justifies high fees and the hospital becomes private. If the hospital's clientele is poor, much of its revenue must come from the county budget and budget crises will necessitate reducing costs and increasing "throughput" per day by rushing patients through treatment, often prematurely. Amenities will not translate into profits. The disposition of resources thus is geared to speed and thrift and avoiding embarrassment or lawsuits—not to comfort or care.

The influence of money over county policy gives rise to a "sensible" passivity among most of the population in capitalist Jefferson Park. With less time free from the daily struggle for survival, and county officials already beholden to wealthy donors, county politics reduce the majority of the county's people to ignorance and apathy regarding important decisions. This apathy is interrupted by occasional outbursts of rage at corruption, incompetence, or a tax burden grossly out of proportion to benefits received. The result is that most of the populace has little say in deciding whether a hospital should be constructed, what its design should be, and whom it should serve. The same holds for construction and repair of roads, fire stations, airports, the location of factories, the location and quality of schools, libraries, recreation centers, and health clinics, and the mixture and incidence of taxes to pay for all these. Most capitalist Jefferson Park consumers never know what issues are at stake, what alternatives they have, that they could do something other than leave decisions to government bureaucrats.

Conservatives insist that the solution lies in taking decisions out of the hands of government—whose decisions are often corrupt and biased and "necessarily" coercive—and leaving them to the market, where "all choices are voluntary and freedom is preserved." But decisions about parks, roads, schools, and fire protection affect large numbers of people. Even mainstream economists have long recognized there is nothing efficient or democratic about leaving such decisions to market allocation. Such decisions should be collectively made, preferably in a way that properly values available options and guarantees everyone an equal and effective opportunity to participate without wasting their valuable time.

The Participatory Case

In hypothetical participatory Martin Luther King County (MLK), all citizens belong to their neighborhood council, their ward council, and the MLK council, as well as to still larger and more encompassing councils. With this structure, not all ward or county council members need to attend all ward or county council meetings. For really important issues, it is agreed, in our hypothetical case, that decisions are made by a referendum of all members with whatever voting system is warranted. Other times, it may be that only representatives sent by neighborhood councils to ward councils or by ward councils to county councils deliberate and vote. Meetings are always open and televised, with very prominent notice before referenda occur. In addition, one county workplace is the Collective Consumption Facilitation Board (CCFB), which is empowered to facilitate decision-making regarding county collective consumption. The CCFB is governed by the same participatory rules as any other workplace. Each neighborhood and ward council has its own smaller CCFB to facilitate their collective consumption decisions, and the same holds for cities, states, and regions.

So we see decisions being made at the various levels of individual, neighborhood, ward, and county. To fully understand collective consumption requires relating it to the planning of all economic decisions. Here, however, as a first step, we emphasize relevant local institutions and the logic of some of their procedures.

MLK county determines short- and long-term collective consumption priorities and plans. It chooses between projects like new athletic complexes, cultural centers, hospitals, schools, and bus systems, or no new efforts at all. The county council makes decisions by referendum of the whole council, using methods they agree on for a variety of proposed projects. Competing collective consumption alternatives arise out of communications between the CCFB and county council representatives or just messages from neighborhood councils. Again, we are not trying to provide a detailed blueprint that must be adhered to by all parecons, not only because most of the details of a new economy will only be learned via the experience of creating it, but also because there will be no such detailed universal blueprint. Different parecons in different countries and different workers' or consumers' councils in a given parecon can in many instances arrive at different approaches even for doing similar things, depending on their histories, situations, and preferences. It is only the broad values and the overarching structures that are universal from parecon to parecon and within one parecon from unit to unit. At any rate, in this hypothetical descriptive account of a particular parecon's operations, the CCFB has data about the prior years' plans as well as projects that were not approved last year. A first set of options includes a continuation of plans in progress, a listing of other plans previously desired but delayed, and a list of proposals for possible new collective consumption projects received by the CCFB throughout the year from neighborhood councils, individuals, and workplaces.

Participatory planning procedures then refine these many possibilities into more precise options or pass them up to more encompassing councils for choices to be made by appropriate voting procedures. Although additional participation by citizens requires that more of their time go to managing collective consumption than under capitalism, it is less time than they previously spent compensating for the ills induced by profit-motivated decisions.

In the same way that the county determines its collective consumption preferences, ward and neighborhood councils consider such issues as further improving local day care facilities, scheduling food delivery, re-seeding neighborhood parks, changing pool schedules, building a new movie complex, and enlarging the local library. Neighborhood CCFBs facilitate such decisions by listing options and enumerating their likely effects. Instead of the whole county participating, it is agreed that insofar as these decisions have an overwhelmingly local impact, only members of the affected ward or neighborhood will cast ballots, though ultimately each neighborhood's plan is summed into the plan for the whole county, and then summed into the plan for the whole society, and processed through participatory planning, with the possibility of other constituencies weighing in as they are affected.

The difference between capitalist Jefferson Park County and participatory Martin Luther King County should be clear. In the capitalist case, collective consumption succumbs to the will of government bureaucracy and powerful private interests. The definition of options and their refinement into final choices rests with "professionals" subject to pressure from private lobbies. Most citizens are estranged from decisions, since the process and outcomes accommodate only the wills of powerful elites motivated by a desire to maximize their own profits and status.

In Martin Luther King County, individuals, neighborhoods, and interest groups submit ideas for collective consumption projects. Workers serving on the CCFB refine these options into coherent possibilities whose effects can be compared. Their workplaces are structured so that CCFB workers have no economic vested interests channeling their work, and in any event, final collective consumption is debated by everyone who wishes to participate and final decisions are made by democratic procedures sensitive to the different effects decisions may have on different constituencies. But what about individual consumption in capitalism and in a parecon?

Individual Consumption

The Capitalist Case

In capitalism, shopping is the quintessential activity. "Live to shop." "Shop 'til you drop." But in capitalism when we consume we know little about what others must do to produce what we consume. Even if we wanted to do so, we have limited ability to temper our requests out of concern for producers. We can only respect the limits of what is available, our personal budget, and our own desires.

But what determines availability in capitalism? The aims and motives of owners, a fact which significantly restricts consumer options. And what tells us what the market offers? Packaging, advertising, and word of mouth, none of which is entirely trustworthy. And what determines our budget? Wages, income, and other forms of grossly unequal wealth. And what additional pressures influence us to buy more of this or that? The norms of gender, class, and culturally circumscribed behavior, the requirements of work, the pressures of seeking status through consumption, and, in the absence of viable social alternatives, the need to find almost all enjoyment from private commodities.

The absurdity of consumption under capitalism is difficult for those of us living inside the system to recognize. In *The Dispossessed* (Avon, 1974), science-fiction writer Ursula LeGuin has a character named Shevek who comes to earth from a moon habitat devoid of consumerism to visit a capitalist shopping mall. His reaction is as follows:

> Saemtenevia Prospect was two miles long, and it was a solid mass of things to buy, things for sale. Coats, dresses, gowns, robes, trousers, breeches, shirts, umbrellas, clothes to wear while sleeping, while swimming, while playing games, while at an afternoon party, while at an evening party, while at a party in the country, while traveling, while at the theater, while riding horses, gardening, receiving guests, boating, dining, hunting— all different, all in hundreds of different cuts, styles, colors, textures, materials. Perfumes, clocks, lamps, statues, cosmetics, candles, pictures, cameras, hassocks, jewels, carpets: toothpicks, calendars, a baby's teething rattle of platinum with a handle of rock crystal, an electrical machine to sharpen pencils, a wristwatch with diamond numerals, figurines and souvenirs and kickshaws and mementos and gewgaws and bric-a-brac, everything either useless to begin with or ornamented so as to disguise its use; acres of luxuries, acres of excrement. ... But to Shevek the strangest thing about the nightmare street was that none of the millions of things for sale were made there. They were only sold there. Where were the workmen, the miners, the weavers, the chemists, the carvers, the dyers, the designers, the machinists ...? Out of sight, somewhere else. Behind walls. All the people in all the shops were either buyers or sellers. They had no relation to the things but that of possessions. How was he to know what a goods' production entailed? How could they expect him to decide if he wanted something? The whole experience was totally bewildering.

The Participatory Case

Citizens in MLK county have a wide variety of living arrangements. Some live alone, some in couples, some with a partner and children, some in communes. Some live with a few friends and others live in "co-housing communities" where many dwellings band together as a larger whole to collectively share various resources and responsibilities. All these different kinds of living units and many others, no doubt, are part of neighborhood consumption councils.

As one of the more collective forms of living group, what might a co-housing community be like? The hypothetical Emma Goldman community (EG) might have 67 members, of whom 35 range from a few months to 17 years old. Of the 32 "adults," 24 are "coupled" and eight "uncoupled." Eight of the children have biological parents living as a couple in the complex. Another 12 have both biological parents living in the complex but not "coupled." Nine of the remaining 15 children have one biological parent with them and the other either deceased or living elsewhere. Four children have biological parents who live elsewhere, but none in the complex.

EG has households of various types. A quarter of the couples are gay and many people live in extended families. The complex has a children's section and an adult section so that children and adults can enjoy privacy from one another. The community's households all have pleasant individual living quarters and adequate kitchen facilities, but EG also has a collective dining hall, collective sports equipment, a large library and entertainment center, a collective laundry room, and a well-outfitted computer center.

The community meets regularly to adopt and update consumption plans, and to coordinate schedules for day care, shopping, and other tasks where people can benefit from economies of scale. Clearly, the advantages of the co-housing community lie in this collectivizing feature—the sharing of tasks and responsibilities, the ready availability of assistance, baby sitters, friends, and project partners, and the benefits of not wasting personal consumption allowances on goods that can be enjoyed much more cheaply, efficiently, and ecologically when shared collectively.

So what is the situation of the individual consumer? First, he or she considers individual consumption in light of already determined collective plans for the county, neighborhood, and co-housing community, since these collective decisions may greatly affect needs for private consumption. Of course, carefully planned collective consumption does not relegate private consumption to the ashcan of history. There is plenty left to decide personally, and we must ask how this differs from consumption under capitalism.

Lydia belongs to the EG community. She likes it because its membership (which changes as some people leave and others are accepted by a vote of the whole complex) is in tune with her own tastes. As with most communities, there is no smoking. People of diverse ages, sexual preferences, and cultural backgrounds are included. Most of the members of EG are into theatre, film, music, or writing. Their collective consumption decisions are made accordingly, so EG has less athletic equipment, science labs, and crafts rooms than co-housing communities which feature those pursuits, but enjoys a very nice theatre, above-average sound systems, photo labs, and well-equipped music rooms.

Lydia determines her personal consumption needs by taking collective requests into account. She also considers the implications of her requests for workers with the aid of information generated by parecon allocation procedures. Beyond being able to consciously affect and take account of collective decisions, Lydia is also privy to the general character of her community mates' anonymous private consumption choices because she is allowed to question those that seem dangerous or otherwise antisocial at planning sessions whenever it is evident that someone has proposed to consume more than a fair allotment or whenever it is clear that someone's consumption request is of such a character that Lydia (or anyone else) feels that it is potentially harmful either to the consumer or to the co-housing community as a whole. Of course, the same holds for Lydia's requests, which are also put into the public hopper, though no one knows who in particular is requesting what because in Lydia's council it is agreed that unless absolutely necessary, consumption requests are anonymous.

The fact that Lydia has to propose her consumption yearly doesn't mean she cannot change her requests when the need arises. Participatory consumption welcomes regular updates of plans. Yet Lydia must get her food, furniture, clothes, and other goods somewhere. Primarily, she will get it at local outlets in her neighborhood although she can also make purchases at outlets elsewhere should she want to. She has a kind of credit card, that incorporates her plan, budget, and choices, and allows regular updating in light of changes in her preferences and patterns.

Consumption Planning

Assume that all higher-level consumer federations have already arrived at collective consumption plan. Let's follow the consumer calculations of two residents of MLK county, Arundhati and Tariq.

Determining County-Level Collective Consumption

Consumption planning begins with collective consumption projects, starting at the highest level and working down, and culminating in a vote on an entire collective consumption package. We look in on this process at the point where individuals present requests for county-level collective and individual consumption.

Of course, all of last year's data is available and MLK residents pay particular attention to records of their requests and final plans from last year, to their county's status as a borrower or creditor, to IFB projections for this year's average consumption, and to the county consumption facilitation board's summary of collective consumption projects members have suggested.

The CCFB proposes various options. But consumers are not hit suddenly with a menu of collective consumption options they know nothing about, have not discussed, and have no opportunity to alter. On the contrary, consumers are periodically informed regarding the formation of these proposals and can intervene at any time with comments, suggestions, and alternate proposals of their own.

Afer having spent time evaluating the various CCFB proposals, each living unit discusses them, suggests alterations, and registers preferences. Individuals weigh the benefits of proposed collective consumption requests against their estimated social costs and estimates of county consumption within their region. People also consider the implications for individual consumption of collective consumption for which they will be "charged" their fair share.

For example, Arundhati who lives with her husband and their three children as members of EG co-housing community, considers how options vary in terms of their social costs and benefits. She considers how much a new county cultural center would reduce the need for personal cultural products, what strains it would place on workers, and how much it would diminish each county resident's personal consumption budget.

Of course a particularly large county collective consumption request need not reduce individual consumption budgets drastically in the same period. The "debt to society" can be spread over time through county borrowing and saving. This is not only reasonable but essential if any large-scale collective consumption is to occur. In any event, Arundhati and others deal with these issues with the aid of the information made available by the CFBs and computers that quickly and conveniently provide information on the implications for average consumption bundles and make comparisons with other units and past plans. Consumers manipulate software that helps them evaluate the implications of alternative collective consumption choices. For example, Arundhati can see data describing how a new community athletics center would reduce what is available for individual consumption but permit greater access to exercise equipment, basketball and volleyball courts, pools, etc., for herself, her husband, and her children.

After receiving feedback from all the households that make up the county council, the CCFB modifies its list of proposed collective consumption projects and resubmits it for households to consider. After discussion, each household ranks the revised proposals, including explanations for its preferences. At this point, the CCFB proposes four possible collective consumption agendas, explaining the implications of each for overall plan possibilities.

Households, co-housing communities, and other living units then vote on the four collective consumption bundles, dropping the least popular with each vote until one remains. This voting is "live"— living units and representatives are linked by computer and TV hook-ups so that votes can be inclusive and tabulated immediately. In this example, as in most other voting procedures, representative structures facilitate making amendments to incorporate as many viewpoints as possible. Then all citizens can vote on the amendments because of the speed with which votes can be tallied.

The above is but one possibility. But there is no one right way to undertake collective consumption. Different counties would employ different procedures. Guidelines for transparency, participation, self-management, and proper valuation, are the universals.

Once MLK and other counties have settled on their collective consumption requests, these can be massaged in light of one another and summed into state and national collective consumption requests. Rather then pursue that in detail, next we describe how neighborhood and personal consumption requests can be developed.

Determining Personal Consumption Proposals

Since neighborhood collective consumption mirrors the logic of county collective consumption, we move to personal consumption requests. To develop a personal consumption plan, Tariq consults the IFB's estimates of indicative prices, assessments for collective consumption for members of his neighborhood, and average personal consumption estimates, and settles on a "borrower/loaner" status. To simplify, similar products of comparable quality are grouped together so Tariq needs to express preferences for socks, but not for colors or type of socks; for soda, books, and bicycles, but not for flavors, titles, or styles of each. Statistical studies enable facilitation boards to break down total requests for generic types of goods by the percent of people who will want different types of records, soda, or bicycles. There are no competing companies producing products, only "product industries" creating diverse styles and qualities of goods for different purposes, all with the intention that everyone get what is best meets their needs.

Tariq has under-consumed relative to his allowance in the past two years and has decided to even up the balance a bit this year. On the other hand, his county, MLK, has requested a higher than average county collective consumption bundle, some of which is being borrowed, but some of which will be "paid for" now by reducing the consumption of MLK residents this year. Tariq knows there is no point being too modest in his initial proposal—the iteration process will compel him to lower his final request as necessary. But he doesn't want to make requests that are outrageously immodest, either, since that would only lengthen the bargaining process and do nothing to increase his final consumption.

Tariq knows his selections have social implications. It is not that his choice of a particular kind of food implies that everyone else should get the same amount of that product. People have different needs and tastes. But the total of Tariq's consumption calculated according to the IFB-generated indicative prices and adjusted for MLK's above-average collective consumption request and his individual status as a borrower against past savings implicitly expresses what he thinks is a reasonable average consumption bundle for all members of society. It would be pointless for Tariq to suggest a value too far in excess of what the IFB has anticipated, unless he thinks the IFB has made a gross underestimation.

So Tariq takes his turn at a computer terminal to try out various combinations of different goods, checking on the total value of his proposed bundle. The computer contains anticipated averages, indicative prices, and so on, as well as qualitative descriptions of the products (which he can also see at outlets) and of the work that goes into their creation. The information helps Tariq assess whether rote or dangerous methods are employed to produce the goods he wants.

Tariq knows that if he requests a lot of goods that require work at below-average job complexes, he is implicitly changing the societal average work complex and his own labor requirements. Self-interest and collective solidarity argue against such a request unless he thinks the benefits of consuming the good in question are worth the extra drudgery. In any event, getting detailed information about production relations only requires a few minutes.

As Tariq completes his first proposal, so do other consumers, and all are submitted to the societal planning data bank where they are collected and processed by IFBs. New summaries are presented including updated projections of anticipated indicative prices, average consumption, and the current status of each good, all to be discussed next chapter.

13

Allocating

> Freedom is not merely the opportunity to do as one pleases; neither is it
> merely the opportunity to choose between set alternatives. Freedom is, first
> of all, the chance to formulate the available choices, to argue over them—and
> then, the opportunity to choose.
> —C.Wright Mills

In the two prior chapters we discussed the institutions of participatory planning and the direct situations of hypothetical workers and consumers in hypothetical workplaces and communities. What remains is to discuss the more detailed dynamics of participatory planning, some of its content and its character. For one thing, up to now we have assumed long-run projects were decided before annual planning, and that at the outset of the yearly planning process each economic actor had access to important information. How is this accomplished? Other topics we address in this chapter are the handling of information, the tasks and procedures of the facilitation boards, and a description of the personal experience associated with planning.

Long-Term Plans

Should society make a qualitative change in coal mining that drastically improves health and safety? Should it update existing steel plants, build a new high-speed rail line, or transform agriculture to conform to ecological norms? All may be desirable, but presumably, given limited resources, not all can be done at the same time. That is the meaning of long-term investment choice and the problem it poses. Which projects are worth doing and which are not? In what order should they be done? And how fast should we tackle the list—which is to say, how much present consumption are we willing to sacrifice for future benefit?

Long- and short-term investment projects differ in regard to how many years' resources must be committed for the project to reach fruition. Large- and small-scale investment projects differ also regarding the magnitude of commitments and the breadth of efforts required. One approach to long-term planning would be to handle this issue before yearly planning begins. At this time, all previously agreed to long-term projects could be reviewed and updated so that the commitment of resources necessary for this year could become part of subsequent planning calculations. After national projects are settled, large regions could settle on their new long-term projects, and so on, down to the smallest units. In each case, alternate proposals could be aired, preferences expressed, implications assessed, new alternatives broached, options eliminated and improved, and final decisions made after due deliberation, all by participatory procedures similar to those described in our earlier discussion of county-wide planning.

A procedure that could shorten the process would be to first decide the proportion of economic resources we want to commit to investment. Debate about options could then be made knowing roughly what productive resources were available. Formulation, presentation, and modification of long-term investment options could be made and updated by the investment facilitation boards, who could base their proposals on submissions from units, also as outlined in the earlier county example.

It is important to recognize the advantages of collective, participatory investment planning. In capitalist or market coordinator economies, each unit assesses potential investments according to norms imposed by the market and class system. In the workplace, the decision to switch from one technology to another is made by assessing likely profit/loss and capital/labor or coordinator/labor bargaining implications. But this is most definitely not the same as deciding on the basis of social cost and social benefit. Only the benefit of owners, coordinators, and stockholders is taken into account. Moreover, investment decisions in market economies are not even planned in coordination with one another. For example, the steel plant that decides not to introduce new technology because it appears unprofitable might have decided differently were they better able to foresee how innovations in other industries would dramatically alter the cost of inputs or the demand for steel. Or, since there is a premium on corporate secrecy under capitalism, two firms might make a decision to invest in a new plant when society only needs the output of one.

In participatory planning, on the other hand, coordinated planning in light of social costs and benefits is possible. Each potential investment stands or falls not because of contemporary relationships alone, but because of conditions most likely to prevail once all innovations are available. Whatever criteria society uses to determine whether to enact particular investments, the participatory planning system will produce a more accurate assessment of social costs and benefits than would capitalist or coordinator systems. In addition, in a participatory system judgments will emphasize the impact of choices on the whole economy's social relations from the point of view of improving the quality of life of all workers and consumers, rather than just the circumstances of elite classes. But what about planning more broadly?

Preparing Data for the First Round

How do iteration facilitation boards estimate overall production and consumption for the coming year? How do they come up with initial indicative prices that economic actors can use, and what exactly do these prices convey? Most important, does proposing likely outcomes and indicative prices make a lie of our claims that no single agent has greater say than others? Can facilitation workers exert undue influence on planning?

Various planning boards begin by reviewing last year's results, including what inputs generated what outputs in every unit. They know the final indicative prices and therefore can calculate the value of last year's production. Moreover, qualitative information is included in extensive reports from all units and federations and quantitative information can be accessed using terminals that allow users to see the inputs required for outputs desired.

Facilitation boards modify last year's data to estimate this year's likely outcomes based on comprehensive demographic reports regarding likely changes in population by age and gender, the distribution of people between city and country, and so on. They know which investment projects have been completed and how these investments should affect production potentials. As a result, facilitators can make educated guesses about changes in production work levels and indicative prices.

We could provide more detail, but nothing about this type of data manipulation warrants it. The techniques are well known and noncontroversial—tedious, but not difficult. Facilitators are merely taking last year's data and massaging it in light of projections about investments that have come to fruition, growth of the labor force, and changes in tastes—the latter being estimated from last year's interchanges and from polls of particular constituencies.

Facilitators could could follow only prescribed steps for massaging their data, or they could take some latitude for discretionary and hopefully creative adjustments. In the former case, facilitators would have no ability to influence outcomes, but might provide less than the best possible guesses. In the latter case, there is greater risk of subjective bias, but also potential for better projections. We will talk more about this trade-off later when we discuss examples, but here we make four preliminary observations:

1   It is hard to see any way facilitation board workers (whom we call facilitators for short) could gain by maliciously biasing data even if they went about their work without supervision.

2   The choice between using more flexible but also more subjective techniques and using less flexible but also less creative techniques lies in the hands of society, not facilitation board workers.

3   There is no reason facilitators' discretionary calculations could not be checked by anyone who wished to.

4   Facilitators' projections are, in any case, only guidelines to help economic actors make decisions.

Facilitators themselves don't make any production or consumption proposals (other than their own), nor do they revise, veto, or approve any proposals (other than their own). Indeed, facilitation could be automated, with computers taking last year's data and altering it according to rules that tell what changes to make. Facilitators would then only update the program rules as they better understand how variables affect one another. A less formulaic approach would allow facilitators to use their experience to refine automatic projections. But in either case, facilitators make no decisions about what the economy will do. They only provide information whose formulation is open to public scrutiny and which economic decision makers are free to ignore if they mistrust it.

At the outset of planning everyone in society has access to projections for indicative prices and production and consumption at every level, including summaries of related assumptions. Individuals use this information as they please in developing their own plans for the year. It is therefore hard to see how facilitators could bias outcomes even if society chose, as we think wise, to give them leeway in their means of calculation and projection. Of course facilitators, like all other workers have balanced job complexes and are remunerated only for effort and sacrifice.

Revising Data in Subsequent Iterations

The tasks of facilitators in subsequent iterations are not particularly complex. After each economic council and federation submits its first proposal, facilitators respond by preparing new data for the coming round. They no longer have to guess based on last year's results. Once this year's initial proposals are in, IFBs calculate the excess demand or supply for every good and accordingly adjust the indicative price of each good up or down. There is room for practical experience and artistry in making the indicative price adjustments or, if preferred, the changes could be made according to fixed rules. In either case, not every price must be adjusted by the same function of its excess demand or supply. One possibility is that IFB workers with experience in particular industries or with qualitative information indicating whether proposals are relatively soft or hard could expedite convergence by discretionary, informed adjustments. But in any event, in early rounds, IFBs only summarize qualitative information in data banks for councils to assess, calculate excess supply and demand, adjust indicative prices, and revise projections of predicted final outcomes. The updates of predicted final outcomes are still guesses, but they are based on more information with each new round of planning. Reports of excess demand and supply and qualitative information, however, are a matter of accurate record-keeping.

It is important to note, however, what it is that facilitators would be "updating" in each round. Before planning commences, IFBs use last year's results, including information about investment projects, polls taken during the year, and various demographic data to project anticipated results for the coming year. Of course actual initial proposals will not be identical to IFB projections. Once the year's planning begins, IFBs are revising information based on the most recent set of proposals submitted. So at the outset of round two, workers and consumers receive summaries of qualitative information, new indicative prices, the percentage of excess demand and supply for every good, and new projections of what average consumption and the average social benefit to social cost ratio will be for workplaces this year. Workers and consumers use all this data, as we have discussed, to modify their requests in subsequent rounds.

During the planning process, facilitation boards at different levels would regularly communicate with one another and with plant boards regarding logjams, requests that remain unusually far from expected averages, reluctance among producers or consumers to compromise, and especially changing labor requirements that require transfers of workers.

But facilitators carry out only communicative tasks and never make decisions for others. Whether they do their job well affects the final plan, but it is hard to see exactly what motive IFB workers might have to intentionally bias outcomes or even how they could do it, and it is certainly possible to have oversight mechanisms.

In later iterations, in addition to adjusting indicative prices and providing new projections, IFBs could generate alternative feasible plans for councils to assess and vote on. Indeed this is the case in the version of participatory planning we have been describing. This approach would increase the potential for IFBs to influence outcomes since in late iterations they would be actually formulating options. It is conceivable, for example, that IFB workers might present five internally consistent plans but not a possible plan that would actually be most preferred. But notice that the only reason for having IFBs present options for a vote is to reduce the number of iterations required to reach a final plan. It is a matter of practical convenience, and, should councils be suspicious or unsatisfied with what IFBs present, the councils and federations can always choose to continue the iterative process as they had been. In other words, this stage of the planning process can be postponed until the councils feel that the time saved warrants any diminution in the quality of results. Moreover, the idea is that this time-saving part of the procedure would only begin when the major part of the plan has already been settled on. We are talking about final moves after the essential outcome is no longer in doubt. Moreover, councils could always insist that an additional alternative plan be included with those generated by the IFBs to be voted on.

Finally, for those who fear that computers could become the new dictators, the programs are socially evaluated and improved each year. The computer is acting on data emerging directly from the social planning process and the preferences expressed by it participants. The computer uses socially determined data and rules and only carries out data manipulation and calculations. Moreover, all the scenarios we have outlined for producers and consumers to make their choices allow for amendments. Neither consumers nor producers need accept computer projections.

Society could have IFB workers play a substantial role in refining options to embody people's preferences, but as with other procedural choices, there is no one right way. If a society chooses a more mechanical approach, the need for special oversight to guard against bias is minimized, but planning might take more time. If IFB workers are given more leeway, the possibility of human error or bias is increased and provisions to correct for it become more important (though significant self-interested bias is hard to imagine given that facilitation workers benefit only if average job complexes or overall productivity increase, just like all other workers). But workers and consumers probably save planning time.

Whatever combination of automatic procedures and human discretion is adopted for IFB work, unlike in coordinator and capitalist economies, no aspect of participatory planning is immune to social evaluation. Nor is any part of the plan finalized without being filtered through the social barter process where everyone's preferences, evaluations, and opinions interact. Nor is any individual in a position to systematically advance personal or group interests against social interests.

The difference between participatory and central planning is that in the latter, "planners" generate the plan, submit it to those who will carry it out, get feedback about whether actors can or cannot accomplish what planners propose for them to do, and then impose a plan. More, they occupy a different class position and enjoy material and job related advantages which can be defended and enlarged via plan choices. In participatory economics "plan workers" only facilitate the process whereby workers and consumers propose, haggle over, and revise their own plan, making their own decisions. And if facilitators formulate any proposals, it is only after all the important decisions have been made. And facilitators are not in a separate class and do not have larger incomes or better work conditions to defend or advance against others' interests.

Working at a Facilitation Board

Working at a facilitation board is not much different than working anywhere else in the economy. Work is partly conceptual and partly executionary, and work complexes are balanced by the usual approach of combining diverse tasks. IFB work may be more desirable and more empowering than average work complexes in the economy as a whole, but, if so, greater than average desirability would be compensated for just as it would in any other workplace— that is, by assignments to less desirable tasks elsewhere. Greater than average empowerment might even require rotating people in and out of IFBs after some time period, in addition to general balancing. Likewise, since working at an IFB is particularly likely to enhance people's understanding of the interlocking complexities of economic possibilities, it makes sense to rotate this work, taking the efficiency implications of experience and training into account as well. Finally, depending on society's political structures, a case can be made for working to have IFB staffs be politically balanced across a spectrum of views, avoiding any biases on that score.

Qualitative Information

Consumers need to be able to assess the implications of their requests for workers. Producers need to know why consumers want what they are working on, not only so they can feel good about their contributions, but also to decide how hard they want to work.

In addition to quantitative estimates of social costs and benefits, average incomes, and average benefit/cost ratios, producers and consumers also need access to qualitative, descriptive information.

Consumer and producer councils can easily write up qualitative summaries of the work they do and the motives for their consumption requests. There is no sense overdoing it. There is no point in everyone saying, "I want milk because it is nourishing." Producers would provide a general description of the quality of work involved in their workplace as well as the desirable and undesirable traits their particular kind of work tends to generate. Consumers would concentrate on explanations of unusual requests. But people trying to assess their own choices in light of other people's qualitative descriptions would want access to summary information at the level of producer and consumer federations. So the tasks are:

1 To develop a database system allowing easy access to all this information.

2 To aggregate the information from lower units into federation-level summaries.

Can we imagine an effective way to do this? First, individuals would need "keys" to extract qualitative information. I would go to a console, and say, "Let me see what goes into producing such and such good," or "What is work like in such and such an industry?" or "What is generating the high consumer demand for refrigerators?" or "Why does a particular neighborhood want so many more bicycles than the national average?" We could also ask, "What are the strengths and weaknesses of such and such a product?"

If we think of all the money spent yearly in the US on advertising —most of which is misinformation—we can see that the information system we need may not be such a burden on time and resources after all. Indeed, it may require significantly less than the total resources and energies currently allotted to less comprehensive and less truthful, though more repetitive and wasteful advertising.

Though the information-handling capabilities of such a system would have to be quite powerful, only the system's scale distinguishes it from databases already used in offices all over the country. The problem of storing and accessing descriptive information is nothing new for programmers, nor is establishing a system for easily updating or otherwise refining such a database, giving it a simple query system, or having it provide averages. Moreover, even for a large country, the system we need would not require much more memory and handling than systems currently in use by large credit-card companies.

For the most part, IFBs would oversee the qualitative database system. Summarizing large numbers of individual reports would be demanding, but like other tasks it could be organized to minimize the likelihood that IFBs would accidentally much less intentionally bias the information councils use.

Part IV
Criticism of Parecon

First they ignore you. Then they laugh at you.
Then they fight you. Then you win.
— Mahatma Gandhi

A Judge is a law student who marks his own papers.
—H.L. Mencken

Any economy must allocate goods and resources. Different ways of accomplishing this will naturally differently affect who does what, who gets what, and what will be produced, consumed, and invested.

Someone who believes that civilization is best served by pitting people against one another will opt for allocation via competitive markets. Someone who thinks complicated decisions are best made by experts who should be materially rewarded for their expertise will opt for central planning. In either case, according to most economists, these are the only feasible allocation procedures. We claim this "impossibility theorem" is little more than self-serving prejudice and to prove it we have described how consumers and producers could participate cooperatively in planning and coordinating their joint endeavors—without central planning and without markets.

Can people take control over their own lives, care for one another, and act to enhance their own situations and the situations of their fellow citizens? Can we have an allocation system that promotes solidarity by providing information necessary for people to empathize with one another and by creating a context in which people have not only the means to consider one another's circumstances but also the incentive to do so? Can we have an allocation system that promotes variety at the same time that it creates balanced job complexes and egalitarian consumption opportunities? Can we have an allocation system that promotes collective self-management by permitting every worker and consumer to propose and revise her/his activities? Can we develop an allocation system that promotes equity rather than class division and hierarchy?

Other economists deny that all this is possible but advocates of parecon believe economic activity can be made equitable by ensuring that desirable and undesirable tasks are shared equally. Fulfilling and rote work can be mixed to create equitable work complexes. Consumption bundles can be balanced to ensure equal access to consumption opportunities. And decision-making authority can be assigned in proportion to how decisions affect people. Ironically, deep prejudices based on years of experience in oppressive circumstances make seeing that all this is possible the most difficult step in achieving a better economy. Those who hesitate to undertake the tasks of designing such an economy do so not because the tasks are so difficult, but because doing so challenges ingrained prejudices and undermines elite interests.

At any rate, after reading this far, hopefully you agree that participatory economics is a well-conceived system which could be implemented and which would enhance equity, diversity, solidarity, and self-management. The big question, however, is whether we have overlooked some criticisms regarding these aims or whether parecon would have deleterious affects on other values people hold dear which would dramatically offset its virtues.

We assumed many chapters ago that our choice of guiding criteria would suffice to define a truly inspiring and desirable economy. But were our guiding values as well chosen, as we claimed so that having met our goals, other problems will prove minor? For example, what if parecon is wasteful or doesn't elicit sufficient effort to attain acceptable levels of productivity or yields damning reductions on output for other reasons? Or what if it stifles creativity? Or obstructs merit? Or prevents serendipitous discovery? Or what if it eliminates privacy, or makes our lives too frenzied by imposing excessive responsibilities? Or what if it disorients economic attention by exaggerating the importance of individuals as compared to collectives, or vice versa? Or what if it sacrifices quality, produces chaos, or is ecologically unsustainable? Or what if it conflicts with other non-economic institutions that we desire, or is too dull to inspire support, or is impossible to attain?

Any of these problems might outweigh the virtues built into parecon and cause a potential supporter to decide that while parecon is in many respects better than capitalism (or market or centrally planned coordinatorism or bioregionalism), in some respects parecon it is so much worse that it would have to be rejected. Given that possibility, we need to address each possible criticism in turn as our focus for the remainder of this book.

14

Efficiency

Do Parecon's Incentives Motivate Optimally?

Thus capitalism drives the employers to do their worst to the employed, and
the employed to do the least for them. And it boasts all the time of the
incentive it provides to both to do their best! You may ask why this does not
end in a deadlock. The answer is it is producing deadlocks twice a day or
thereabouts. The reason the capitalist system has worked so far without
jamming for more than a few months at a time, and then only in places, is
that it has not yet succeeded in making a conquest of human nature so
complete that everybody acts on strictly business principles.
— George Bernard Shaw

Efficiency means not wasting assets even as we pursue desirable
ends. In economics, we do not want institutional arrangements that
squander resources, time, labor, talents, or any other assets used to
produce outputs to enhance people's lives. That doesn't mean we
want to exploit all assets mercilessly with no concern for the values
we hold dear. It means we want to meet needs, develop potentials,
and foster preferred values, and also avoid wasting assets.

The dictionary tell us an incentive is "something, such as the fear
of punishment or the expectation of reward, that induces action or
motivates effort." The linkage between not wasting assets and good
incentives is simple. The threat or reward of incentives is precisely
meant to induce behaviors that utilize assets appropriately.
Incentives contribute to the extent outcomes are efficient or not.

Even among those who accept that rewarding effort/sacrifice is
morally superior to other alternatives, many might reasonably
wonder if there is an unfortunate trade-off between rewarding effort
to attain equity and having appropriate incentives to attain
efficiency. Is this a trade-off that we must navigate by adopting a
reasonable system of rewards that strikes some kind of
compromise? Does parecon do that? Do we need to moderate our
desire to reward only effort/sacrifice by incorporating other
incentives that less admirably promote our equity values but that
better motivate laboring activities to avoid wasting assets?

The question is fair but a little surprising because it turns out
that the case for rewarding only effort/sacrifice on efficiency

grounds is, if anything, more straightforward than the case for rewarding only effort/sacrifice on grounds of equity or morality.

Differences in productive outcomes arise from differences in talent, training, job placement, tools, luck, and effort/sacrifice. Once we clarify that "effort" includes personal sacrifices incurred in training, and assuming training is undertaken at public rather than private expense, the only one of these factors influencing performance over which a person has any individual discretion is his or her own effort. By definition, a person cannot enlarge his or her innate talent or luck to get a reward. Rewarding the occupant of a job for the contribution inherent in the job itself or for the good tools employed in that job also does not enhance the occupant's performance, so long as productive jobs and good tools are promoted by the economy more generally. Thus the only factor we need to reward to enhance individuals' performance is their effort/sacrifice. This claim certainly turns common wisdom on its head. As we revisit below, not only is rewarding only effort/sacrifice consistent with efficiency (assuming appropriate accompanying methods exist to elicit good allocation of energies and tools and so on), but rewarding either talent, training incurred at public expense, job placement, or tools has no positive incentive effects. These rewards are literally wasted. We cannot change our genetic endowment because someone offers us a salary incentive for our output, nor can we change our luck, nor the quality of our workmates, nor the tools available.

As a practical example, in a very inexact but nonetheless revealing analogy, suppose we wanted to induce the fastest race we could from runners in a marathon. Our goal is to get everyone in the race to run as fast as possible. Should prizes be awarded according to outcome, rewarding those who go fastest the most, and so on, down to those who go slowest, or according to effort, perhaps by examining improvements in personal best times?

Rewarding outcome provides no incentive for poor runners with no chance of finishing "in the money" and no incentive for a clearly superior runner to run faster than necessary to finish first. In fact, no one has any incentive to go much faster than the person they are barely beating, assuming they cannot beat the person finishing ahead of them. On the other hand, paying in accord with improvements in personal best time—that is, paying in accordance with effort as measured by this index—gives everyone an incentive to run as fast as they can and in that way produces the fastest overall time. So why, we might wonder, do so many people believe that seeking equity by rewarding only effort/sacrifice conflicts with attaining efficiency and productivity? Three reasons typically arise:

1   People tend to believe that if consumption opportunities are equal other than for differences in effort expended, people will have no reason to work up to their full talents or capabilities.

2   If payment is equal for equal effort, there is no incentive for people to train themselves to be most socially valuable.

3   Effort is difficult to measure accurately, while outcome is not, so rewarding performance is the practical option.

Responding to reason one, in situations where solidarity or pride in one's work is insufficient to elicit effort without reward, and where greater consumption opportunities are the only effective rewards, it will be inefficient to award equal consumption opportunities to those exerting unequal effort. That much is correct. But that is not what we have proposed. We do not rule out correlating consumption opportunities with effort/sacrifice made at work, but precisely the opposite. The parecon approach is that everyone should have a right to roughly equal consumption opportunities because the parecon vision of production is that all should exert roughly equal effort/sacrifice in work. To the extent job complexes are balanced so no one is required to make greater personal work sacrifices than anyone else, effort is largely equalized and therefore consumption should be largely equalized as well. But this is not to say that variations cannot occur. Individual variations of effort and therefore consumption are perfectly acceptable and anticipated in a participatory economy. People can choose to work harder or longer, or perhaps to take up some onerous tasks that have not been allotted but need doing. Alternatively, people can choose to work less hard or less long to earn less. In short, people can work less and consume less, or work more and consume more, in each case in proportion to the effort/sacrifice involved.

But if there is no sky to reach for, you may be asking—if there is no vast advantage in consumption opportunities to be sought and won—will people lift their arms to work at all? It is one thing to say it is morally proper to remunerate only effort/sacrifice. It is another to say that doing so will elicit enough effort to yield efficient productivity. Would effort incentives elicit efficient productivity?

In a society that makes every attempt to deprecate the esteem that derives from anything other than conspicuous consumption, we shouldn't be surprised that many people feel that great income differentials are necessary to induce effort. But to assume that only the accumulation of disproportionate consumption opportunities can motivate people because under capitalism we have strained to make this so is not only unwarranted, it is self-deceptive. In the first place, very few people attain conspicuous consumption in modern capitalist societies. And those that do not are, for the most part, among the hardest working in the level of effort/sacrifice expended. Normal working people currently work hard in order to live at a modest level of income, not to consume conspicuously. People can therefore obviously be moved to exert effort and endure sacrifice, even sacrifices greater than they ought to have to put up with, for reasons other than a desire for immense personal wealth. Moreover, family members make sacrifices for one another without the slightest thought of material gain. Patriots die to defend their country's sovereignty. And there is good reason to believe that for non-pathological people wealth is generally coveted overwhelmingly as a means of attaining other ends such as economic security, comfort, useful artifacts for pursuit of desirable hobbies, social esteem, respect, status, or power. If economic security is guaranteed, as in a parecon, there will be no need to accumulate excessively in the present out of fear for the future.

We need not debate the point at length, but wish merely to note that if accumulating disproportionate consumption opportunities is often a means of achieving the more fundamental non-material rewards, as we believe, then there is every reason to believe a powerful system of incentives need not be based on widely disparate consumption opportunities. If expertise and excellence are accorded social recognition directly, there will be no need to employ the intermediary device of conspicuous consumption to get people to engage in areas of work where their talents are best displayed. If people participate in making decisions, as in a parecon, they will be more likely to carry out their responsibilities without recourse to excessive external motivation. If the allocation of duties, responsibilities, sacrifices, and rewards is fair, and is seen to be fair, as in a parecon, one's sense of social duty will be a more powerful incentive than it is today. And if a fair share of effort/sacrifice is in any event demanded by workmates who must otherwise pick up the slack, and additional effort/sacrifice are appreciated by one's companions, recognized by society, and also awarded commensurate increases in consumption opportunities, why should anyone doubt that incentives will more than adequately elicit needed involvement and effort? The fact that there won't be motivation to undertake excessive production for useless or egotistical ends would be a gain, not a loss.

But what about reason two? What incentive will people have to train themselves in the ways they can be most socially valuable if remuneration is only for effort/sacrifice, not output?

Since Mozart could contribute more by composing than being an engineer, it would have been inefficient for society in terms of lost potentials had he studied engineering. And if Salieri would have made an even worse engineer than composer, the same holds true for him. Society benefits in accruing more valuable products if people develop the talents in which they have comparative advantages, and this means society benefits if its incentive systems facilitate rather than obstruct this outcome. If Mozart would be inclined to pursue engineering over composing by preference, it would be desirable that society provide enough incentives for him to compose concertos rather than design bridges so that he would happily follow that path. But the query embodied in issue two is how will a parecon do that if by composing Mozart would get the same rate of pay for the same effort/sacrifice as he would for designing bridges? Won't we lose out on the remarkable compositions we could get from someone with the innate talents of a Mozart, with society suffering thereby?

First, there is good reason to believe that people generally prefer to train in areas where they have more talent and inclination rather than less—unless there is a very powerful incentive to do otherwise. Does anyone truly think that offered the same pay for using a lathe or a piano, Mozart would choose the lathe unless someone threatened convincingly to make his life utterly miserable were he to opt for the piano? In other words, in most instances, incentives are not even needed to get people to utilize their greatest talents, we just have to avoid disincentives, and there are no such disincentives in a participatory economy. Those who could become wonderful composers, playwrights, musicians, and actors (or dentists, doctors, engineers, scientists, or what have you), will not pursue other avenues of work in which they are less apt to excel in pursuit of greater material reward because there is no greater material reward elsewhere. Nor will people in a parecon shun training that requires greater personal sacrifice since this component of effort will be fully compensated. Second, for those cases where a little extra benefit of some sort would be needed to propel a person into his or her most productive pursuits, a parecon increases direct social recognition of excellence as compared to other economies. In a participatory economy, indeed, the best, and in some sense, the only way to earn social esteem related to one's economic activity is to make notable contributions to others' well-being through one's efforts. Since working in accord with one's talents can best do this, there are powerful incentives to develop innate talents. The only thing a parecon prohibits is paying ransoms to superstars. Instead, a parecon employs direct social recognition and thereby avoids violations of our deeply held values. Will some prospective Mozart or Einstein, knowing their potential, opt to become an engineer or a violinist rather than a composer or physicist? It could happen, but it seems unlikely. Would this happen more frequently than in class-divided economic systems which squash most people's talents due to imposing on people harsh poverty and robbing them of dignity and confidence? To ask is to answer. Not to mention that in capitalism many people with great potential squander their talents anyway by opting for the huge rewards they can gain from doing things like becoming a corporate lawyer whose main function is to help big firms avoid paying taxes—an outcome that is socially harmful, though of course beneficial to those with money.

What about reason three, the difficulty of measuring effort as compared to performance? While economic textbooks speak blithely of marginal revenue product in infinitely substitutable models, the real world of social endeavors rarely cooperates. There are many situations where assigning responsibility for outcome is ambiguous, and where determining who really contributed what to output is effectively unknown. As those who have attempted to calibrate contributions to team performance can testify, there are some situations where it is easier than others. Sports teams are certainly more suited to such calibration than production teams. But even there it is more difficult to calibrate individual contributions in football and basketball than in baseball. And even in baseball, arguably the easiest case of all, there are never ending debates over different ways of measuring direct contributions to victory in individual games, not to mention the difficulty of assessing a player's impact on team chemistry.

Nor is measuring effort always so difficult. Anyone who has taught and graded students knows there are two different ways—at least—to proceed. Students' performances can be compared to each other (output), or to an estimate of how well the student could have been expected to do (effort). Admitting the possibility of grading at least in part according to personal improvement (grades are not, in fact, rewards, but also measure absolute attainment as in mastery of some subject matter) is tantamount to recognizing that teachers can, if they choose, measure effort—and they can do it even though they are not in the dorm rooms of their students, monitoring their hours of study.

Now consider your workmates. They not only know your past productivity, which means they can compare your efforts to your past by comparing its product, they can actually see you exert each day. So co-workers are in a far better position to judge each person's effort than a teacher is able to judge the effort of students. Indeed, who is in a better position to know if someone is only giving the appearance of trying than people working with him or her in the same kind of labors? It is actually not only more just to remunerate effort/sacrifice than output for all the reasons we have explored, but particularly in an economy with balanced job complexes, it is actually quite a bit easier. Errors will by definition be much smaller. Methods can be, and in a parecon would be, democratic and mutually acceptable. Entanglement of effects and factors is not a problem. And it is not nearly so easy to pull the wool over the eye's of one's workmates as it is to do so with a supervisor, as people do today.

15

Productivity

A Destructive Labor/Leisure Trade off?

> I would rather have roses on my table
> than diamonds on my neck.
> — Emma Goldman

One might admire the moral and logical structure of participatory economics, and even the incentive structure of its remuneration scheme, yet nonetheless still have fears about parecon's output being too low. Chapter 14 addressed critical dimensions of productivity, but one issue that some critics have emphasized still remains. Will parecon lead to a steadily declining output or even to stagnation and decay due to people choosing to work too few hours?

The concern is not as odd as it might seem. In a parecon it is true that people self-consciously decide the labor/leisure trade off and do so free from compulsion. That is, in each new planning period each person has two priority decisions.

1 How much, overall, do they want to consume?

2 How much, overall, do they want to work?

These two decisions are connected in that the sum total work in an economy creates the sum total output. In turn, the sum total output determines the average consumption per capita. We each consume that average tweaked in accord with our effort/sacrifice rating. It follows that to consume more either I must work more or harder than average, or the average amount that everyone consumes must rise. Thus, aside from any increases in productivity gained from technical or social innovations, if I wish to consume more, I need to work more, pure and simple. And so, as one of their largest choices, all society's actors in the participatory planning process decide their own level of work and simultaneously the average level of work and overall productive output and thus the average consumption bundle across the economy. And not only do I have to work more if I want to consume more, but, if I wish to work less, then I will consume less.

The productivity complaint is therefore that people will collectively work many fewer hours in a parecon than in capitalist economies, and total output will drop compared to what it would have been had people worked longer hours or more intensely. The complaint is likely correct, we think, in that people will probably reduce the average time and intensity they work in a participatory economy as compared to that which they endure in a technologically comparable capitalist economy. But is this alteration worthy of complaint or compliment? It is tempting to answer snidely and leave it at that: Presumably, we should also oppose unions because under their influence workers went from ten-hour days to eight-hour days. Indeed, perhaps we should look back on the twelve-hour day sweatshops of the early Industrial Revolution era as a near utopia. But, setting aside this easy reply, let's explore further.

The sense in which the purported complaint is instead a compliment ought to be clear enough. The complaint highlights that parecon is more democratic than existing economies. In a market system more work is compelled even if literally everyone would prefer to slow down. Competition demands that each workplace maximize profits. But profits go up when employees work longer and more intensely. Owners and managers therefore seek to compel, cajole, entice, or otherwise generate longer and more intense work by employees, and endure similar pressures themselves, even if their personal preferences run in the opposite direction. Marx described this central attribute of markets with the pithy admonition that for capitalists their drive was to "accumulate, accumulate, that is Moses and the Prophets." Juliet Schor in her book on work and leisure in America provides an instructive indicator. Considering the US from the period after WWII—the golden age of capitalism—to the end of the twentieth century, Schor notes that per-capita output approximately doubled. She points out that an important decision should have been made in conjunction with that increase in productive capability. That is, should we maintain or even expand the work week to enjoy the much bigger social product that increased productivity made possible? Or should we retain the per capita output level of the 1950s, using the increase in productivity per hour to reduce the work week by establishing a schedule of working one week on and one week off, or working just two and a half days a week, or a month or a year on and a month or a year off, with no reduction in overall output per person. You do not have to decide which option you prefer to note that in fact no such democratic decision ever took place because the issue never arose. The market ensured that work pace and workload climbed as high as they could without causing the system to reach a breaking point.

It is the market itself and not a conscious collective and free choice that yielded the outcome. So the sense in which the complaint about parecon's citizens making a work/leisure choice that diminishes output is a compliment is that in the transition from markets to participatory planning we recapture conscious social control over determining what labor/leisure trade-off we prefer, rather than having market competition impose on us a singular and very debilitating outcome.

But then what is the complaint part of the observation? Presumably it is that humanity will make this labor/leisure trade-off choice stupidly. In other words, given that parecon permits us to choose between labor and leisure, we will opt to work so little that the fall in output will be horribly damaging to the economy as a whole. Either we will not produce enough to have pleasurable lives now—and will not realize that we can rectify that by working more—or, more subtly, while we may ourselves do fine in the short run, future generations will suffer dramatically compared to what might have been with more labor expended on our part today.

The first half of this logic is not worth serious discussion. It says that given the democratic choice between labor and leisure we will conduct ourselves so moronically that we will starve our stomachs on behalf of our time off, making ourselves suffer more from the hunger than we benefit from the leisure. We need to be compelled— this argument believes—by some outside agency, to work sufficiently to have even the level of short-term consumption that we ourselves desire in order to be presently fulfilled. Even without noting the change in quality of work time and circumstances that a parecon brings, and thus the improvement in work rather than its further debasement, as well as the improved relevance of output to human well-being and development as compared to enhancing firstly profit for the few as under capitalism, this humans-are-idiots logic cannot be at the root of a serious productivity complaint.

But the second half of the logic is more disturbing. Consider ancient Egypt, that is, in 4,000 BC or so. At its outset, Egyptian society was remarkable in many respects relative to others at the time, but over a period of roughly 4,000 years it was overwhelmingly stagnant. Life was essentially the same for each new generation as in the past, with little application of human insight to creating new conditions better than those enjoyed by one's parents, or grandparents, or even great great (and repeat that word great 100 times or more) grandparents. The lack of change in ancient Egypt is literally mind-numbing in its scale. For a comparison, in 1900 the average life expectancy in the US was approximately 45, and in 2000 75, and we had gone from just a few people having barely functional telephones to omnipresent high-tech labor-saving and sensory enhancing tools throughout society. Of course the lack of change in Egypt had nothing to do with a labor/leisure trade-off since most people worked horribly long proportions of their bitterly short lives, but it does show at least the possibility of the condition of large-scale and enduring stagnation that parecon's critics fear. That is, the complaint's supposed dreaded condition, stagnation, is not impossible in real historical situations. In fact, it existed for most of human history so we must take seriously the accusation that stagnation could arise again with transition to a parecon. So would parecon be stagnant or not?

The complaint assumes that without the compulsion of competition to propel productivity, humanity will fail to recognize the benefits of increasing output, seeing only the debits of increased workloads. This is an assumption, and a poor one at that. First, work is part of what makes us fulfilled humans. We do it not only to meet immediate needs, but also to express potentials and to open new future opportunities. In parecon, there will be people whose work is to focus on innovation via investment. They will not earn if they do not work, with duties that would include clarifying the benefits of innovations to society to induce willingness among people to undertake them.

Most people under capitalism hate their jobs—and with good reason. But some auto workers who hate their jobs enjoy working on their cars after hours; some people with deadening careers serve in the local volunteer fire department. People don't mind work—it gives their lives meaning—what they hate is alienated labor. And jobs in parecon are designed precisely to minimize the alienation of labor and maximize creative and empowering work. Moreover, do parents not understand that the lives of their children will be improved by contemporary investments and will they not, therefore, allot some of their energies to improving future prospects? Consider how parents now choose to spend their meager incomes as between their own pleasures and those of their children. Is it remotely plausible that with improved conditions of work, improved dignity at work, improved quality of life from the products of work which are justly distributed, and greatly enhanced educational opportunities turning us all into confident agents and decision-makers, that we should decide not only to work less—which is reasonable enough—but, year in and year out, to work so much less that we and our children will suffer because of the choice? Is this a serious prospect at all, much less one that should cause us to doubt the desirability of replacing markets with participatory planning as a means to increase equity, solidarity, diversity, and in particular self-management?

Everyone has to decide for themselves, of course, but consider Schor's example mentioned earlier. Suppose in 1955 the US had adopted a participatory economy. What would have been the impact on total volume of work and output—and derivatively on progress—even ignoring other benefits? The quality of work for 80 percent of the workforce would have improved greatly. Waste production of all kinds would have diminished and disappeared. Needless and excessive production would have disappeared as well. Innovations would have aimed at bettering the quality of work and consumption, not maximizing profit. And then there would have been the reductions in military, advertising, and luxury expenditures, and the gains in education and talent thereby made available for scientific, engineering, artistic, aesthetic, and other advances. So let's call the total output in 1955 Y. What would have happened in the 40 years after WWII if we assume a parecon rather than a capitalist economy? Productivity per person would have doubled in our hypothetical example (though in reality it would do much better, not least because of increased creativity and talent devoted to the issue, but also because instead of innovation aiming at profit it would aim directly at fulfillment). As well, there would have been more public goods, of course. Less output need have been devoted to cleaning up pollution and curing socially caused diseases and to managing resistant workers, because all these adverse features would have been diminished or eliminated. Less would have gone into advertising to sell goods for reasons that have nothing to do with benefitting those who buy them because there would no longer have been any interest in doing that. Less would have gone to projecting military power, and to providing luxuries to the rich, and to incarcerating the poor, for similar reasons. This would all have occurred, in other words, because there would have been less pollution since we would have assigned proper values to external effects, fewer conditions that sicken citizens for the same reason, no managers above workers or workers below managers due to parecon's balanced job complexes, no incentive to produce and distribute other than to meet real needs, no accumulation compulsions, no world to subjugate in order to profit by ripping off resources and energies from other countries, no rich to luxuriate, no poor forced to steal, and so on. The point is, in addition to per-capita productivity doubling (or more) in the forty years in question, since much of Y in 1955 had nothing to do with human well-being in the first place and would have been replaced by new outputs that do benefit human well-being, not only would output per person have doubled due to technical innovations, but the relevance of output to fulfillment would have also gone dramatically upward, let's say, very conservatively, by another 25 percent due to useless and pointless and even destructive production being removed, and desirable production put in its place. With just distribution it then would follow that the population could have opted to work in 1995 not only half as long as in 1955, as Schor suggested, but a bit more than a third as long, and still have the same per capita output relevant to meeting real needs and to expanding worthy potentials. At the same time, investment in innovation could have gone on all along at the same rate it did in 1955 under capitalism. So the workweek could go from 40 hours to about 13, in that scenario, over a run of 40 years, with no loss in fulfillment or in output earmarked to engender socially beneficial progress. Does anyone think that humanity is so blindingly lazy that it would opt to cut back work that is no longer alienated even that far, much less to cut it back still further? Isn't it far more plausible that humanity would, in fact, opt for a lesser cutback, say from 40 to 30 or perhaps 25 hours, with, as well, a considerable number of those saved hours going to highly productive hobbies, volunteer pursuits, and self-education? In short, looked at in full context, the productivity complaint is not a serious one, but instead a compliment in disguise.

16

Creativity / Quality

Does Parecon Sacrifice Talent?
Does It Subordinate Quality To Equity

Between persons of equal income there is no social distinction except the distinction of merit. Money is nothing: character, conduct, and capacity are everything. Instead of all the workers being leveled down to low wage standards and all the rich leveled up to fashionable income standards, everybody under a system of equal incomes would find her and his own natural level. There would be great people and ordinary people and little people; but the great would always be those who have done great things, and never the idiots whose mothers had spoiled them and whose fathers had left them a hundred thousand a year; and the little would be persons of small minds and mean characters, and not poor persons who had never had a chance. That is why idiots are always in favor of inequality of income (their only chance of eminence), and the really great in favour of equality.
— George Bernard Shaw

In our experience, every time participatory economics is described, musicians, writers, painters, performers, playwrights, actors, dancers, and many other creative artists raise a ruckus. This sector of workers feels immediately profoundly threatened. They worry that parecon will sacrifice the benefits of talent, or, even worse, will mistreat the talented, particularly in the realm of art and creative expression. We need to address their concerns.

Parecon takes for granted and celebrates the fact that different people have different inclinations and capacities in a very wide range of ways. Some are artistic, some not. Some are mathematical, some not. Some have great bodily coordination or strength, some not. And even among people with special competence in any one area—say some particular mathematical facility, music composing abilities, or whatever else—there will be a wide range of abilities. There are Einsteins and mediocre physicists, Mozarts and mediocre composers. Additionally, there is no cause to be upset by any of this variation. Diversity of orientation and talent means life is far more varied and rich than it would otherwise be. We all benefit from the existence of diverse talents and ranges of talent, both because we can enjoy its products and vicariously enjoy the processes as well.

We contend that parecon celebrates and creates a context conducive to the full discovery and development of diverse talents— not solely in a few lucky people born "well," but in everyone, and not solely where the talent can yield profits for elites but wherever it can have social benefit. At the same time, by its remuneration norms and balanced job complexes, parecon precludes such differences in talents from imposing hierarchies of power or wealth that corrupt sociality. We get to have our cake baked, and baked to perfection, and we get to eat it, and we suffer no nasty side effects.

Musicians, writers, and other artists of diverse kinds have two different negative reactions to parecon. One is no different from a reaction that a surgeon, lawyer, professor, or engineer might have (or a professional athlete, for that matter). That is, they say "wait a minute, you are saying I will have to do my fair share of more onerous work, and I would rather not." This is an understandable but unworthy sentiment. It is like capitalists saying, "wait a minute, you are implying that I must forego my golden-egg machine, my ownership." Correct. Parecon says both that owners must forego their ownership and that coordinator class members must forego their monopoly on empowering work and take on a balanced job complex, and we have argued at length why—for example, to remove class division, to attain equity, to allow and promote self-management, and so on.

A different concern of artists, often mingled with the above class defensiveness, is that somehow they will not be allowed to engage in artistic pursuits at all, or at least as they prefer, even if they are happy to work in a balanced job complex, which many artists already largely do, by the way, cleaning up for themselves, preparing their tools, and so on. Their worry is that the participatory economy will decide that music or video or movies or art or whatever else should not be produced other than in cases where there is a great immediate public demand for it. They worry that experimentation, exploration, and investigation of new avenues that are initially not widely understood, much less appreciated, will be ruled out in a parecon. But this concern is unwarranted, for artists and others too.

Consider people who produce bicycles or who do surgery. If they could not experiment with new designs and methods, we would never get new features on bicycles or new surgical procedures. And it is the same for making computers or conceiving tools for building houses, software, or furniture. Progress in any domain, not just art, requires not only innovative thinking, but the opportunity for it to be discovered, refined, tested, implemented, and appreciated.

Likewise, innovations in bicycles or in surgery do not have to be only for all riders or for everyone who needs an operation to be worth pursuing or adopting. There could be an innovation that greatly benefits a small number of people that most other people don't utilize at all but that is worth pursuing, of course, if the social benefit that the few gain is more than the social cost of the innovation.

No one encountering a description of parecon worries that bicycle workers or surgeons will be precluded from thinking about how to make advances in their fields under a parecon. This is just a part of each job. Of course a bicycle worker who has an idea for an innovation doesn't automatically get to spend a lot of time pursuing it at work, nor does a surgeon, for that matter. If others in the field think it is nonsense and refuse to respect the undertaking, the person with the idea may have to pursue it in spare time or sometimes not at all. But even though everyone knows this can sometimes lead to errors, everyone also knows it is a very sensible approach. Who better to judge whether an innovative idea deserves support than others in the same field, especially given the shared motivations and institutional context?

What is different about artists, one wonders? In a word, the answer is, however surprising to some it may be, nothing.

Consider video, literary, or any other type of artistic work in artistic workplaces. It could be schools. It could be conservatories. The artists and others involved—film makers, painters, whatever—would have councils, like other workers, and of course they would undertake balanced job complexes. They would get effort ratings. If they needed inputs, new equipment, or whatever else, the requests would be part of their workplace plan.

Will a musician be kept on as an employee if he or she wishes to pursue some unusual idea? Unless it is lame-brained, why not? Why should we be confident of this? Because not only the artist's fellow artists but the whole population has no trouble understanding the desirability of wide-ranging artistic exploration.

The problem many artists have with parecon is an odd kind of projection. They project from the current situation—where there are right-wing and profit-seeking sponsors who undeniably bend artistic endeavor to commercial ends and subordinate it to narrow tastes—to parecon, where decisions would be made by their fellow artistic workers and the broad public in a context that would lack such commercial drives, profit-seeking, and narrow-minded conformist ignorance. The concern is misguided, as we conclude from all the experience and reason we have.

But let's suppose, against all contrary argument, that there is some truth here. Suppose that in exchange for security, respect, classlessness, an end to subordination to profit, a redirection of production and consumption—some excellent and deserving artists sometimes have to pursue their creative dreams in their off-hours because they cannot get their fellow artists and consumers to recognize that their ideas are socially/aesthetically worthy. Even in this unlikely eventuality, we are, at worst, on this score and this score alone, back to where we have typically been in capitalist and otherwise hierarchically organized societies all along.

It is therefore hard to see how it can be even a slight, much less a serious problem to trade from a system where profit-seeking capitalists arbitrate what art is worthy, to a system in which fellow artists and consumers are the judges. And the same broad analysis as for artists holds, by the way, for innovative mathematicians, or for special athletes, and so on.

Parecon fosters quality and justice for humanity via balanced job complexes plus remuneration for effort and sacrifice for socially valued productive labor. In other words, parecon does not pursue equity by trying to attain a common denominator of accomplishment. Quite the opposite, parecon promotes the fullest possible development and utilization of diverse talents in creating the richest and most diverse art attainable, but it also preserves equity of remuneration and circumstances, as well as self-management. Each of these aims, we might add, is essential to maintaining an environment in which artists can best express themselves and the public can best appreciate their labors.

17

Meritocracy / Innovation

Does Excellence Get Its Due?
Is Progress an Important Product?

Surely there never was such a fragile china-ware as that of which the millers of Coketown were made. Handle them ever so lightly, and they fell to pieces with such ease that you might suspect them of having been flawed before. They were ruined, when they were required to send labouring children to school; they were ruined, when inspectors were appointed to look into their works; they were ruined when such inspectors considered it doubtful whether they were quite justified in chopping people up with their machinery; they were utterly undone, when it was hinted that perhaps they need not always make quite so much smoke. Whenever a Coketowner felt he was ill-used – that is to say, whenever he was not left entirely alone, and it was proposed to hold him accountable for the consequences of any of his acts – he was sure to come out with the awful menace, that he would `sooner pitch his property into the Atlantic'. This had terrified the Home Secretary within an inch of his life, on several occasions.
— Charles Dickens

According to the dictionary, a meritocracy is "a system in which advancement is based on individual ability or achievement." The virtue is that excellence gets its due. Is parecon meritocratic? Similarly, progress depends on incorporating new means of meeting needs and expanding potentials while also expanding gains bearing on less economic values. Does parecon enhance or somehow subvert the possibilities of progress?

Merit

Of course, any system that rewards having a deed to property in one's pocket but doing nothing or that rewards having lots of bargaining power but doing nothing is not a meritocracy. But what about genetic endowment, doesn't that come under the rubric of individual ability? And what about contribution to output? Isn't one person's contribution (even if enhanced by better tools or the luck of producing something in greater rather than lesser need) part of individual achievement and merit? In our view, rewarding merit ought to mean rewarding us for what we've earned; but, as we've argued previously, good genes are no more earned than noble birth. Nevertheless, we must admit that in everyday language genes and contribution to output are considered part of merit. So if rewarding these can only mean remunerating them materially or with access to enhanced formal influence over decisions, then in that sense parecon is not a meritocracy. On the other hand if it were satisfactory to appreciate these contributions and to convey respect and thanks for them, but not to convey power or wealth for them, parecon would still qualify as a meritocracy. Since we are rebutting a criticism, we will assume the generally accepted definition of meritocracy, making the criticism correct. Is it damning?

To feel this is a serious problem for parecon, you either have to feel that individual contribution to output should be rewarded in principle and on moral grounds—which we don't, as we have argued—or that in not rewarding it, some other outcome will have a negative effect on your system so that excellence will not be sufficiently promoted by the economy and we will suffer its loss.

Parecon is designed to maximize the motivating potential of non-material incentives. There is every reason to hope jobs designed by workers will be more enjoyable than ones designed by capitalists or coordinators. There is every reason to believe people will be more willing to carry out tasks that they themselves proposed and agreed to than assignments handed them by superiors. There is also every reason to believe people will be more willing to perform unpleasant duties conscientiously when they know the distribution of those duties as well as the rewards for people's efforts are equitable.

But all this is not to say that there are no material incentives in a parecon. One's peers—who have every interest in seeing that those they work with fulfill their potentials—will rate one's efforts. No one can manifest genetic endowment or utilize advantageous tools or training without exerting effort, and the incentive to exert effort is therefore also a material incentive to manifest these, even if not as large an incentive to do so as remunerating for output would be.

It is true we do not recommend paying those with more training higher wages since we believe it would be inequitable to do so. But that does not mean people would not seek to enhance their productivity by becoming more knowledgeable. First of all, education and training would be public expenses, not private. So there are no material disincentives to pursuing education and training. Secondly, since a parecon is not an "acquisitive" society, respect, esteem, and social recognition would be based largely on "social serviceability" which is enhanced precisely by developing one's most socially useful potentials through education and training. In a parecon you do not rise in the eyes of your neighbors or peers due to owning more, but for your personal qualities and achievements. And then there is of course the simple personal inclination to do what one can do well in order to express one's greatest capacities, and enjoy the satisfactions that come from doing so. In other words, merit gets its due, appropriately.

Innovation

The same logic as evidenced above applies to innovation, which explains why we lump meritocracy and innovation in a single chapter. A parecon does not reward those who succeed in discovering productive innovations with vastly greater consumption rights than others who make equivalent personal sacrifices in work but discover nothing. Instead a parecon emphasizes direct social recognition of outstanding achievements for a variety of reasons. First, successful innovation is often the outcome of cumulative human creativity so that a single individual is rarely entirely responsible. Furthermore, an individual's contribution is often the product of genius and luck as much as diligence, persistence, and personal sacrifice, all of which implies that recognizing innovation through social esteem rather than material reward is ethically superior. Second, underneath the protestations, there is really no reason to believe that with changed institutional relations social incentives will prove less powerful than material ones. It should be recognized that no economy ever has paid or ever could pay its greatest innovators the full social value of their innovations, which means that if material compensation is the only reward, innovation will be under-stimulated in any case. Moreover, too often material reward is merely an imperfect substitute for what is truly desired: social esteem. How else can one explain why those who already have more wealth than they can ever use continue to accumulate more?

Nor do we see why critics believe there would be insufficient incentives for enterprises to seek and implement innovations, unless they measure a parecon against a mythical and misleading image of capitalism. Typically, in economic analyses of markets it is presumed that innovative capitalist enterprises capture the full benefits of their successes, while it is also assumed that innovations spread instantaneously to all enterprises in an industry. When made explicit, however, it is obvious that these assumptions are contradictory since in capitalism for a company to reap the full financial benefits of an innovation it must keep all rights to it, even secretly, yet for other companies to benefit they must have full access. Yet only if both assumptions hold can one conclude that capitalism provides maximum material stimulus to innovation and also achieves maximum technological efficiency throughout the economy. In reality, innovative capitalist enterprises temporarily capture "super profits" also called "technological rents" which are competed away more or less rapidly depending on a host of circumstances. This means that in reality there is a trade-off in market economies between stimulus to innovate and the efficient use of innovation, or a trade-off between dynamic and static efficiency. It can't be that firms monopolize their innovations, on the one hand, and that all innovations are utilized as widely in the economy as is beneficial for output and operations, on the other hand. But the former needs to occur for maximum incentive and the latter for maximum efficiency, in a market system.

In a parecon, however, workers also have a "material incentive," if you will, to implement innovations that improve the quality of their work life. This means they have an incentive to implement changes that increase the social benefits of the outputs they produce or that reduce the social costs of the inputs they consume, since anything that increases an enterprise's social-benefit-to-social-cost ratio will allow the workers to win approval for their proposal with less effort, or sacrifice, on their part. But adjustments will render any local advantage they achieve temporary. As the innovation spreads to other enterprises, indicative prices change, and work complexes are re-balanced across enterprises and industries, the full social benefits of their innovation will spread equitably to all workers and consumers.

The faster these adjustments are made, the more efficient and equitable the outcome. On the other hand, the more rapidly the adjustments are made, the less the "material incentive" (other than that afforded to the effort/sacrifice involved) to innovate locally, and the greater the incentive to coast along on others' innovations. While this is no different than under capitalism or any market arrangement, a parecon enjoys important advantages. Most important, direct recognition of social serviceability is a more powerful incentive in a participatory economy than a capitalist one, and this considerably reduces the magnitude of the trade-off. Second, a parecon is better suited to allocating resources efficiently to research and development because research and development is largely a public good which is predictably under-supplied in market economies but would not be in a parecon. Third, the only effective mechanism for providing material incentives for innovating enterprises in capitalism is to slow their spread at the expense of efficiency. This is true because the transaction costs of registering patents and negotiating licenses from patent holders are very high. Capitalist drug companies claim there is no incentive for them to develop new drugs unless they can reap vast profits by patenting their products. This may be true under market capitalism, but the patents that induce them to innovate also often keep the drugs out of the hands of those most in need, so this is hardly an efficient system. In a parecon, on the other hand, investment decisions are made democratically—so research and development will occur wherever there is a need, and no one has any incentive to keep innovations from being adopted by others—so there is maximum diffusion of new products and techniques.

Of course, in a parecon, the rules of the game are subject to democratic adjustment. If it were determined that there was inadequate incentive to innovate—which we doubt—various policies could be tweaked. For example, the recalibration of the work complexes for innovating workplaces could be delayed (to allow those workplaces to capture more of the benefit of the innovation, or extra consumption allowances could be granted to innovators for a limited period of time. Such measures would be (in our view) a last resort, but would in any event depart from equity and efficiency far less than in other economic systems, and in no systematic recurring fashion.

In general, much of what parades itself as scientific opinion about incentives is plagued by implicit and unwarranted assumptions predictable in an era of capitalist triumphalism. One should be neither as pessimistic about the motivational power of nonmaterial incentives in an appropriate environment as many people otherwise critical of injustice have become, nor should one see any obstacles to the deployment of limited material incentives specifically for innovation in a parecon should its members decide they are needed. In the end there is no reason to doubt the efficacy of a mixture of material and social incentives during the process of creating an equitable and humane economy, with the balance and mix chosen to further equity, diversity, solidarity, and self-management for all— rather than simply generating advantage for a few.

18
Privacy / Frenzy

Do Parecon's Citizens Lack a "Room of Their Own"?
Does Anyone Have Time for Anything But Economics?

People's lives are in turmoil. There is a sense of crisis for men as well as for women, and for children too. Do we have an idea or even a glimmering about how people can and should live, not as victims as in the past for women, nor as atoms just whirling around on their own trajectories, but as members of a human community and as moral agents in that community?
— Barbara Ehrenreich

Any economy on some counts is good, of course, but if it is really bad on other counts, it can lose much of its luster. Does parecon achieve equity and its other virtues by sacrificing people's privacy or by imposing unreasonable pressures on people to participate when they would rather be doing other things?

In "A Roundtable Discussion on Participatory Economics" in *Z Magazine* (July/August 1991), Nancy Folbre referred to this problem as the "tyranny of the busy-body" and the "dictatorship of the sociable." In a class my frequent co-author taught at American University, this issue came to be known as "the kinky underwear problem." Folbre also cautioned of the potential inefficiency of groups dominated by the sentiment "Let's not piss anybody off." David Levy observed in a *Dollars and Sense* (November 1991) book review that while the 1991 book on parecon that Robin Hahnel and I authored, *Looking Forward,* reminded him in some respects of Ursula LeGuin's novel *The Dispossessed* readers should be warned that LeGuin's subtitle was "An Ambiguous Utopia" because "reliance on social pressure rather than material incentives create a lack of initiative, claustrophobic conformity, and intrusiveness." In comradely private communication, radical economist Tom Weiss-kopf cautioned against "sacrificing too much individuality, specialization, diversity, and freedom of choice." What is the source of these misgivings, and how do we respond?

Parecon recognizes that economic decisions about both consumption and production affect more than the immediate consumer or producer. And parecon also asserts that those affected by decisions should have proportionate influence over them. Does this yield a situation in which everyone is so continually subordinate to oversight by others that privacy disappears? Does it empower only those who enjoy being involved in planning and making decisions and disempower those who are less socially concerned? Does it impose too many meetings and, even after reducing the work week, leave us all spending too much time hassling over economic choices?

A Busybody Economy?

For us it is important to distinguish between misgivings that any and all participatory processes may be too intrusive into people's private lives, and the criticism that particular measures which may or may not be adopted in a specific parecon are more socially intrusive than they need to be. First, let us reiterate features of our model designed to protect the citizenry from tyrannical busybodies.

Beside being free to move from one neighborhood (or job) to another, and besides being able to make consumption proposals anonymously, consumption proposals justified by one's effort rating cannot be easily vetoed. While there is always, of course, nothing but a motion to close debate or at least silence the loud mouth to prevent a busybody from carrying on uselessly about someone else's consumption request, it is difficult to understand why people would choose to waste their time expressing or listening to views that had no practical consequence. And the fact that individuals can make anonymous consumption requests if they do not wish their neighbors to know the particulars of their consumption habits keeps this from becoming a serious problem at all.

All societies have to face a tension between leaving people alone and taking care of those who need it. Should a society sponsor public service announcements pointing out the harm of cigarette smoking, for example? People with strong views will hope to persuade other people to do what they think is in their best interest even if they cannot (and would not even want to) force them to do so. In a parecon, animal-rights folks, if they live in a community with meat eaters, may get up at meetings and urge their fellows not to slaughter innocent, sentient creatures for their "Big Macs." If the meat-eaters respect others they will listen to their arguments, though perhaps ultimately reject their views. But neither side will go through this over and over, and no doubt political or economic deliberative assemblies in a parecon might establish guidelines to separate out serious issues from harassment. But the same problems exist in a capitalist democracy: I can picket outside a McDonald's denouncing meat-eating or outside a fur-coat store—or outside the Gap for selling items using child labor, even confronting buyers personally. Would we rather a society that was less intrusive even than that, and that did not permit picketers to criticize buyers and sellers at all for their choices?

Dictatorship of the Sociable

In workers' councils balancing job complexes for empowerment should alleviate one important cause of differential influence over decision-making. Rotating assignments to committees also alleviates even temporary monopolization of authority. On the other hand, we stopped short of calling for balancing consumption complexes for empowerment and refused to endorse forcing people to attend or remain at meetings longer than they found useful. An apt analogy is the saying "You can lead a horse to water, but you can't make it drink." Parecon has every intention of leading people to participate, but no doubt, some will drink more deeply from the well of participation than others, and those who do, will—other things being equal—probably influence decisions disproportionately. And likewise, folks who continually have very good ideas about decisions might have their ideas adopted more often (which is not the same, however, as having more weight in the decision-making itself—in a parecon people have proportionate say). But even those who are more sociable, or who regularly have good ideas and who as a result more often influence the views of others and thus the outcomes of decisions, would have a difficult time benefitting materially from their efforts, and the less social should suffer no material penalty as a result. In any case, while we find the complaint more amusing than worrisome, certainly even someone who agrees with its orientation would have to also agree that it would be better to have a dictatorship of the sociable with no material privileges accruing to them, than a dictatorship of the propertied, of the bureaucrats and party members, or of the better educated, all with great material privileges accruing.

We also fail to understand why parecon does not seem to all who consider it as thoroughly libertarian as we intended. People are free to apply to live and work wherever they wish, and society may have very stringent rules about rejecting people on unwarranted grounds (such as race, gender, etc.). People can ask for whatever consumption and services they desire and can distribute their consumption over their lives however they see fit. People can apply to whatever educational programs they want. Any individual or group can start a new living unit, a new consumer council, or a new worker council, with fewer barriers to overcome than in any traditional model. The only restriction is that the burdens and benefits of the division of labor be equitable. That is why people are not free to consume more than their sacrifice warrants. And that is why people are not free to work at job complexes that are more desirable or empowering than others. It may be that some chafe under these restrictions or consider them excessive. Once upon a time people chafed at the idea that slavery would be abolished and their "freedom to own slaves" eliminated. We believe the logic of justice requires the pareconish restrictions on "individual freedom" just as the logic of justice places restrictions on the freedom to profit from private ownership of productive property or of slaves.

Too Many Meetings?

It is not uncommon that when told that workers and consumers will cooperatively plan economic outcomes in their own workplaces and consumption councils as well as interactively for the whole economy, people throw up their hands and say—sure being more just, more equitable, more this and more that is nice, but not if I have to live my life in interminable meetings.

Part of the reason for this reaction may be that people are already enduring too many meetings and that the meetings people now endure are horribly alienating. Pat Devine, a radical economist from England who proposes a more mixed approach to allocation than we favor but encounters a similar complaint, reports that:

> In modern societies a large and possibly increasing proportion of overall social time is already spent on administration, on negotiation, on organizing and running systems and people. This is partly due to the growing complexity of economic and social life and the tendency for people to seek more conscious control over their lives as material, educational, and cultural standards rise. However, in existing societies much of this activity is also concerned with commercial rivalry and the management of the social conflict and consequences of alienation that stem from exploitation, oppression, inequality, and subalternity. One recent estimate has suggested that as much as half the GNP of advanced western countries may now be accounted for by transaction costs arising from increasing division of labor and the growth of alienation associated with it.

The implication of this insight is interesting. Perhaps a good economy can not only increase equity and self-management but even reduce the aggregate time devoted to running the economy, though, in Devine's trenchant words, "the aggregate time would be differently composed, differently focused, and, of course, differently distributed among people."

David Levy reviewed *Looking Forward* in *Dollars and Sense* (November 1991). He makes a similar point to Devine.

> Within [current capitalist] manufacturing firms we find echelons of managers and staff whose job it is to try to forecast demand and supply. Indeed, only a small fraction of workers directly produce goods and services. The existing system requires millions of government employees, many of whom are in jobs created precisely because the market system provides massive incentives to engage in fraud, theft, environmental destruction, and abuse of workers' health and safety. And even during our 'leisure time' we must fill in tax forms and pay bills. Critics of Looking Forward's complex planning process should examine the management of a large corporation. Large corporations are already planned economies; some have economies larger than those of small countries. These firms supplant the market for thousands of intermediate products. They coordinate vast amounts of information and intricate flows of goods and materials.

In sum, "meeting time" is far from zero in existing economies. But for a parecon we can divide the issue into meeting time in workers' councils, consumers' councils, federations, and participatory planning.

Conception, coordination, and decision-making are part of the organization of production under any system. Under hierarchical organizations of production relatively few employees spend most, if not all, of their time thinking and meeting, and most of the rest of the employees simply do as they're told (or try not to do as they are told). So it is true, most people would spend more time in workplace meetings in a parecon than in a hierarchical economy. But this is because most people are excluded from workplace decision-making under capitalism and authoritarian planning. It does not necessarily mean the total amount of time spent on thinking and meeting rather than on working would be greater in a participatory workplace. It is important to remember that in a parecon decisions are taken at appropriate levels of organization. The whole workplace doesn't meet to decide everything, of course. Rather some things are decided widely, others more narrowly, though each within a framework established at a more inclusive level. And while it might be that democratic decision-making requires somewhat more overall meeting time than autocratic decision-making, it should also be the case that a lot less time is required to enforce democratic decisions than autocratic ones. It should also be clear from our discussions of the daily circumstances and behavior in participatory workplaces that workplace meeting time is part of the normal parecon workday, not an incursion on people's leisure.

Regarding the organization of consumption, we plead guilty to suggesting that these decisions be arrived at with more social interaction than in market economies. In our view one of the great failures of market systems is that they do not provide a suitable vehicle through which people can express and coordinate their consumption desires to everyone's greater good. When you enter a five-story apartment building with no elevators and see old people on the top floors and young ones on the lower floors, when you enter a community and see huge numbers of appliances that are rarely used with the redundancy of their parallel dormancy eating up budgets and preventing people from having the wherewithal to get more fulfilling luxury items, and when you consider what can be accomplished by replacing isolated individual choices with mutually concerned collective ones, you get a feel for the material reason—in addition to the participatory and self-managing reason—for consumption councils. It is through a layered network of consumer federations that we propose overcoming alienation in public choice and the isolated expression of individual choice that characterize market systems. Whether this will take more time than the present organization of consumption will depend on a number of trade-offs, but in any event, in our view this would not be too high a price to pay.

Presently economic and political elites dominate local, state, and national public choice. For the most part they operate free from restraint by the majority, with periodic time-consuming campaigns mounted by popular organizations to rectify matters that get grossly out of hand. In a parecon people would vote directly on collective consumption issues. But this would not require a great deal of time or mean attending endless meetings. Expert testimony and differing opinions would be aired through democratic media. People would become empowered through participation, and meetings would have concrete outcomes so most people would want to participate. If it turned out that most people didn't bother to attend (like typically occurs now in union meetings) then we could conclude there was something wrong with the institutions. But still, people would be free to pay as much or as little attention as they wished.

We actually believe the amount of time and travail devoted to consumption decision-making in our model would be less than in market economies. Consumer federations could operate exhibits for people to visit before placing orders for goods that would be delivered directly to neighborhood outlets. Research and development units attached to consumer federations would not only provide better information about consumption options, but a real vehicle for translating consumer desires into product innovation. While the prospect of proposing and revising consumption proposals within neighborhood councils might appear to require significant meeting time, we tried to describe in detail how, with the aid of computers and rather simple software packages, this need not take more time than it takes people currently to prepare their tax returns and pay their bills. In any case, nobody wouldn't have to attend meetings or discuss their neighbors' opinions regarding consumption requests if they chose not to; individuals could choose whether to utilize or ignore the greater opportunities for efficient social interaction prior to registering consumption preferences; and time necessary for consumption decision-making would be treated like time necessary for production decision-making—as part of one's obligations in a parecon, not part of one's leisure time. And perhaps most intangibly, yet very importantly, the core activity of life would no longer be to "shop till you drop," including finding stores, comparing competing items with negligible differences, fighting traffic, and making purchases for reasons having little or nothing to do with real freely-developed need and desire. This might make sense in a capitalist society that curtails other options for fulfillment and lumps social intercourse and modes of attaining dignity and status overwhelmingly into market mediated consumption. But it would make no sense in any sensibly-organized society. Reducing the centrality of atomized consumption-related activities in people's lives should more than compensate for any additional time required for consumption decision-making, even ignoring other benefits.

But how much meeting time does participatory planning require? Contrary to critics' presumptions, we did not propose a model of democratic planning in which people or their elected representatives, meet face-to-face to endlessly discuss and negotiate how to coordinate all their activities. Instead we proposed a procedure in which individuals and councils submit proposals for their own activities, receive new information including new indicative prices, and submit revised proposals until they reach a point of agreement. Nor did we suggest meetings of constituents to define feasible options to be voted on. Instead we proposed that after a number of iterations had defined the major contours of the overall plan, the staffs of iteration facilitation boards would (mechanically) define a few feasible plans within those contours for constituents to vote on without ever having to meet and debate these at all. Finally, we did not propose face-to-face meetings where different groups would plead their cases for consumption or production proposals that did not meet normal quantitative standards. Instead we proposed that councils submit qualitative information as part of their proposals so that higher-level federations could grant exceptions should they choose to.

But while we do not think the criticism of "too many meetings" is warranted, we do not want to be misleading. Informed, democratic decision-making is different from autocratic decision-making. And conscious, equitable coordination of the social division of labor is different from the impersonal law of supply and demand. We obviously think the former, in each case, is greatly preferable to the latter. But this is not to say we do not understand that this requires, almost by definition, increases in meaningful social intercourse.

19

Individuals / Society

Does Parecon Over-Privilege Individuals
Above the Community Or Vice Versa?

Why should workers agree to be slaves in a basically authoritarian structure?
Why shouldn't communities have a dominant voice in running the
institutions that affect their lives?
— Noam Chomsky

Part of the complication of conceiving a good society, or any good social institutions, is the subtle relationship between individual and collective. On the one hand people are social beings. We depend on others. We influence and are influenced by one another. Our acts need to be compatible with those of others in ways that make the interaction beneficial. On the other hand, we each have our own wills and preferences and we each want room to move and choose as individuals, and even to run up against and differ from one another.

One can imagine economies that err on either side of this divide. An economy could privilege individuals and therein lose track of the need for mutuality and collectivity. It could generate actors isolated from one another and too often at odds with one another. It could cause us to fail to benefit from possible but foregone collectivity. Or an economy could privilege collectivity and therein deny individual freedom. It could subordinate each individual to overarching features that negate personal preferences. Does parecon suffer either of these ills?

Privileging Individuals?

Some have suggested that parecon overly concentrates on popular participation in small and local decisions at the expense of larger social issues. They say it privileges individual participation undervaluing the need for larger collective consistency. Since democracy is not costless to practice, we should economize on its use, they argue, while parecon overdoes democracy locally at the cost of under-attending larger issues.

Such critics are right that we should reject a model that diverts people's participatory energies from more important to more trivial issues. More, it is easy to see how a presentation of parecon that focuses on local councils and provides only summary descriptions could lead some to conclude that parecon attaches too little importance to long-term investment. But the missed reality is that parecon's procedures of participatory planning are not only appropriate for local involvements but also appropriate for long-run and large-scale involvements. The options are:

1   To relegate long-run decision-making to the vagaries of the marketplace.

2   To entrust long-run decision-making to a political and technical elite.

3   To permit councils and federations of workers and consumers to propose, revise, and reconcile the different components of long-run economic involvements.

Of course, we favor the third option, given our prioritization of self-management. Laissez-faire market systems are unarguably least appropriate for long-run development decisions. Even the terribly flawed Soviet version of central planning demonstrated important advantages over market economies in that regard. Moreover, every historical case of successful development by a late comer to the world arena has been an example of the efficacy of planning rather than laissez-faire competition. Even in predominately market economies, a cursory look shows that a huge proportion of long-run production takes place under the purview of the state including most high tech innovation in the US, or of massive private institutions operating more or less in the manner of the state, which is to say, employing planning.

If we reject the vagaries of the marketplace for long-run decision-making, of course, if a political and technocratic elite is not chosen democratically, the dangers are obvious. But even supposing we chose those who we opted to entrust to conceive and negotiate a long-term plan democratically, there would be less room for popular participation and less resemblance to real self-management than under participatory planning. Since we agree with those worried about over-privileging the local that choosing between transforming coal mining to dramatically improve health and safety and replacing highway travel with a high-speed rail system or transforming agriculture to conform to ecological norms vitally impacts people's lives, we also agree that popular participation should be maximized in these matters just as in deciding daily consumption options.

So, as always, the issue comes down to how can ordinary people best become involved in decision-making? In our view the federations of coal miners, rail workers, automobile makers, and agricultural workers, and the transportation, food, and environment departments of the national federation of consumers should all play a prominent role in formulating, analyzing, and comparing long-run options like those mentioned above. In parecon, the skilled staffs of iteration facilitation boards and skilled workers in R&D units working directly for involved federations would play an active role in proposing long-term options. But the main point is, in parecon with the aid of accurate indications of social costs and benefits, workers and consumers, through their councils and federations of councils, can decide long-term planning just as they can decide annual planning and manage their own work and consumption. Large-scale and small-scale decisions are treated the same. The former is certainly not subordinated to the latter.

Over-Privileging Society?

Just as an economy could overlook the global in seeking to address the local, an economy could also do the reverse, subordinating individuals to a stifling national conformity and regulation. Does a parecon have this failing?

It is hard for us to credit this criticism seriously. Parecon, after all, affords each individual as much freedom as one can imagine short of trampling on the comparable freedom of others. Nonetheless there is a sense in which this concern arises, in particular, for some anarchist critics—ironically so, given that parecon is basically an anarchistic economic vision that eliminates fixed hierarchy and delivers self-management.

Still, for some anarchists the whole idea of institutions or even of society itself is an irritant. Their justified and appropriate anger at structures that subordinate most people's human potential to the elite advantage of a few somehow extrapolates into the feeling that institutions *per se* are oppressive. In this view, parecon is too social precisely because it has institutions like councils and balanced job complexes, with specific structures and roles. One either plays by parecon's rules or suffers exclusion, they feel—which is true enough—and they find this oppressive.

Such critics, in our opinions, overstate the extent to which we privilege society. But beyond that, they feel that it is a mark of the underdevelopment of human possibilities to have institutions at all. For them, every encounter, every interaction, should be free of prior assumptions, and thus there should be no lasting norms, rules, or roles, but only spontaneous generation of always new and utterly free relationships. For us, however, this is just taking the atomization of humanity to its ultimate debilitating conclusion and making believe that the antisocial result is in fact wholesome.

Humans are social. To fulfill functions, meet needs, and expand possibilities, we interact and mesh our choices. We enhance what each of us can contribute by interlinking what all of us undertake. It is true that having lasting expectations about one another's activities in the form of lasting social institutions can reveal a humanity that is not yet freed—as in our subordination to markets, private ownership, or other oppressive structures—but lasting social institutions can also reveal a humanity meshing its individual and social sides seamlessly, to the advantage of each. The solution to bad institutions is not no institutions, but good institutions.

If parecon has institutions that enhance sociality, get needed functions done, further preferred values, and uplift human possibilities, that's good. If parecon instead narrows our options, that is not good. But that there are institutions at all can't be taken as a sign of failing. It is, instead, merely a sign that humans are present.

Parecon enlarges rather than restricts human possibilities. It rules out the choice to be a wage slave, to have an unbalanced job complex, and to wield disproportionate decision-making influence. But in doing so parecon creates a context suitable to the freest and fullest elaboration of each person's potentials and aspirations subject only to the constraint that others enjoy the same range of possibilities.

20

Participatory?

Is Participatory Planning New, Or Is It Just Another Name for a Mix of Markets and Central Planning?

In 1806 Pfuel had been one of those responsible for the plan of campaign that ended in Jena and Auerstadt, but he did not see the least proof of the fallibility of his theory in the disasters of that war. On the contrary, the deviations made from his theory were, in his opinion, the sole cause of the whole disaster, and with characteristically gleeful sarcasm he would remark, `There, I said the whole affair would go to the devil!' Pfuel was one of those theoreticians who so love their theory that they lose sight of the theory's object—its practical application. His love of theory made him hate everything practical, and he would not listen to it. He was even pleased by failures, for failures resulting from deviations in practice from the theory only proved to him the accuracy of his theory.
—Leo Tolstoy

Some critics say participatory planning is a system of exchange using prices and equilibrating supply and demand. Doesn't that make it largely a market and therefore subject to many ills that afflict markets? Other critics ask, aren't parecon's facilitation workers just central planners? Don't they disproportionately influence outcomes and won't they bias results on their own behalf, thereby becoming a ruling coordinator class?

The sentiments behind these complaints are very much in tune with our own values and aims. It would be very disturbing, therefore, if the claims themselves were accurate.

Market Allocation By Another Name?

It is certainly true that participatory planning has numeric indicators that we call indicative prices and that people and institutions in a parecon consult these indicative prices to make their decisions. And it is also certainly true that the mix and match of the decisions that people make in participatory planning come into accord, via a meshing of supply and demand.

Some deduce from these facts that participatory planning must therefore be a disguised market system. It turns out this is mostly a matter of confused terminology, not substance.

If one means by market system, a system in which there are prices and in which supply and demand come into accord during allocation, then, yes, participatory planning would be a market system. But with that definition, all non-trivial allocation systems would qualify as market systems (even including central planning) and instead of markets being a specific kind of allocation mechanism with its own particular properties, the word market would be a synonym for allocation itself, and we would need a new word for what economists more typically call a market system.

When commentators use the term markets in that encompassing way, it makes folks think that what we have in the US, Italy, India, Australia, and Brazil ... is essentially inevitable. After all, any economy will value items and try to avoid gluts or shortages by equilibrating supply and demand in accord with its valuations. So any economy must employ "markets," if they are so defined. The next step, of course, is to say that we have markets, therefore there is no need for change. It is a powerful sleight of hand, generating passivity in the face of contemporary economic problems.

Suppose you looked at the Soviet Union some time back. You would have seen the same thing that causes these critics to identify parecon as some type of market system. Economic items in the old Soviet Union had a price. Supply and demand came into proximity with each other by a process that in large part took note of people's responses to prices. So was the old Soviet economy a market system? Only if we use a very misleading definition, of course.

Any economic system beyond personal barter includes some kind of mechanism for people to compare options (some kind of prices, perhaps accompanied, as in parecon, by qualitative information as well). And if the economy isn't horribly wasteful, any such system will also have supply and demand coming into proximity of one another, as occurred in the old Soviet economy. But no one would mistake the old Soviet economy for a market economy. Why?

Of course, it is because the old Soviet institutional framework and its components, and in particular the allocation roles for each actor established by those institutions, were quite different than those promoted by what we call market exchange. In the old Soviet Union the prices were ultimately set by central planners (who did, however, consult people's reactions to those prices). The workers—through their managers—had only to respond regarding their ability to fulfill instructions and to convey information about available resources, as well as to obey instructions. The planners had only to calculate and set prices and issue marching orders.

Managers had to administer as well as obey. Consumers had to go to the store and pick what they wanted, paying the established price and keeping within their budget—seemingly quite like at any supermarket. But there was no competition among buyers and sellers leading to competitive prices which prices in turn contoured the competition.

The point is that yes, parecon has, among other features, a kind of budgeting, and a meshing of supply and demand, as does any complex economy. But, nonetheless, parecon does not incorporate a market, because, among other factors:

- Participatory planning doesn't have buyers and sellers maximizing their own advantage each at the cost of the other.

- It doesn't have competitively determined prices.

- It doesn't have profit or surplus maximization.

- It doesn't have remuneration according to bargaining power or output.

Rather, parecon has other features entirely contrary to these, as noted throughout this volume. For example, it has far better estimates of true social costs and benefits, and very different incentives and rewards, different apportionment of influence over outcomes, and different personality and preference implications, as discussed in prior chapters.

The critic might not relent so fast. If participatory planning persists as intended it is very different from markets, agrees the critic. But won't market behavior intrude? Won't people pursue market exchanges for personal advantage—black markets—until markets have subverted the participatory planning process? Isn't parecon vulnerable to re-emerging market allocation?

The logic of the complaint goes like this. Let's say that a country has a parecon. A very skilled tailor finds that people appreciate his work and that he can charge them for favors. The tailor does so, and soon the tailor has made such a profit that he can employ other tailors to do his work on a larger scale, benefitting from his special knowledge. After a while the talented tailor has established an industry. With his profits, his empire can freely expand. Markets and capitalism return.

Technically this is called a black market. One can imagine lots of different approaches to this type of finagling in different participatory economies. At the extremes:

- One society might decide that this is such a minuscule problem that they will simply ignore it institutionally, letting normal operations reduce it to a trivial annoyance, but taking no special steps.

- Another society might take a diametrically opposite approach and beyond allowing the barter of goods among actors, as in my trading a shirt for a pair of gloves of yours, make transfers of goods outside planned transactions illegal, including punishing violators.

To decide which of these positions to favor, or something in between ... one might want to take into account a few things.

1 The second part of the problem, hiring wage slaves with gains from black marketeering, is simply not an option in parecon. At an absolute minimum, the economy will not allocate resources to a production unit assembled in such a fashion—not to mention, why would anyone work there?

To test the above claim, let's make the problem more real. One country goes parecon, another does not. A rich person from the latter country comes into the parecon and advertises for wage slaves to work in a factory that he wants to build in the parecon country. He offers a high pay rate, let's say, using his assets from without. This cannot happen, of course, but why not?

On the one hand, if you believe in parecon, you think most people will look at this guy like he's the devil and want nothing to do with him. On the other hand, what if some people, for whatever reasons, want to give up balanced job complexes and remuneration according to effort and sacrifice and proportionate impact on decisions and council democracy and so on, for the better wages this owner offers? It still cannot happen because society just doesn't allow it. The planning process will not provide the newcomer's firm with inputs, and it will not accept its outputs. (Even earlier, there is the matter of whether this owner from abroad could possibly make big profits paying wages sufficient to attract people away from parecon firms.)

2 But what about the first part of the problem: individuals benefitting by selling their talents? For example suppose I have these wonderful ornaments that I make in my spare time from road kill, or stuff I find in the trash. (It cannot be made from inputs that I would have to get from the economy because the economy will not provide such inputs for

profit-seeking.) Or, to make it more real … I am a mind-bogglingly good tennis player or pianist and I sell lessons on the sly. Why won't this corrupt the system?

Well, it is correct that in a parecon this is technically possible, but it is also important to realize that it is very hard in practice. For one thing, you cannot transfer income—actual money—because (a) there is no cash money to transfer and (b) even if there were, the black marketeer could not enter the planning process to consume with it without revealing, by its magnitude, that he/she was cheating the system. So the black marketeer has to be paid in goods just as if he traded his sweater for his neighbor's shoes, but in this case he or she would be trading a service, like tennis lessons. It is very clumsy, to say the least, and this puts a lid on the problem even without taking into account the social onus. But if, in fact, the black marketeer manages to get people to pay for lessons, how does she explain her resulting abundance? The social ostracism that would accompany any ostentatious consumption that revealed cheating (and what other source could their be for wildly excessive consumption?) would be a very high price to pay for income above and beyond the already quite comfortable and socially rich existence parecon typically provides. And there is not only a social and moral loss to be incurred by this type behavior in a parecon since much consumption is collective, and that would be lost as well.

So even without legal penalties, on the one side there is great difficulty in carrying off black market behavior and in accruing much by way of it, and on the other side, there is considerable loss in being identified as a social ingrate (which is almost impossible to avoid if you are benefitting significantly).

Returning to the original social choice, believing all the above, one might figure it is not worth society's time to worry about this problem because it is easier to turn the other cheek and if some folks manage a little extra lucre, so be it. Or one might decide, instead, that the dangers are significant (like the dangers of outright theft, which is outlawed) even with the social obstacles to such behavior, so that society ought to police the matter. Or, perhaps, one might move from the latter view to the former view as the system develops and as parecon values become commonplace. In any event, there is not, lurking here, a slippery slope back into markets.

Still, the persistent critic might wonder, is it right for a person to not have the option—because society precludes it—to garner the highest income possible by trading his/her talents?

This revisits points already addressed, but, of course if one thinks people should be remunerated according to what they can extract via their bargaining power—which is what markets foster—or according to their contribution to output —as markets are supposed to achieve—then one would not want parecon in the first place because it remunerates according to effort and sacrifice. But if one does favor remuneration for effort and sacrifice, then why should the existence of societal restrictions be a debit? There is no such thing as "anything goes" in any society. It cannot be anything goes for you and me when I want to do X which precludes your doing Y and you want to do Y which precludes my doing X. We cannot both implement our preferences once my anything conflicts with your anything, so it is not possible to say "anything goes."

More importantly, if we have institutions in a society—and there is no society that doesn't have institutions—then by virtue of the roles the institutions embody and those they do not embody, even before considering laws and enforcement, there are restrictions.

For example, we do not allow slave-owning in the US. It is not permitted. It doesn't matter if I come to you with a million dollars and say sign here, be my slave—it is not legal. In fact, however, it is not really an issue. The law is relatively moot because save for interstices where one can operate without being visible, no one wants to be a slave and no one wants slaves. The social opprobrium on both sides is too great relative to the gains even for venal folks to attempt it. Now, having wage slaves is another matter—that is acceptable and therefore pursued with vigor and in fact taken as a given in capitalism. But in a parecon, in contrast, having wage slaves is not an option. You cannot be a part of a parecon as a wage slave or while employing a wage slave. You would not get inputs and your outputs would not be distributed. And trying to do it on the sly would be like trying to own a slave in capitalism on the sly: unacceptable and unlikely to succeed to any significant degree.

Parecon does not perfectly eliminate—whether by definition, by incentives, or by consciousness-raising—every violation of its own morals that someone might entertain. And so this question is an apt form of a broader one—does parecon make most violations of its values so counter productive as to be not worth pursuing even if one could get away with it, and can it prosecute other violations when they occur as successfully as any other model prosecutes violations?

Parecon's claim is that the answer is yes on both counts—actually better than other systems on both counts. And if the next question is, well, what about murder, theft, and other crimes—or what about the black market if you decide to prosecute actors for that? Do these require police, and if so won't that lead right back to old-fashioned coercion and hierarchy? The answer is yes, a society with a parecon is like any other society in that it has to deal with abuses of individuals and of society, and yes that entails—in fact it defines—a "police function." But no, this does not imply old-fashioned political coercion and hierarchy any more than the fact that parecons have a "production and allocation function" implies old-fashioned market or corporate-based class division. But discussing how to accomplish police, judicial, legislative, or other political functions is a matter for a presentation about political vision outside the scope of this book, though it could be pursued by a similar approach—settling on needed functions, worthy values, and finally desired institutions.

Central Planning By Another Name?

The critic of participatory planning now takes an opposite approach. Aren't the facilitators just central planners? Isn't this not really a new system, but the same old authoritarian one, at least in practice?

The planning process, and thus the role of "facilitation boards" is, remember, more or less like this. Each actor (which is sometimes an individual, sometimes a workplace, or sometimes a consumption council), submits a proposal for what they wish to consume or produce, that is, their economic activity. The proposals of course do not mesh into a workable plan immediately. For most goods more is sought for consumption than proposed as supply even when people try to make sensible proposals based on projections of the likely average income for the coming period and awareness of their past period's actual results. Demand is brought into touch with supply and vice versa by a decentralized process of refining proposals in light of data from prior rounds of proposals as well as technical data about capabilities and other factors we have described.

Facilitation boards are, in this process, just workplaces like any others in the economy. They include various tasks combined into balanced job complexes. If the facilitation board's average job complex rating is better than the average for society, people working in a facilitation board have to work at sub-average options outside as well. If the facilitation board job complex is worse than for the rest of society, facilitation board workers have to work at better than average tasks outside the board as well.

As to what a facilitation board does—there are different kinds, with different purposes, but basically they either accumulate proposals and information, prepare data for access by others, and with various socially agreed-upon algorithms cull insights from data, passing back into the process the resultant information, or they facilitate meeting people's preferences, such as by helping people find new places to live or work. And that's it. Facilitators make no decisions other than about their own circumstances. What facilitators do can be checked by anyone at any time since all information is freely available. Moreover, virtually everything facilitators do could be largely and perhaps completely automated—though in practice this would likely be inefficient.

The critic hears all this and is not swayed. Surely you are starting to imply a coordinator class, just by having people working in an institution whose role is to decide who is affected by a certain decision and to what degree, are you not?

To answer, one has to look further at the model, taking into account what it does and doesn't address. The planning process has no need for anyone to play the role the critic indicates and indeed explicitly precludes it. The proportionate impacts on outcomes for different actors emerge organically from their involvement at various levels of the planning process and not from being decreed by some person or group from above.

However, suppose such estimates did have to be made by someone specially assigned to the task, which in fact they do not. That would still not mean that there is a coordinator class in the economy any more than the fact that there is a managerial function in many industries in a parecon implies that there is a separate coordinator class there, or the fact that there is an engineering function, or a surgical function, or a need to have agencies that do calculations or that summarize information means that folks involved in those activities will be a separate and privileged class. It is not the existence of important technical or conceptual tasks *per se* that engenders class division, but rather how those tasks are distributed among the populace.

If everyone has a balanced job complex, then no one has disproportionately more empowering work than others. Moreover, if there are no ways to make aggrandizing decisions to advance oneself or one's class at the expense of others, then systematic abuse of even temporary powers is virtually impossible. If your work group needs to have a "conductor" and Leonard gets the nod next week, he can be good or bad at it, and can even be a pompous ass or an exemplary genius at it, but he cannot use the position to enrich himself or some class of actors. That option doesn't exist because remuneration and circumstances are beyond his or anyone else's capacity to privately manipulate.

The critic is steadfast. Suppose I work in an institution that controls some of the critical levers of the economy, she says. Then even if I have a balanced job complex within that institution, I may still have an unbalanced job complex with regard to economic power and the broader community, right?

No, at least not in a parecon, because if you worked in the type of institution just described, as part of your job complex you would have to work part time elsewhere, to attain a balance.

But more important, which institution is it that the critic has in mind as providing a base for abuse? And what advantages does it bestow upon a worker there, such that he or she and others like him or her will become a class with advantages to defend and expand?

The worry is valid in the abstract, of course, but then we have to look to see whether in any particular kind of economy this problem exists in practice. For example, if someone was a central planner in a centrally planned economy, they would be able to bend and massage economic outcomes to serve all planners and also all folks with relative monopolies on decision-making power in workplaces by further enlarging the advantages that such folks enjoy. They could accomplish this by promoting investment patterns that enhanced information centralization and thus further aggrandized coordinator class privilege, not to mention by directly decreeing greater rewards for such folks. So here the claim would be right. These individuals, by virtue of their central planning positions, would have means to advance their interests contrary to the interests of other actors. But, none of this exists in a parecon.

Yes, there are boards or bureaus in a parecon that disseminate and even summarize information, but there is no way for anyone working in one of these boards (or doing other highly valued or conceptual functions as a part of their balanced job complex, for that matter) to benefit themselves, either in isolation or collectively, by doing anything other than what is also in everyone else's interest—that is, by doing their work as well as they can. For one thing any deviation would be obvious. But, even more important, there could be no self-serving deviation in ways that were not trivial, such as direct theft. It is precisely this kind of attribute that is striking about parecon, in fact.

The idea behind this claim is pretty simple. In a parecon or really any economy at all, to improve one's economic lot one needs more income or better circumstances (or more power since that facilitates the other two). But in a parecon everyone gets a share of income based on the effort and sacrifice they expend in their work (or based on their need if they cannot work) which means there is no way to gain more for oneself or for a group other than by working harder or longer, which, in fact, benefits everyone. For me to get ahead, the total product must grow or I have to expend more effort and sacrifice in producing that product, which is fair enough. I cannot get ahead at the expense of others by grabbing a bigger share than I am entitled to and leaving them with less than they are entitled to.

Similarly, since we all have balanced job complexes, my work situation only improves if the society's average job complex improves so that everyone's situation at work benefits. Yes, I can select from among balanced job complexes one I prefer over one that doesn't suit me, and of course I will do so and I should do so, but that has no broad class implications and is as it should be for everyone.

Could a class of fakers arise who make believe that they cannot work, who consume the average bundle, but who do not work the normal load? It is hard to imagine, but more important than being far-fetched, it would be a minimal achievement and they would not have any authority over anyone, and since they would have to show all the signs of a work-preventing ailment, on balance they would gain little, if anything, at considerable risk.

At any rate, participatory planning is neither a market system nor a centrally planned system precisely because it has different defining institutions and roles than each and because in theory and also in practice there is no tendency for it to devolve into either.

21

Flexibility

Should A Parecon Incorporate Limited Markets

When we should have been planning switches to smaller, more fuel efficient, lighter cars in the late 1960s, in response to a growing demand in the marketplace, GM refused because "we make more money on big cars." It mattered not that customers wanted the smaller cars, or that a national balance of payments deficit was being built .... Refusal to enter the small car market when the profits were better on bigger cars, despite the needs of the public and the national economy, was not an isolated case of corporate insensitivity. It was typical.
— John DeLorean

The idea in this chapter is different than in the rest of our critical chapters. The hypothetical critic in this chapter accepts that parecon is a fine idea. She accepts that markets and central planning are horribly flawed. She accepts the desirability of councils, balanced job complexes, self-management decision-making norms and procedures, and remuneration for effort and sacrifice. She accepts that participatory planning fosters all those features and has additional virtues as well, and she supports it for those reasons. But, even with all that celebration, she worries about it being too doctrinaire.

Okay, markets for all our allocation is a horrible idea, but why not just for some of it, she urges. Why not try to capture the benefits markets have for those items where its benefits will be greatest and where we can curtail accompanying debits? She claims markets are responsive. They react to shocks quickly and they can update weekly, daily, or even hourly. Participatory planning cannot re-plan repeatedly, she says, so can't we therefore benefit by using markets to augment or along with or even in place of pareconish approaches, at least for the items where speed of reaction is needed?

In other words, can't we have a slightly mixed economy? Can't we take the essence of participatory economics and strengthen it by adding some limited attributes of other economies—in particular, some market mediation of exchange? The critic continues, you have some product that you know will have frequent innovation. When you plan it in the participatory planning process at the outset of the year, you get a very fine assessment of its true costs and benefits (or exchange value) at the start of your year. The procedures support the economy's broad values. They respect and foster self-management, and so on. But what happens when innovations occur for the item in question well before the next planning period comes around, say only two or three months into the year?

I know the system handles modest typical preference changes fine, says the critic, including those arising from changes in the product, but what if there is a really large change because an innovation makes the product really much better or perhaps due to a massive fire destroying lots of production potential, and, as a result, many more people want the product than planned to get it (well beyond what slack planning can handle)? Wouldn't it be good to let the consumers and producers of the item operate as they would via a market, so that the price would move quickly and in the correct direction, and so that demand would properly fall? Wouldn't this improve on having to replan the whole economy?

Our answer to this very fair question comes in two parts.

First, if in such cases the only option was to persist with the plan as conceived in the initial planning period or to incorporate market features, we would favor the former. The loss in efficiency induced by having to wait to adjust until the next planning period would be quite modest compared to the debits of ushering market allocation back into the system. The short of it is that moving quickly by markets from wrong prices to still wrong prices by methods that subvert all the values we hold dear is not improving matters.

But, second, this is not the actual situation. There is no reason why parecon consumers should have to sit tight with the initially planned exchange rates and allocations, rather than correct for surprising innovations or calamities, even for large ones such as is hypothesized here. To compare, suppose an innovation or a calamitous destruction of productive potential occurs in a market economy. The conditions prevailing have changed. Old prices no longer clear markets properly. How do prices and material choices by actors respond?

With markets, buyers and sellers try to get as much benefit for themselves, regardless of the effect on others, in the new situation, just as in the old one. The market response, in other words, will likely go in the right direction, but the motive driving the correction, as at all times with markets, will be pursuit of profit/surplus and advance of competing actors via enlarging market share. The process will ignore the will of agents not directly involved in the exchange. It will impose antisocial motives, and other failings, as we have discussed at length about markets in general.

Additionally, the idea that markets respond well to shocks and changes is, in any event, only a mathematician's assumption. In fact, the rippling changes percolating from an unexpected major change in demand or supply take time to unfold and the assertion that they will inevitably occur quickly and accurately (even if we set aside other reasons for market prices diverging from true costs and benefits and market outputs diverging from accurate repre-sentations of people's unbiased preferences) conveniently ignores a host of disequilibrating dynamics that actually afflict market systems and that may mean that the initial markets affected by the shock do not re-equilibrate quickly, or at all; and/or that inter-actions between interconnected markets produce a disequilibrating dynamic that pushes all markets farther from a new equilibrium.

Thus re-equilibration in a market economy typically requires a change in some initial market affected by the unforeseen event followed by changes in any markets where supply or demand is affected by the change in the first market, followed by changes in other markets where supply and demand is affected by changes in the second tier affected, and so on. How much of this re-equili-bration takes place how quickly is anybody's guess. Market enthusiasts assume it all happens very quickly, and that market prices are good in the first place and good after re-equilibration as well. Of course in reality only some of it happens. None of it happens instantly. And worst, market prices diverge from accurate valuations of true social costs and benefits both before and after any shock. In sum, to the extent that re-equilibration does not reach all markets, and to the extent that markets which do eventually re-equilibrate do not do so instantaneously, market systems will perform inefficiently and inequitably in response to the unforeseen event even if its prices were efficient before and wound up efficient after the shock. Of course, when its prices aren't efficient before and don't wind up efficient afterward, things are that much worse.

For such reasons, we would not want to have some items handled by market processes in a parecon even if it were an otherwise plausible option, but more, we really could not sensibly do so even if we wanted to. Having a little markets in a parecon is a bit like having a little slavery in a democracy, though even less tenable. The logic of markets invalidates the logic of participatory planning and of the whole parecon, and it is also imperial, once it exists trying to spread as far and wide as it can. You cannot have some workplaces seeking market share, trying to induce purchases regardless of impact on consumers and society, ignoring external effects, trying to elevate remuneration according to power or output or surpluses, and expect those firms to interface congenially with the rest of the participatory economy. So, in contrast, if we have to live or die with it in full, what about participatory planning's responsiveness?

Again an innovation occurs, this time in a parecon. The unforeseen event significantly affects demands and valuations so that the original plan—which was efficient and equitable before the shock—is no longer efficient and equitable. The optimal solution, at least regarding the choice of material inputs and outputs and their valuation and thus distribution, is to redo the entire planning process and arrive at a new plan perfectly efficient and equitable in light of the new conditions. Doing so is in that sense the analog of a market system jumping from allocations before the shock all the way to allocations after all of the interconnected markets re-equilibrate, without any misallocations in the interim. But wait says the critic, this answer won't do because re-planning is impractical except in cases of huge unforeseen events with large enough impact to merit that big an undertaking, even if I will admit that in such cases nothing would prevent redoing the plan—which would be much simpler than planning from scratch. My point is, says the critic, most of the time deviations are important yet not worth cranking up the entire planning process involving all workers and consumers councils, federations, and IFBs. To appease me regarding parecon's flexibility, you need to have something more convenient, even if a little less perfectly efficient and equitable, than entirely replanning the whole economy.

In short, when a shock requires significant adjustments, how do we tide over with appended alterations until the next scheduled planning period fixes things "perfectly"—never more than 12 months away? The answer is that different instances of parecon might have different approaches to doing this. Here is one.

Workers in a parecon industry notice markedly changed demand or valuations. Many more people than planned come to want some product. The easiest adjustment is if the original plan allowed for production of a certain amount extra of the good in question, so that unexpected increased demand can be met by actualizing this extra potential. The name for a plan with no extra potential built in is a "taut plan," and the name for a plan with extra potential built in is a "slack plan," with the amount of "slack" varying for the economy and its industries. This is exactly analogous to business inventories in a market system, whether kept on hand, or able to be generated.

But suppose workers notice that the increased demand will take them beyond the available slack. As a result, they begin to contact facilitation boards seeking extra workers and begin consulting suppliers for additional inputs. If this can be had to the extent needed, they report the results and the facilitation boards calculate the effect on final prices. The predictions are made available to all consumers. If assets for the desired production can't be had, supply won't rise sufficiently and, instead, decisions will have to be made regarding allocation of the limited available products. Of course all the usual methods and motives of parecon operate at each step, whatever specific approaches a particular parecon might employ.

Let's pick a simple unforseen event. An unprecedented warm spell dramatically increases people's desires for air conditioners beyond what was planned plus available slack.

An easy possibility is to ration the existing supply of air conditioners at the level set by the original plan. This could be done in a variety of ways. (1) Give everyone seeking air conditioners only X percent of the what they they asked for, where X equates demand with available supply. Of course, this is not possible for items that are not divisible. So (2) give air conditioners only to those who asked for one in the original plan and only in the quantity they asked for. Do not accommodate new demanders or increased demands. But another option is (3) raise the price of air conditioners until the excess demand disappears, i.e. employ increased prices to ration air conditioners. In this case we would have to have an IFB in place to adjust indicative prices during the year. Or we could have the national consumer federation and the national air conditioner industry federation make the price adjustments. If we adjust the price of air conditioners to eliminate the excess demand we have to charge users the higher price or their demand will not fall to the existing level of supply. Those who get the air conditioners and are charged the higher price now must either reduce the amount of some other goods they consume—not picking up all they ordered in their original plan—or they must increase borrowing which is monitored in a participatory economy by their consumer federation.

But of course as this example intentionally makes evident, a more desirable adjustment to the unforeseen event would be increasing production of air conditioners. We now know that more of society's scarce productive resources should be devoted to air conditioners than the original plan called for, and therefore by implication, less of society's scarce productive resources should be devoted to producing other goods and services. Adjusting production of air conditioners is in this event more complicated than simply rationing the existing supply in any of the above ways, but to do so also better meets real needs, and is therefore more efficient.

The simplest way to increase production is to ask the air conditioner federation to increase output via overtime. If the workers can produce more by working more hours without needing significantly more inputs, the only remaining issue is an equity matter—how much to compensate them for their extra sacrifice. They will re-rate themselves and presumably claim sacrifices equal to the extra hours plus extra sacrifice they consider the after hours nature of their work to be. They will produce more air conditioners credited to their firm's social benefit to social cost ratio.

But what if more air conditioners cannot be produced without more non-labor inputs which must be obtained from other workers' federations? Then a fuller and more efficient mid-plan adjustment requires renegotiation between the air conditioner federation and the workers' federations who supply them. This is just the percolating and spreading implication of a shock in an entwined economy, the same as would occur were allocation handled by markets. But in all cases of all involved parecon firms the choices about (1) rationing and (2) adjusting production schedules, simply repeat themselves. How much mid-term adjusting to do—rather than just waiting for the new planning period to get inputs and outputs all "perfect" again; and then how much of that mid-term adjusting to do simply by rationing, i.e. adjusting consumption only; how much to by adjusting production of the initial item affected and/or of other items that are inputs, etc.; and which of the various options to use in any part of an adjustment, including whether or not to recalibrate prices, are all practical issues to be decided by those who work and consume in a participatory economy following general norms and procedures applicable in specific cases, though not via one single right norm or procedure that must be followed always in all cases and in all parecons, we would guess.

In any event, there is no reason to think that the proliferating adjustments in a participatory economy are any more difficult or cumbersome than in market economies—unless one makes the unrealistic assumption that markets adjust infinitely quickly to their new equilibria. And so the overall difference from a market system is increased rather than diminished flexibility, in that options can be consciously chosen, the elimination of various (competitive) causes of spiraling divergence from equilibrium, plus, of course, that the procedure's guiding motives are social rather than profit seeking, the valuations are accurate rather than distorted, and the influence of actors is proportionate to the degree they are affected rather than enormous for ruling classes and minuscule for subordinate classes.

Thus, with a large change in desirability of a product or some other major shock in a parecon that goes beyond what slack can accommodate, everyone who wants some affected good could be supplied, or only those who originally placed orders could be, or only those willing to pay a new higher price could be. In any of these events, there would be some change in the real price, rising above or falling below the planning period's indicative price. A parecon can handle all these matters in numerous ways.

Indeed here is another angle from which to think of the whole situation. Think in terms of the year's end. Suppose you got everything you sought, exactly as you sought it. But suppose the total value assessed at year's end was less than the total you allotted from your budget—final prices for the year changed from planned prices so that the total cost of all that you consumed was less in final fact than it was in your initial planning. Then you would be entitled to a refund, or else you would have unfairly lost out. Or suppose the total value of what you consumed in final prices turned out higher than originally indicated in planned prices. Then you would owe some, or would have received more than you deserved. But parecon has no trouble correcting in regard to either result. It can properly allot credit or debit to your account.

The only difficulty in the above trivially simple approach is that you would not have had a chance to reassess your choices based on the accurate prices. But a parecon can meet this problem too. It need only provide monthly updated price estimates based on the year's unfolding patterns, so that you can, in fact, continually reassess your remaining choices against slightly altering price projections. With slack and the averaging of different consumers' choices, the amount of replanning would likely be very modest.

The main point of all this, however, is that speed of response is not all that much of a virtue in the first place, nor do markets possess as much speed as people think, nor do they speedily arrive places where people should knowingly wish to go in any event—and certainly that speed of response should never be "bought" by incurring costs that are way more damning than the modest gains achieved.

22

Elevating Need?

Does Parecon Honor or Denigrate Need?

Reason, or the ratio of all we have already known, is not the same that it shall be when we know more.
–William Blake

In a participatory economy remuneration is for effort expended and sacrifice endured in work. Does this mistakenly reject providing according to needs? Does it prevent needs from being properly met? Does it elevate a self-interested calculus denying more social motivations? Does it induce individualist rather than social inclinations? Even supporters of parecon wonder about these questions. How do we respond?

One issue is does parecon address the needs of people who cannot work? Yes, parecon provides an average income to those who cannot work. What about people with special health needs? Health care is a free public good in a parecon. What about calamity victims? Insurance is also a public good, so again parecon provides appropriately. What about children? Do parents have to take less social product for themselves in order to clothe, feed, and otherwise provide for children? No, an average income goes to children, by right of being human. Children do not have to work to get their fair share. Parecon remunerates effort and sacrifice but that doesn't impede meeting needs of those who cannot work because if you cannot work in a parecon, you get an income anyhow. And if you have added health needs, those are met as well.

But wondering about needs-based allocation might involve more subtle matters. Suppose there is a severe cold snap in your region. Should you have to pay for needed heat out of your income, thus leaving less budget for desirable goods than you anticipated just because of bad luck regarding the weather? Should bad weather diminish you budget for getting goods to enhance your life? Or should the cost of heating to withstand the cold snap be provided socially?

Ultimately, we are asking what counts as a health or a calamity request handled outside one's budget—and what counts as our responsibility within our budgets. No single answer universally applies. Different countries could arrive at different norms. So could a single country at different times or even different regions inside a country. The self-managing choices of the polity and/or workers and consumers councils decide. But it's plausible to predict that pareconish people will have a bias. To the extent society can protect everyone against harsh circumstances without abrogating other values and without incurring undue expense and disruption, I would imagine pareconish people will likely agree that adjustment policies should reduce any serious suffering for external unforeseeable circumstances, not only in the case of catastrophic calamity, but in lesser cases, as well. In any event, that's my bias. It seems to me that there is no moral reason to allow some people to fall victim to unpredictable but truly harmful bad luck, while others relatively benefit. But this choice is not built into parecon as an abiding norm in the way that balanced job complexes are built in, for example, and different possibilities exist for how to try to fulfill this aspiration and for the degree to seek to fulfill it, and these differences will be explored differently in different cases, no doubt.

The critic worried about providing for needs may yet be unappeased. His or her concerns may have a different logic. Isn't there something wrong when an economy rewards our labors with remuneration rather than simply giving us what we need by virtue of our being human? Why do we have to earn a share? Why isn't a share ours by right? For that matter, why do we need an incentive to work? Why do we need to get a share of output for our labors, withheld if we don't do them, rather than each of us working simply because it is our social responsibility to do so—and getting whatever we need, simply by right of our humanity?

The description sounds exalted, but imagine being ship-wrecked on an island with fifty other folks. We have a lot of toys salvaged from our ship. There is a beautiful swimming area. There are games to be played, music to be performed and heard, relationships to explore, poetry to write, nature to experience, and so on. There is also, however, a need to build housing, grow and harvest food, pot fresh water, maintain single fires, and so on. So there is hard, boring labor, and there is fun and enriched leisure time.

Suppose I announce that I need a dwelling, fresh water, food, a luxurious carved flute, and some newly made clothes. My happiness, sanity, and fulfillment depend on having all that, I say. I need it. But I also announce that I would rather not work producing that stuff or anything else. I enjoy swimming and hanging out too much to give time to anything more onerous each day. I need a lot of leisure. That is just me.

Does anyone seriously think my announcements should be honored? But what else does it mean to say that I ought to get what I need regardless than that these announcements are acceptable? If it means, as I suspect it always does, sure, you get what you need, but you have to work the fair amount for it, and what you need isn't what you say it is but instead what society somehow agrees on in context of what you say, then the phrase "getting what you need unconnected to labor" is misleading rhetoric.

In practice, moreover, in addition to being utopian regarding the amount of output available—we cannot all get all that we want and isn't what we want in fact what we need?—rewarding need without labor (for those who can work) is actually not equitable at all. And if the assumption is that we will behave to make it equitable, how do we do that without an allocation mechanism which tells us what is a fair amount to work and consume? Likewise, even if I do a fair share of work, should I be able to say I need more than my correlated fair share of food or housing or carved musical instruments just because I determine that it would make me happier? If that is not my unilateral right, then how is appropriate need assessed?

The answer should be that a social process decides what is appropriate, with each actor having proportionate input, and with the decision made in light of an accurate understanding of the full social costs and benefits of the creation and utilization of each product, including of the labor involved. This, of course, is precisely what parecon delivers by accounting for time and effort in production as well as the value of outputs and processes. The point is, for an economy to respect the needs of each actor in the same degree as it respects the needs of all other actors requires that the economy arrive at proper valuations of full social costs and benefits of work and its inputs and outputs and that it apportion shares of output in accord with effort and sacrifice expended, with allowance, of course, for special cases of the sort noted earlier.

So it is precisely because parecon is geared to meet needs and develop potentials that parecon remunerates as it does, determines values as it does, and involves actors in decisions and apportions work responsibilities as it does. If we break the relation between work and income we eliminate the possibility of people knowing what is greedy and what is appropriate, even assuming everyone wants to abide such guides spontaneously, and also of knowing the direction people wish the economy to go in.

And there is another point to be made. A critic may worry that remunerating effort and sacrifice rather than providing for needs irrespective of work will propel actors to seek personal income rather than care about one another. But, in fact, as we have seen, parecon creates a context in which to get ahead personally, even someone who starts out quite self-interested, greedy, and dismissive of the needs of others, has no choice but to address the needs of others. In a parecon we enjoy improved work conditions if society's average job complex improves, which means we must favor not all changes in our own work place, irrespective of impact outside, but only changes in the whole economy that make the largest gains in quality of life implications of work, even if none of those changes are situated in our own workplace. And the amount we get per hour of average labor at average intensity goes up, likewise, if the whole social product goes up, again imposing on actors attentiveness to society and not just self.

Ironically, therefore, it turns out that giving people what they declare they need with no attention to their participation in production does far less to produce social concern and mutual awareness than rewarding effort and sacrifice, since the former says we need only concern ourselves with assessing our own desires in determining what we want and receiving it, while the later requires that we pay attention to the well-being of the whole community even if we are solely interested in advancing our own well-being. That is, giving people from the social product simply for what they proclaim to be their needs promotes an individualistic, anti-social calculus in everyone, whereas rewarding effort and sacrifice and operating via participatory planning from within balanced job complexes literally requires that we pay attention to the entire social condition, including the situations, needs, and possibilities of others.

23

Compatibility

Can a Parecon Accommodate and Be Accommodated By Other Institutions?

> I wish that every human life might be pure transparent freedom.
> — Simone De Beauvoir

> My notion of democracy is that under it the weakest shall have the same opportunities as the strongest ... no country in the world today shows any but patronizing regard for the weak ... Western democracy, as it functions today, is diluted fascism ... true democracy cannot be worked by twenty men sitting at the center. It has to be worked from below, by the people of every village.
> — Gandhi

Humans are social beings and we do not live by bread alone. Economics is neither the sole nor even the sole centrally important aspect of life. It is critical, but so are culture, politics, kinship, ecology, and international relations. The good society we aspire to will have a transformed economy but very likely also transformed kinship, polity, and cultural relations, transformed relations with nature, and transformed relations among societies.

In fact, what makes some part of social life central? The answer is that it depends on your purpose. Central relative to what? We are interested in changing society for the better. So our question is, what makes some domain of society central to the effort to change society for the better?

One answer is that centrally important means (a) providing pervasively influential pressures on the way society is and the way it could be, and (b) impacting broad constituencies so that they can potentially act in light of their aims to try to make desirable changes. The economy does this, of course, by defining how we produce, consume, and allocate and by exerting pressure on other areas of our lives via its impact on these other functions and by demarcating us into the capitalist, coordinator, and working classes, which, by virtue of the different roles they play in economic and social life can both perceive the economy's importance and also develop interests and agendas to perpetuate or to change its features. But the polity also does all this, though with respect to adjudication, legislation, and the implementation and enforcement of shared programs. And what we might call kinship also does it, regarding procreation, nurturance, socialization, and other functions related to the creation and emergence of each new generation. And the culture does it as well, regarding the way communities define their mutual relations, celebrations, and broad identities.

Each of these four realms of social interaction defines centrally important features in societies and demarcates conflicting social groups, and each sphere can generate movements seeking new structures critical to the definition of a new society. So all are central, not only one or another, not only economics. But if a good society is one where all these domains emanate liberating influences, is a parecon compatible with a positive vision we may adopt for other spheres of social life? Does it emanate pressures that will foster their logic? Do they emanate pressures that will foster parecon's logic? If not, can parecon be modified by tweaking it without losing its benefits or undercutting its operations?

This question can only be answered definitively by setting forth visions for other spheres and evaluating the interrelations. We know, obviously, that many models for other spheres would conflict with a parecon—for example those that would involve hierarchies of privilege or restrictions on freedom, including those with racist cultures, sexist kinship relations, and authoritarian politics, or, for that matter, relations to ecology denying human well being and development, and relations among nations contrary to equity, diversity, solidarity, and self-management. Institutions existing alongside a parecon will have to respect balanced job complexes, remuneration for effort and sacrifice, and self-management and to the degree that they need inputs and render outputs, will have to interface with participatory planning. A parecon, operating alongside other domains of life, will likewise have to respect and mesh with their operations.

The idea is relatively simple. Major institutions in society have roles that people fill and that in turn influence people's beliefs, aspirations, and expectations. You cannot have people propelled toward type "a" beliefs, desires, and expectations in one major part of their lives, and toward type "b" beliefs, expectations, and desires in another major part of their lives when the implications of "a" and "b" are strongly at odds. For an obvious case, you cannot have home lives or educational systems producing new recruits for a parecon who lack the confidence and learning to participate in it, nor, for that matter, can you have homes or schooling producing new recruits for a capitalist economy that have too much confidence and learning to accept the subordinate roles they will play in it. And vice versa, you can't have an economy producing hierarchies and expectations in men and women, or in people of different races and cultural communities, or in citizens playing various roles in the polity, that are contrary to what the kinship, cultural, and political institutions of society require to function.

So are the people parecon presents to the rest of society the kind of people who will be compatible with and thrive in institutions designed to eliminate racism, sexism, heterosexism, political authoritarianism, environmental degradation, and global imperialism? Models for such institutions still await development, but we believe that we can provisionally answer this question in the affirmative, given that people in parecon feel solidarity, are used to participation, expect and seek equity, have practice with and value self-management, and anticipate and appreciate diversity.

24

Human Nature

What About Jaundiced Humanity?

"Incapacity of the masses." What a tool for all exploiters and dominators, past
present and future, and especially for the modern aspiring enslavers,
whatever their insignia ... Nazism, Bolshevism, Fascism, or Communism.
"Incapacity of the masses." This is a point on which reactionaries of all colors
are in perfect agreement... and this agreement is exceedingly significant.
— Voline

Some critics of parecon base their objection on the grounds of human
nature. "A better economy? Don't be silly. Human nature precludes
it. Humans are greedy, avaricious, self-seeking, consumerist,
individualist, antisocial, authoritarian, order-givers and takers.
You cannot build a house out of sand. Neither can you build a utopia
out of humans. We lack the right stuff."

The claim that "humans are rotten" may be a rationalization that
hypocritically propels self-interest or it may be truly believed. In
either event, it operates with great power.

When I was a college student at MIT in the class of 1969, I was
very active in the anti-war movement. As part of my organizing
efforts I spoke to a great many students, sometimes one-on-one,
often in large groups. Discussions would go on long into the night.

The mood would be very intense since, after all, these folks took
school very seriously and not only were matters of great social
consequence on the agenda, but also such matters as whether they
would have classes to go to or classes would be shut down. In these
meetings I would refute misgivings and misconceptions about the
anti-war movement's view of history and society, one after another,
but for many folks these facts were actually secondary, a kind of red
herring. The rock-bottom line of defense against having to commit to
stopping the war in Indochina was, for most, a variation on one
theme. Finally, someone would express this argument explicitly:
"Why bother opposing it? Even if we were to curtail this war, there
would just be another one. Even if we reduced, temporarily, the
destruction, massacre, and indignity, these would return and make
up for lost time. That is the nature of humanity." The speaker would
continue: "People are greedy violent animals, so what more can you

expect? Let me go back to my classes, let me avoid all this distraction. Stop berating me with it. There is nothing I or anyone can do. Human nature sucks."

I think this was then and is still now a bedrock logic of both repression and capitulation. It is hammered into our every pore from every direction for a good part of our lives. How does an advocate not only of ending a war or some other atrocity, but of attaining a just world, rebut such cynical views?

The short answer I like to give I first heard from Noam Chomsky. Imagine you are in an upstairs window looking out over a nearly empty street below. It is a scorching hot day. A child below is enjoying an ice cream cone. Up walks a man. He looks down, grabs the cone, and swats the child aside into the gutter. He walks on enjoying his new cone. What do you think, from the safety of your distance from the scene, about this man? Of course, you think this fellow is pathological. You certainly don't identify with him and think, that's me down there, I would do that too. Instead you would be horrified and you would likely even rush down to comfort the child. But why?

If humans are greedy, self-centered, violent animals wouldn't we expect that all humans, confronted with the opportunity to take a delicious morsel at no cost to themselves, would do so? Why should it horrify us when we see someone do it? Why should we find it pathological? The answer is that we actually do not think that people are innately thugs. We only gravitate to that claim when it serves our purposes to rationalize some agenda we hold for other reasons entirely, such as when we ignore widespread injustice because to do otherwise would be uncomfortable, costly, and even risky.

For my second answer, I ask an advocate of the view that "humans suck" to consider from personal experience if there is some exception to this otherwise general rule. Do you suck, I ask? Are you greedy and avaricious, concerned only for yourself? If you are, okay, but do you know anyone who isn't? Some relative, an acquaintance, a hero from history, anyone? Just one such person? And then I ask, how did this one social rather than antisocial person arrive at their concern for and solidarity with others?

To confused stares I say, well, think about it. We live in a world with institutions that propel greediness and self-centered calculation. The messages all around us foster these antisocial attitudes rather than countering them. It is easy to explain selfishness arising in us in this context. In our world selfishness is the way to get ahead and we even often get punished in our own lives if we care so much about others that it diverts us from personal advancement. Indeed, it is easy to explain even gross proportions of greed and narrow individualism in our world. After all, if we merely have the capacity to drift in that direction, then given our environments, there is no surprise that we will do so, some of us more than others. But what about the one person you have conjured into mind, or the millions I can think of, almost everyone in various parts of their lives, who displays more social and empathetic behavior? From where do their mutually supportive acts and feelings arise? If people suck as you say, and they suck due to a wired-in disposition that we cannot hope to transcend even to the degree of ending war and starvation, then these better attributes should not exist at all, and if they happened to accidentally arise in some modest dose, surely they would be buried out of existence by the overwhelming pressures of our circumstances. Therefore for social caring to be as prevalent as it is—and in truth, we know it is very widespread—perhaps it is the trait that is wired-in, rather than its opposite.

This argument begins not with a look at human nature itself, as if we could peer down and see the immensely complex implications of our genes, but from a look at what human nature must embody to get the outcomes we see in the context of the antisocial structures we endure. Your good niece or grandmother, the good person in history, and the good inclinations you yourself have, all these could not possibly have emerged if the view that we are innately horrible is correct. Innate evil plus surrounding institutions stifling sociality and enlarging greed would not yield even one good grandma.

The long answer is different—more erudite, but ultimately no more conclusive than what goes above. It rebuts social Darwinism, discussing the actual logic of inheritance, evolution, and so on. It rarely has any real bearing on why people hold the views they do, because people decrying human nature as abysmal rarely if ever are doing so due to actual views about the mechanics of the evolution of human nature. At any rate, we know so little about such matters that in fact there is no conclusive scientific argument about human nature, starting at the genes. We know from experience that human nature is such that greed and violence and worse can emerge from human beings. After all, we have all seen this, or know of it, for ourselves. We also know that human nature is such that love and loyalty and respect and caring can emerge from human beings. The cynic says there is too much disposition toward the former for any institutional structure to prevent the baser tendencies from emerging and dominating. One thug with a club can wreak havoc, forcing others, even against their inclinations, to wield clubs in return. This is not an entirely crazy fear, though it is hard to understand why it leads the cynic to favor institutions that virtually compel people to pick up clubs. The optimist says that given circumstances that foster and reward their better selves, humans can engage in mutually beneficial social relations with means for handling what little violence and anti-sociality arise in the normal order of events, and without tumbling down a slippery slope of greed or destruction. We urge this, and provide parecon as a set of relevant economic structures. So who is right?

One important answer to offer the cynic is that since we do not know for certain who is right, why are you betting on the depressing outcome being the case? How can you not favor acting on the possibility that we can develop institutions which would foster the best in us, and in the context of which, therefore, we would be social and caring and the horrible artifacts of competition and self-centered violence would be eliminated? Why are you betting against the efficacy of having institutions which less aggressively promote self-centeredness and greed, much less foster their opposite?

The answer the cynic offers is generally, "but they tried that, in Russia, in China, and so on, and it failed horribly. Out with the old boss, in with the new. Out with the old horrible outcomes, in with new ones, as bad or worse. You cannot do it."

The activist reply has got to be, yes, what you say about those historical efforts not yielding a truly just and equitable new society is the case, but what was implemented was not, in fact, new institutions fostering the best in us. It was, instead, new institutions still fostering antisocial outcomes, class divisions, and all the old crap, as the saying goes. It doesn't prove that we cannot have desirable social structures that institutions with predictably horrible implications—Leninist political structures, central planning apparatuses, etc.—had the expected horrible effects.

Yes, you are correct that if we institute structures like those of parecon and if, against the socializing pressures of these new institutions, people still en masse strive to subjugate and oppress one another in ways that subvert equity and justice, you will then have a real argument for the impossibility of these goals. But until then, it is nothing but unfounded cynicism.

Another way to put this is to ask folks, who do you want to be right? When a cynic rebuts desires for a better world by claiming human nature precludes it, it always seems that he or she really wants it to be the case that people are innately evil. The cynic's whole manner, their demeanor in the discussion, their advocacy, and their stubborn refusal to even consider other possibilities, all reveal a disposition to want their claims to be true—and I ask them, how can this possibly be? Why, I wonder, do you have a vested interest in being right about human nature precluding sociality? Why don't you weep over your belief, if, as you say, you think it means we will have murders and wars and hierarchies of hunger until the end of time? What can it be about this belief being right that so rewards you that you actually want it to be the case? And could it be that whatever benefit you enjoy from the belief is what makes you feel as you do?

Of, course, what I have in mind is what Voline addressed in the quotation opening this chapter—the need to rationalize injustice, whether to enjoy its fruits without remorse, or to avoid remorse over being immobilized by fearing the consequences of battling it.

25

Asset or Debit?

Does Vision Produce Sectarianism?

One cannot escape the feeling that these equations have an existence and intelligence of their own, that they are wiser than we are, wiser even than their discoverers, that we get more out of them than was originally put into them.
—Heinrich Hertz

There is a surprisingly prevalent type of criticism of economic vision as extensive as parecon that we have yet to address. It doesn't charge that parecon is unable to meet human needs by reason of poor incentives, or impossible requirements, or anything else explicitly identified. Quite the contrary, it finds no fault on this score. And it doesn't charge that parecon is deficient because despite being able to effectively accomplish economic functions, parecon subverts values that we aspire to, whether by accidental omission or willfully. Quite the opposite, this criticism praises the values and sometimes even the structures of parecon. This critical response resists aggressively advocating parecon, in fact, precisely because parecon has every appearance of being an economically and socially positive vision. Parecon is resisted, that is, because it appears to be so good. How can this be?

Any kind of vision, these critics claim, is detrimental to improving society, because however wonderful it may seem vision is never truly perfect and also because vision inevitably leads to closed-minded sectarianism, which entrenches its faults. These critics argue as follows.

- First, society and people are too complex to perfectly predict. Thus, in some fashion all efforts to project future institutions, however insightful, must fall short of optimal and be flawed compared to what would be ideal. Experience is the only corrective, and to have instructive experience requires experimenting and evaluating practical results, step by step, without prejudging possible destinations. We should not adopt a full vision until we implement one. Preconception of a full institutional vision, rather than just of clear values, overextends our capacities.

- Second, in espousing a set of institutional aims and trying to get people to share them, people will inevitably become invested in those aims. Identities will become wrapped up in their worthiness. Energies will go to defending them irrespective of actual logic and evidence. Inflexibility will set in. Arrogance will arise. Advocates of fully formulated institutional vision will lose the ability to learn and will begin to mechanically impose their aims even on the supposed beneficiaries of vision. Little attention will go to alteration, improvement, addition, or reconstruction, as compared to if we were guided by practice alone, not preconceived vision.

These critics of preconceived vision conclude that the right way to attain vision is through the experience of everyone experimenting, without detailed pre-envisioning and without sectarianism-inducing espousal of compelling, encompassing aims, and without efforts to get widespread shared agreement. We should say only very general things about what we want—such as that the future should be just, equitable, reduce hierarchy, and so on.

We agree that error and sectarianism are both possible faults. But how should we respond to these insights? Consider two opposed approaches.

The first approach employs what ecologists call the "precautionary principle," which says that in the face of uncertainty and inevitable human subjectivity, we should be aware of our limitations and should act very cautiously to minimize tendencies toward negative consequences.

The second approach we call the "red-light principle." It says because of uncertainty and possible sectarianism, we should stop any attempt to pre-envision the future. We should not develop and share full and compelling vision like that put forth in this book, whether for economics or for any other sphere of social life, because such vision will not serve as an aid to moving forward, but as an obstacle.

I believe the precautionary principle is far more appropriate than the red-light principle.

For one thing, before stopping the pursuit of compelling vision, we ought to understand the cost of doing so.

Suppose a movement obeys the red light principle and chooses to forego a widely shared compelling vision that reveals how new defining institutions would operate, why they would get their assigned tasks completed, and why they would yield vastly superior outcomes than current institutions.

First, this movement will not have a good notion about what experiments to undertake to learn as it proceeds. Just as scientists need theoretical frameworks to guide their choice of experiment, so too political activists need overarching vision to guide their choice of social experiment.

Second, lacking widely shared vision to inspire membership, generate hope, sustain commitment, and provide coherence and identity, the red-light movement will not have a sufficiently wide base of membership and participation to grow beyond a small scale.

Third, lacking a widely shared compelling vision will not mean there will be no such visions operating on the left. Quite the contrary, those who don't care at all even about the precautionary principle will still develop and employ vision, most likely with market coordinatorist values and aspirations, which will then guide (and limit) experiments in new relations as well as strategies for winning change. There will not be an absence of vision if those attuned to not overreaching our experiential and conceptual bounds and to not being sectarian entirely eschew vision, but instead there will be a vision developed and held by narrow elites who don't have such concerns. So the movement that doesn't seek shared public vision will either fail to inspire support sufficient to win significant gains (which is our prediction), or if it does inspire such support, it will implement a narrowly held vision contrary to all but elite aspirations.

So yes, inaccurate prediction and sectarian attachment to vision are indeed possible problems of pursuing shared vision. But we believe that stop-light advocates have chosen the wrong solution to averting these problems: namely, dismissing serious and compelling institutional vision entirely. This "solution" repeats a more common mistake that operates in many venues. Here are two related examples:

- Someone sees that technologies, medicine, and science can oppress people. Their proposed solution: dump technology, medicine, and science.

- Someone sees that many reforms in practice coopt dissent and legitimate existing oppressive structures. Their proposed solution: dump reforms.

In these cases, as with vision, there is an unwarranted leap from justified precaution to red-light debilitation. A true critical characterization of some instances of technology, science, medicine, reforms, or (in our case) seeking vision, wrongly extrapolates into a rejection of these things outright.

Of course many technologies are oppressive, including destructive weapons, pollution-generating cars, and alienating and disempowering assembly lines, not to mention nuclear or biological weapons. But these are not the only technologies we have, and there are other technologies that are positive– shoelaces, cooking utensils, aspirin, eyeglasses, solar generators. The whole category—technology—isn't, in fact, infected. Moreover, the reason that many technologies are oppressive isn't that there is something intrinsically harmful in creating innovations of design that incorporate knowledge of laws of nature. Rather, the harm arises from social relations that create sectors of people able to produce and use technologies to harm some constituencies to the advantage of others. More, the choice to do without technologies is even worse than the problem of having many defective ones. If implemented, it would plunge us into a range of suffering that would be unfathomable. What ought to be ruled out is therefore not technologies (or medicine or science) *per se*, but oppressive technologies (medicine and science), and what ought to be sought is ever more effective means of producing desirable technologies while guarding against their misuse as well as against the harmful elitist trajectories imposed on technology creation and use. Following the precautionary principle in this case, in other words, doesn't lead us to suicidally reject all technologies but to carefully pursue desired technologies so as to maximize positive effects and avoid ill effects. Yes, of course we should have humility before the complexity of technology. But we should not have so much humility that we entirely cut off our capacities to innovate. Paralysis is not progress.

Consider now the example of reforms. Sure a reform's accomplishments can be insufficient to warrant the effort expended to win it. And certainly a reform's desirable consequences can be outweighed by the extent to which it dulls dissent or ratifies existing oppressive structures, or by intended or even unintended negative consequences. But to notice these potential problems and in response rule out reforms *per se* would mean ruling out all changes that fall short of entirely transforming social relations. It would mean not fighting against unjust wars, not seeking better wages, not trying to gain more power for grassroots constituencies and their organizations, and not attempting to diminish racist or sexist relations, and in these ways, it would lead to becoming a callous movement that ignores immediate suffering and therefore deserves little support.

So the problem is not reforms *per se*, but pursuing reforms as the best gains that we can possibly hope for and thus in ways that presuppose maintaining underlying injustices. The problem is not reforms, that is, but reformism. And the alternative to reformism is not to dump all reforms (following the red-light principle), but to fight for reforms in ways that not only seek worthy immediate gains, but increase movement membership, deepen movement commitment, enrich movement understanding, develop movement infrastructure, and in short, create preconditions for winning still more gains and ultimately fundamental change.

The above examples may seem a needless digression, but I suspect that those who reject technology, those who reject all reforms, and those who reject compelling institutional vision are all making essentially the same error. A real problem is rightly identified. In the case of vision the problem is that we can have incomplete, inadequate, or wrong vision and we can misuse desirable vision. But it is wrong to propose as a solution that we dump vision. We should abide the precautionary principle by trying to develop and employ vision well, not put up a red light.

So how can we make serious, compelling, shared institutional vision an asset rather than a debit? We can work to ensure:

1   That vision illuminates the new society's defining features but does not overstep into utopian wish fulfillment or pursue details that transcend what we can reasonably imagine.

2   That vision is accessible and becomes widely known, understood, and publicly shared, so that vision's creation, dispersal, and use is itself a participatory phenomenon fostering a growing movement of informed, careful, and always learning advocates.

3   That vision is debated, dissected, refined, and improved as thought and experience permit. That is, it is not statically defended, but instead steadily enriched. Vision is not seen as an end point, but as a source for continuing creation, innovation, experiment, and development.

4   That flexible, evolving, and enlarging vision is rooted in careful thought and experience and helps guide current

programs so that our contemporary efforts lead toward what we desire for the future.

In this book we have sought to pose a particular vision clearly and accessibly, based as best we could not only on our own logic and experience, but on that which has accumulated during the history of leftist struggles in past decades. We have tried to respect the limitations of social prediction and the dangers of dogmatism by promoting a critical, evaluative, experimental, and open process. But as to the future trajectory of pareconish vision, there is a little ditty that applies nicely:

> The viewer paints the picture,
> The reader writes the book,
> The glutton gives the tart its taste,
> And not the pastry cook.

Put differently, the implications of a vision depend ultimately on movement responses. It is not books that will determine how vision is used, but those who read books and extend, alter, apply, and utilize their offerings.

26

Excitement / Attainability

Can We Have A Parecon, Or Is History Forever Capitalist?

I see in the near future a crisis approaching that unnerves me and causes me to tremble for the safety of my country ... corporations have been enthroned and an era of corruption in high places will follow, and the money of the country will endeavor to prolong its reign by working upon the prejudices of the people until all wealth is aggregated in a few hands and the Republic is destroyed. I feel at this moment more anxiety for the safety of my country than ever before, even in the midst of war.
—Abraham Lincoln

Is participatory economics exciting enough to attract abiding support? Are conditions bequeathed to us by past history conducive to allowing us to win against existing obstacles and thereby attain participatory economics?

Excitement

Lacking "excitement" may seem like an odd criticism, but from an activist standpoint, it is not. It is not enough that goals posited for our future be desirable or even wonderful. They must also attract support. If not, they will exist on paper, but not in deeds. Words that lack excitement might inform or brighten the lives of a few who study them, but they are unlikely to transform the lives of all those who work and consume (or of all those who nurture the next generation, who teach or learn, who celebrate and identify, or who create laws, who adjudicate disputes).

Yes, parecon is a good model if it is a wonderful economy: viable and desirable. It is a good social vision, however, only if it is a good model and also attractive to widespread and growing constituencies. This is the "excitement" factor. But if parecon is viable and desirable, then the excitement factor is overwhelmingly a matter of how parecon is communicated. Its contents are certainly consistent with the possibility of exciting expression. More justice is more inspiring than less justice. More democracy is more inspiring than less democracy. More equity, diversity, and self-management are more inspiring than less equity, diversity, and self-management.

The particular words one person uses to talk about parecon may not be overly inspiring—something of which I may be guilty. But the solution to that is for others to do better both in further refining and improving the model, and especially in conveying that it is a worthy practical vision and making it so.

Attainability

What about attainability? Is parecon an attainable aspiration for the populations of countries like the United States, Brazil, Italy, Venezuela, Greece, England, Australia, Russia, Mexico, France, India, Indonesia, South Africa, Argentina, Haiti, and Japan, etc.?

Normal citizens feel two very important obstacles to undertaking social change efforts:

1   The fear that even if they were to win a new world, it would turn out to be just like the old world—or worse.

2   The doubt that they could ever do anything that would win a new world.

This book directly addresses point (1), at least regarding economics. It argues that if we manage to attain a parecon it will be vastly superior to capitalism and it will not devolve or degenerate back into the oppressive modes we now know, but will instead prosper and evolve positively, consistent with its guiding values. The model is thus viable and worthy. Attaining it would be worth it.

But can we attain it? This is a very different question. Ultimately the only proof is to succeed. Short of that the only argument for its possibility is:

1   Recognition that what humanity creates humanity can transcend—feudalism was not forever, slavery was not forever, neither capitalism nor coordinatorism will be forever.

2   Recognition that elements of parecon have already been implemented successfully. At www.parecon.org there are links to organizations that have explicitly implemented pieces of the parecon vision in their practice as well as accounts of those efforts, further discussion of the model, and considerable strategic discussion, as well. For that matter, our own daily lives are full of aspects of the norms and even the logic of parecon which we cling to obstinately

with our better selves against the pressures of the societies we endure.

3 A presentation of a broad set of strategic guidelines, aims, programs, structures, and steps, each of which can evidently be accomplished and which all together reveal a scenario that could end in a participatory economy. Regarding strategic demands and efforts that could accumulate into a process attaining a parecon, we cannot undertake such a discussion here, but in *Moving Forward* (AK Press, 2001), elements of that discussion are the primary focus.

Still, if the proof is ultimately only in the practice, the confidence to even try to attain participatory economic goals that comes from faith in human progress, from experience of expanding successes, and from consciousness of plausible scenarios of change depends first on more people entering the camp of those advocating parecon and trying to make it a reality. This book is obviously an effort to help propel that process.

Brief Bibliography

Titles by the author,
titles referenced in *Parecon,*
and selected titles of special interest

Books by Michael Albert
- *Trajectory of Change* (South End Press, 2002)
- *Thought Dreams* (Arbeiter Ring Press, 2002)
- *Moving Forward* (AK Press, 2000)
- *Thinking Forward* (AR, 2000)
- *Stop The Killing Train* (SEP, 1994)
- *What Is To Be Undone?* (Porter Sargent, 1974)

With Robin Hahnel
- *Looking Forward* (SEP, 1991)
- *Political Economy of Participatory Economics* (Princeton University Press, 1991)
- *Quiet Revolution in Welfare Economics* (PUP, 1990)
- *Socialism Today and Tomorrow* (SEP, 1981)
- *Marxism and Socialist Theory* (SEP, 1981)
- *Unorthodox Marxism* (SEP, 1978)

With David Dellinger
- *Beyond Survival* (SEP, 1983)

Multi-Author
- *Talking About A Revolution* (SEP, 1998)
- *Liberating Theory* (SEP, 1986)

Additional essays and other materials by Albert, Hahnel, and others, related to economic vision and parecon can be found on ZNet (www.zmag.org) and especially on the parecon subsite of ZNet (www.parecon.org)

Additional Titles Referenced Herein
or of Special Related Interest

- R. C. D'Arge and E. K. Hunt, "Environmental Pollution, Externalities and Conventional Economic Wisdom: A Critique" (*Environmental Affairs* no. 1, 1971)
- Sam Bowles, "What Markets Can and Cannot Do" (*Challenge Magazine,* July 1991)
- Harry Braverman, *Labor and Monopoly Capital* (Monthly Review, 1974)
- Pat Devine, *Democracy and Economic Planning* (Cambridge, 1988)
- Herb Gintis, "Alienation and Power: Towards a Radical Welfare Economics" (Ph.D. diss., Harvard, May 1969)
- Daniel Guerin, *Anarchism* (Monthly Review, 1966)
- E. K. Hunt and R. C. D'Arge, "On Lemmings and Other Acquisitive Animals: Propositions on Consumption" (*Journal of Economic Issues 7,* no. 2, June 1973)
- E. K. Hunt, "A Radical Critique of Welfare Economics," in Ed Nell ed. *Growth, Profits, and Property* (Cambridge, 1980)
- Peter Kropotkin, *Mutual Aid: A Factor of Evolution* (New York University, 1972)
- Oscar Lange and Frederick Taylor, *On the Economic Theory of Socialism* (Monthly Review, 1964)
- Ursula LeGuin, *The Dispossessed* (Harper and Row, 1974)
- Stephen Marglin, "What Do Bosses Do?" (*Review of Radical Political Economics,* 1974)
- Alec Nove, *The Economics of Feasible Socialism* (George Allen and Unwin, 1983)
- Anton Pannekoek, *Workers Councils* (*Southern Advocate for Workers' Councils,* Melbouren, 1951)
- Rudolf Rocker, *Anarcho Syndicalism (http:// flag.blackened.net /rocker/works.htm #Anarchism%20and% 20Anarcho-Syndicalism)*
- Stephen Shalom, *Socialist Visions* (SEP, 1983)
- Jaroslav Vanek, *The General Theory of Labor Self-Managed Economies* (Cornell University, 1970)
- Pat Walker, ed. *Between Labor and Capital* (SEP, 1979)

Index